Handbook of Family Life Education

Handbook of Family Life Education

The Practice of Family Life Education

Volume 2

edited by

**Margaret E. Arcus
Jay D. Schvaneveldt
J. Joel Moss**

SAGE Publications
International Educational and Professional Publisher
Newbury Park   London   New Delhi

For information address:

SAGE Publications, Inc.
2455 Teller Road
Newbury Park, California 91320

SAGE Publications Ltd.
6 Bonhill Street
London EC2A 4PU
United Kingdom

SAGE Publications India Pvt. Ltd.
M-32 Market
Greater Kailash I
New Delhi 110 048 India

Printed in the United States of America

Library of Congress Cataloging-in-Publication Data

Handbook of family life education / edited by Margaret E. Arcus, Jay
    D. Schvaneveldt, J. Joel Moss.
        p.   cm.
    Includes bibliographical references and indexes.
    Contents: v. 1. Foundations of family life education — v. 2. The
practice of family life education.
    ISBN 0-8039-4294-X (v. 1). — ISBN 0-8039-4295-8 (v. 2)
    1. Family life education—United States—Handbooks, manuals, etc.
I. Arcus, Margaret E.   II. Schvaneveldt, Jay D.   III. Moss, J. Joel.
HQ10.5 .U6H36   1993
306.85'07—dc20   93-26637
                                                                          CIP

93 94 95 96 10 9 8 7 6 5 4 3 2 1

Sage Production Editor: Rebecca Holland

Contents

Preface

The *Handbook of Family Life Education* had its genesis in the invitational Symposium on Family Life Education held at Brigham Young University in February 1986. This symposium brought together 20 family life educators from across the United States and from Canada and Spain to discuss selected developmental issues in the field of family life education. The symposium was modeled on the National Council on Family Relations Theory Workshop. Several major papers were prepared by selected individuals and were precirculated to all symposium participants; two discussants were invited to make brief presentations on each paper; and all participants were involved in intensive and extensive discussions of each paper. These formal experiences were further enhanced by small group discussions during luncheons and by the summary discussions that concluded each day.

During these discussions, several developmental issues in family life education were identified that were in need of attention if the field was to grow and prosper. These developmental issues included the need to examine more systematically the definition, the basic assumptions, and the parameters of family life education; the need to address more seriously the theme of values in family life education; the need to link the special and/or unique aspects of educating for family living more adequately to existing theories of education; and the need to ensure that family life education programs were based on a solid, scholarly foundation. The development of a handbook of family life education was identified as one of the ways to address these needs.

There were at least two reasons that this *Handbook on Family Life Education* seemed timely. Although the 1964 *Handbook of Marriage and the Family* edited by Christensen had given some attention to family life education, only a single chapter had been devoted to this topic. This chapter, written by Richard Kerckhoff, was a valuable contribution to the literature, but much has happened in family life education since that time. (The 1987 *Handbook of Marriage and the Family*, edited by Sussman and Steinmetz, was published shortly after the BYU symposium and also gave attention to family life education. But, again, only a single chapter was devoted to this topic.) During the symposium, it became apparent that the themes of family life education (both the developmental issues identified above and the other important topics that had not been addressed in the invited papers) were in need of greater attention than could possibly be provided in a single chapter. Thus symposium participants believed that there was a need for a handbook devoted specifically to the issues and concerns of family life education.

A second reason for such a handbook was that, although there was a burgeoning literature dealing with a variety of family life education topics, there had been no attempt to pull this literature together in any sort of critical or integrative way. It was therefore difficult to determine what kind of progress (if any) was being made on the various issues and concerns of family life education or to decide where the priorities and the energies of the field should be directed. The time seemed right for family life education to synthesize the literature of the field and to do some serious stock-taking.

Because this *Handbook of Family Life Education* is the first handbook to focus specifically on the themes and issues of family life education, it is a bench mark publication documenting the current status of the field. Its primary purpose is to provide an introduction to and a critical perspective on the broad field of family life education, both its major themes and its areas of practice. It is intended to help clarify many of the issues and questions in the field and to serve as a major resource for those who teach, practice, and do research in family life education.

The handbook has been written for use by several different audiences. It would be appropriate for use as a text or as a major reference for graduate and upper-level undergraduate courses in family life education and thus would help to fill a major gap in the family life education literature. It would also be appropriate for use in various in-service education courses and workshops for practicing family life educators. As well, the two volumes of the handbook would be important references for individual practitioners or practitioner units (e.g., community agencies, churches, schools, extension offices) as they enhance their existing areas of service or develop new ones. Finally, because the various chapters in the handbook give attention to needs and new directions in family life education, the handbook would be an important resource for family scholars as they conduct research and develop theory relevant to family life education.

The *Handbook of Family Life Education* is published in two volumes. Volume 1 is subtitled *Foundations of Family Life Education,* and chapters address such topics as the nature of family life education, its evolution as a field of practice, and its process of professionalization. The central theme of values in family life education and the central tasks of planning, implementation, and evaluation of family life programs are examined, as are the important "audience characteristics" that have particular relevance for family life education: gender, ethnicity and diversity, and religion. These topics were selected for inclusion in this volume of the handbook not only because they were central themes in family life education but also because there appeared to be a reasonable amount of literature available on which to base the chapter. Other important topics, such as the politics of family life education, were not included in this volume because there did not appear to be sufficient relevant family life education literature on the topic.

Volume 2 focuses on the practice of family life education. Most of the chapters deal with the content or the subspecialty areas of family life education, with some attention also given to issues relevant to the delivery of family life programs. This volume could have been organized in several different ways, that is, according to topic areas (such as parenting), to settings (such as parent education in community settings, parent education in schools, parent education in churches), or to specific audiences (such as single parents, remarried parents, adolescent parents). A decision was made to focus on topic areas rather than on settings or on audiences for two reasons. First, it would avoid the redundancy that would be likely to occur if several chapters had been written on different aspects of the same topic area. Second, although chapters were not organized according to setting or audience, authors were asked to address these aspects in the development of their chapters. Thus there was the potential for highlighting the similarities and differences that might be a function of either setting or audience. In the view of the editors, this integration across settings/audiences could provide a valuable perspective for practitioners that might be missed if each setting or audience had been addressed individually.

Authors in both volumes were asked to write chapters that were both scholarly and readable. The content of each chapter was to be based on a review of the literature relevant to that chapter and was to take a critical and integrative look at that literature. Because it was not possible within the limitations of the handbook to be exhaustive on each topic, authors were asked to be selective in their use of the literature as they addressed the topic in the context of family life education and to cite what they saw as the best and/or the most important sources so that interested readers could pursue topics in greater depth on their own. Thus an important part of each chapter is its reference list. It should be noted that nearly all authors indicated that their topics could have become an entire book in its own right, and we would agree. The task here was to prepare a chapter for a handbook volume, however, and the development of these ideas into a more extensive publication is a task for the future.

In addition to these general guidelines, authors in Volume 2 who prepared chapters on the topic areas of family life education were asked to address three common purposes as they developed their chapters: (a) to provide a critical and succinct introduction to the relevant content area, (b) to provide a critical review of current educational practice in the content area, and (c) to provide a brief discussion of issues, needs, and new directions in their particular area of family life education. They were also requested to give particular attention to outcome research in the content area, because one of the key questions raised by both family life educators and family life participants has to do with "what works." Each chapter was also to incorporate or address age, gender, and ethnicity issues as these were relevant to the topic area.

The task set for these authors was a tall one and was complicated by at least two limitations. First, there were limits placed by the editors on chapter length. A major criticism of recent handbooks has been that they are too long, too costly, and (sometimes) difficult to use. Thus a conscious decision was made, in consultation with the publisher, both to limit the number of chapters in each volume and to limit the number of pages in each chapter. Authors were asked to write as succinctly as possible so that this limitation would not compromise the quality of the handbook. It was intended that this handbook be user friendly, in size, in cost, and in content.

The second limitation had to do with the available literature. Authors were necessarily limited by the amount and kind of literature that has been published. Some important information simply is not available, but, in our view, it is essential for family life education to compile the information that is available and to identify those areas where further work needs to be done. In many ways, the lack of information is as important as its presence in documenting the current status of the field. Special comment needs to be made about the potential international audience for this handbook. It was not possible for authors to do justice to the relevant literature that has been published in many different countries around the world. Many of the chapters provide specific data on U.S. families, but these were intended to serve as examples only and to indicate to readers in other countries the kinds of family patterns and trends that are relevant to family life education. Both editors and authors have assumed that many of the broad themes and issues of family life education as discussed in the handbook have significance outside the boundaries of the United States.

An important part of the process of the development of this handbook has been the use of one or more external reviewers for each of the chapters. These individuals made many important contributions to the shaping of each chapter and helped to ensure the quality of the overall publication. The editors are indebted to these reviewers for their interest in the handbook, their serious and thoughtful critique of each draft, and their generous sharing of insights and resources with the authors. The editors wish to acknowledge and thank the following individuals who served as external reviewers for one or more of the chapters in this handbook:

Dr. Ruth Brasher—Brigham Young University, Provo, Utah
Dr. Wesley Burr—Brigham Young University, Provo, Utah
Dr. Mary Dellman-Jenkins—Kent State University, Kent, Ohio
Dr. Peggye Dilworth-Anderson—University of North Carolina-Greensboro, Greensboro, North Carolina
Ms. Rosanne Farnden—British Columbia Council for the Family, Vancouver, British Columbia
Dr. Dottie Goss—Oklahoma State University, Stillwater, Oklahoma
Dr. Maxine Lewis-Rowley—Brigham Young University, Provo, Utah
Dr. Nelwyn Moore—Southwest Texas State University, San Marcos, Texas
Dr. Gerry Neubeck—University of Minnesota, St. Paul, Minnesota
Dr. Vicki Schmall—Oregon State University, Corvallis, Oregon
Dr. Barbara Settles—University of Delaware, Newark, Delaware
Dr. Rebecca Smith—University of North Carolina-Greensboro, Greensboro, North Carolina
Dr. Jane Thomas—Vancouver School Board, Vancouver, British Columbia
Dr. James Walters—University of Georgia, Athens, Georgia
Ms. Margaret Young—Utah State University, Logan, Utah

Contributions from several other individuals also need to be acknowledged. First, there are those individuals who provided anonymous reviews of the original proposal for the handbook submitted to Sage Publications. These individuals provided valuable input and insights and helped to shape the thinking of the editors and thus the direction of the publication. As well, colleagues in each of our institutions and communities provided substantial assistance and support to the editors at various stages of the project. These colleagues include Jane

Thomas, Vancouver School Board, and Rosanne Farnden, British Columbia Council for the Family, both in Vancouver, Canada; Margaret Young, Utah State University; and Ruth Brasher and Maxine Lewis-Rowley, Brigham Young University.

The editors also wish to thank Mitch Allen of Sage for his support and encouragement throughout the development and writing of this handbook. He has helped to keep it all on track, and we hope that the response to the publication meets his expectations and justifies his support. Our appreciation is also extended to the production staff at Sage and especially to Rebecca Holland, whose exceptional organizational skills and attention to detail have helped ensure that this *Handbook* is a quality publication.

Finally, no project of this kind succeeds without the support and encouragement of family members. Our heartfelt thanks go to Peter, Karen, and Audra.

1

The Nature and Practice of Family Life Education

Margaret E. Arcus
Jane Thomas

PREPARING INDIVIDUALS AND FAMILIES for the roles and responsibilities of family living is nothing new (Gaylin, 1981; Kirkendall, 1973). Because humans have no built-in knowledge about human development and family living, they must learn it from somewhere. All societies have thus developed ways through which they may transmit the wisdom and experience of family living from each generation to succeeding ones. Some of this transmission occurs through formal events such as puberty or initiation rites, but much of it is learned informally in the family setting itself, as family members observe and participate in family activities and interactions (Hill & Aldous, 1969).

It is only in relatively simple societies, where little social change occurs, however, that families alone can meet the needs of their members for learning about and preparing for family living (Somerville, 1971). In more complex and changing societies, the development of new knowledge, advances in technology, and changes in social conditions all create circumstances where the teachings of previous generations may be neither appropriate nor sufficient.

Because these societal changes may create strains or tensions in individuals and families, disruptions in family living may result. According to Kirkendall (1973), certain family difficulties (such as an increased divorce rate, increased parent-child strife, or shifts in marital and familial roles) have commonly occurred in societies as they become industrialized and urbanized, and these family difficulties have typically given rise to attempts to strengthen the family through the efforts

1

of outside agencies. Over time, these efforts have become increasingly formalized and have led to the establishment of the movement called family life education (Kerckhoff, 1964; Kirkendall, 1973). The general intent of this movement has been to improve family living and to reduce family-related societal problems through family-focused educational opportunities.

The purpose of the two-volume *Handbook of Family Life Education* is to examine the central themes and areas of practice in the family life education movement. In Volume 1 (see Chapter 1 by Arcus, Schvaneveldt, & Moss), chapters focus on some of the foundations of this area of study and practice: the nature, evolution, and professionalization of family life education; the role of values and values education; the development, implementation, and evaluation of programs; and the relevance and influence of religion, gender, and ethnic diversity. The critical overview of the literature provided in these chapters is intended to enhance both scholarship and practice in family life education.

In this second volume of the *Handbook of Family Life Education*, attention is directed specifically to subject matter areas and themes in the practice of family life education. Authors of the chapters in this volume have summarized and critiqued an extensive body of literature to clarify the current status of various subject matter specializations within family life education (e.g., marriage education, parenting education, sexuality education), to raise questions and identify issues in need of attention by family life education practitioners, and to suggest new directions and emergent areas in the practice of family life education.

This introductory chapter in Volume 2 examines both the nature and the practice of family life education and provides the context for the other chapters in this volume. It begins with an overview of the nature of family life education, emphasizing definitions, purpose and content, operational principles, and related areas of specialization. The activities that typically characterize the practice of family life education are then discussed and critiqued, and several issues related to practice are identified. Finally, brief attention will be given to the importance of the family life educator. The chapter concludes by identifying several implications for family life educators as they seek to improve the practice of family life education.

THE NATURE OF FAMILY LIFE EDUCATION

Definitions of Family Life Education

Although the family life education movement is now fairly well established and many activities take place under this name, defining the term *family life education* has been problematic (e.g., Darling, 1987; Fisher & Kerckhoff, 1981; Somerville, 1971). Historically, the term has meant different things to different people, resulting in considerable confusion (and sometimes conflict) about "what counts" as family life education. Although many different definitions have been proposed since the 1960s (see Chapter 1, by Arcus et al., in Volume 1 for a listing of these definitions), most of these definitions have been criticized because they are too vague, too ambiguous, and/or too idealistic. Thus most of these definitions appear to have been of little help to many family life education practitioners.

Considerable concern has been expressed that consensus has not yet been achieved on a definition of family life education (e.g., Arcus, 1986). Although there are some similarities among the various definitions of *family life education* (most, for example, have stated or implied a focus on interpersonal relationships), there are also a number of important differences. As yet, family life educators do not appear to agree on whether family life education should take an individual focus (Gross, 1985; Sheek, 1984) or a family unit focus (National Commission on Family Life Education, 1968), nor are they clear about whether it should be primarily functional family living courses (Cromwell & Thomas, 1976; Smith, 1968) or an area for academic study (Darling, 1987; Herold, Kopf, & deCarlo, 1974). Some have suggested that family life education has a problem-oriented focus (Stern, 1969), while others have emphasized the development of potentials (Barozzi & Engel, 1985). Definitions have also differed in whether family life education is primarily concerned with the development of knowledge (Stern, 1969) or whether it should also include attention to attitudes and skills (Kerckhoff, 1964).

There are several reasons why agreement on a definition of family life education is important (see Chapter 1 by Arcus et al. in Volume 1). Definitions help to clarify thinking about appropriate goals and purposes; they provide a perspective or an orientation to educational practice; they help to delineate the scope of educational activity; and they assist in communicating effectively with others. Moreover, agreement on meaning is an essential step in developing theory about family life education (Fisher, 1986), in preparing family life educators (Gaylin, 1981), and in surveying and evaluating relevant family life education research (Somerville, 1971). When the term *family life education* is *not* defined consistently, it is difficult to compare studies, to accumulate knowledge, and to develop the field conceptually, empirically, and practically. Without a clear definition, it may also be difficult for individual family life educators to identify with and make a commitment to the field of family life education. As well, the lack of clarity in meaning may exacerbate political problems, because individuals may make judgments and decisions about family life education based on different expectations, assumptions, and/or parameters.

One of the difficulties may be that, although definitions may be *necessary* in family life education, they may not be *sufficient*, either to clarify the nature of family life education or to provide the kinds of guidance needed by family life educators as they develop and evaluate programs. Indeed, Thomas and Arcus (1992) have suggested that what is needed at the current time in family life education is *not* further efforts at definition but a systematic analysis of the concept of family life education to uncover more adequately the *meaning* of this term.

In an attempt to move family life education beyond definitions, Thomas and Arcus (1992) used methods of analytical inquiry to investigate the central question of meaning in family life education: *What features must something have to be called family life education?* Their investigation was based on the premise that one needs to be clear about what counts as family life education before important questions (e.g., "Does family life education make a difference?" and "Should family life education be required?") can be adequately answered. Although Thomas and Arcus identified several important features of the concept of family life education that needed analytical attention (i.e., general purposes/intended outcomes, subject matter/content, assumptions, normative beliefs), their analysis examined only the first two of these features: general purposes/intended outcomes and subject matter/content.

The Purpose of Family Life Education

Three different rationales appear to have been central in establishing the purpose of family life education. First was the early rationale underlying the emergence of the family life education movement, that is, the need to help families deal with the social problems of the time. The second rationale was the related and relatively unchallenged assumption that, if only families would learn to "do the right things," then many family problems could and would be prevented. The third rationale for family life education reflected the view of many family life practitioners that, in addition to dealing with and preventing problems, families also needed to have the opportunity to develop their individual and family potentials. (See Volume 1, Chapter 1, for an elaboration of these rationales.)

Based on these three rationales, many different family life education goals and objectives have been developed (see, for example, National Commission on Family Life Education, 1968; National Council on Family Relations, 1970). It is not possible in this chapter to identify all of these goals and objectives, but some of the major ones include (a) gaining insight into self and others, (b) learning about human development and behavior in the family setting over the life cycle, (c) learning about marriage and family patterns and processes, (d) acquiring skills essential for family living, (e) developing the potentials of individuals in their current and future family roles, and (f) building strengths in families. One of the assumptions in family life education appears to be that, if these and other similar objectives are met through family life education programs, then families will be better able to deal with problems, to prevent problems, and/or to develop their potentials.

Many important questions have been raised about the number and the breadth of goals and objectives in family life education. Fisher and Kerckhoff, for example, observed that one agency listed 42 objectives for family life education, and they asked whether it was possible for one profession to have such diverse goals as "to understand the personality of self and others," "to learn to manage the household," as well as "to promote physical health, mental health, democratic family life, and the standard of living" (Fisher & Kerckhoff, 1981, p. 505). Their concern that the goals and objectives of family life education are potentially overwhelming is an important one and a concern that may be shared by other family life educators. In addressing this concern, however, it is important to recognize that some of the goals and objectives of family life education may be ultimate goals or *ends* while others may be subgoals or *means* to these ends. That is, understanding the personality of self and others may be a means to promoting mental health, while learning to manage the household may be a means to improving one's standard of living. Thus the diverse goals and objectives of family life education may be more interrelated than they at first appear. Litke (1976) has developed a process that might be useful in helping family life educators bring some order to the diverse goals and objectives of the field.

In their analysis of the concept of family life education, Thomas and Arcus (1992) focused on the ultimate goals or ends of family life education. They systematically reviewed the family life education literature published since 1960 to determine whether there was reasonable conceptual agreement among family life educators concerning these goals. Based on this analysis, Thomas and Arcus concluded that, at the current time, there was reasonable agreement in the field that the ultimate goal of family life education is "to strengthen and enrich individual and family well-being."[1] This broad statement of purpose not only incorporates some of the subgoals identified above but also appears to reflect all of the rationales previously discussed.

The Content of Family Life Education

According to Thomas and Arcus (1992), there is also considerable agreement among family life educators at the current time concerning the content or subject matter of the field. The most current conceptualization of this content is found in the Framework for Life-Span Family Life Education, developed under the auspices of the National Council on Family Relations (Arcus, 1987; National Council on Family Relations, 1984). One of the strengths of this framework is that it was based on previous literature in the field and was developed over a period of time with the considered input of many family life education scholars and practitioners. Several important criteria guided the development of this framework: (a) The framework was to reflect a broad conception of family life education, consistent with other writings about the field; (b) the number of topics was to be limited so that the framework would be manageable without loss of important ideas or concepts; (c) several broad dimensions of learning (knowledge, attitudes and values, skills) were to be included under each of the content areas; and (d) the framework was to reflect the assumption that individuals of all ages need to learn about family life and to demonstrate that each topic area could be addressed at different age levels (children, adolescents, adults) by varying the focus and the complexity of the key concepts (Arcus, 1987).

The content of family life education as specified in the Framework for Life-Span Family Life Education consists of seven major topic areas (human development and sexuality, interpersonal relationships, family interaction, family resource management, education about parenthood, ethics, and family and society) and three general processes (communicating, decision making, and problem solving). The framework further specifies some of the important knowledge, attitudes, and skills relevant to each major topic area. The topic area of "interpersonal relationships," for example, includes knowledge such as "factors influencing mate selection," attitudes such as "respecting self and others," and skills such as "initiating, maintaining, and ending relationships." Because of its importance not only in understanding the nature of family life education but also in carrying out the associated practical tasks of program design and evaluation, this framework is reproduced in its entirety in the Appendix in this volume.

Although Thomas and Arcus (1992) reported considerable agreement among family life professionals on the content of family life education, they also suggested that it was important to examine even well-accepted ideas in some systematic way, because this agreement in the field may be based on habit or on honest but mistaken beliefs. Thus, as part of their analysis of the concept of family life education, they questioned whether all of the seven topic areas and three processes were indeed essential for this concept. In addressing this question, they first considered what was meant by the term *family life*, because clarifying this term provided the criteria for deciding whether or not a particular content was essential in educating for or about family life.

> The task was not to decide how the family should be defined, but rather to determine what goes on within families as living units (however they are defined) as they go about fulfilling their societal functions. In general, the term "family life" is used to refer to those actions and interactions which occur in families as they bear and rear children; meet the needs of individual family members for support, security, nurturance, affection; produce and consume goods and services in order to support and maintain the family unit; and influence and are influenced by other social institutions and systems such as the economy, education, religion, and the law. (Thomas & Arcus, 1992, p. 5)

Thomas and Arcus then posed the question: "Can we have family life education (that is, can we educate for family life) without this particular content area?" (1992, p. 5). Although it is not possible to repeat all of their analyses here, one example may help to illustrate the process: "Can we have family life education without content in family resource management?" Because interactions and activities in families revolve around such things as developing and using resources to meet basic family needs, making consumer decisions, and establishing short- and long-term family goals, Thomas and Arcus concluded that content in "family resource management" was an essential component of family life and thus was a necessary part of the concept of family life education. They further concluded that indeed all of the topic areas and processes listed in the Framework for Life-Span Family Life Education were essential in educating for family life.

The Framework for Life-Span Family Life Education provides an important resource for family life education practitioners and can be used in several ways (National Council on Family Relations, 1984). For example, it could facilitate program design by helping family life educators to identify appropriate content for new programs or to assess the breadth of content in existing programs. The framework could also be used to identify areas of strength and areas that need attention so as to assess the comprehensiveness of all programs offered within an agency, an organization, or a community. As well, the framework could be a valuable resource in explaining, promoting, and/or justifying broad programs in family life education, an important tool in developing both preservice and in-service preparation programs for family life educators, and a basis for the development and testing of family life education theory. It is likely that creative family life educators may find additional uses for the framework.

The Operational Principles of Family Life Education

Arcus et al. (Chapter 1 in Volume 1) identified several other features of the concept of family life education (derived from a review of the literature of the field) that they termed *operational principles*. Some of these principles are descriptive ones, purporting to describe how family life education *is* practiced, while others are more prescriptive, indicating what family life educators *should do* as they educate for family living. For the most part, these principles have not been subjected to critical reflection, but they appear to be generally well accepted by those in family life education and often serve as guides for professional decision making and action. (For further elaboration on these principles, see Arcus et al., Chapter 1, Volume 1.)

1. Family life education is relevant to individuals and families throughout the life span. Early efforts in family life education were concerned primarily with parent education (or, more technically, with mother education) and thus were directed toward parents (mothers) (see Chapter 2, by Lewis-Rowley, Brasher, Moss, Duncan, & Stiles, in Volume 1). Over time, this focus has expanded to include individuals and families over the entire life span (e.g., Hennon & Arcus, 1993). Hennon and Arcus (1993) have suggested that the impetus for some programs may be related to various normative developments for individuals and families, such as getting married, becoming a parent, or retiring from a job. These normative developments may be age related (attaining puberty), event related (the loss of a family member), or a combination of age and event related (first marriage during young adulthood). Other programs may be based on nonnormative developments, that is, related to the special needs and transitions affecting some but not all individuals and families, such as parenting children with special needs, getting divorced, facing unemployment. The response of family life educators to both normative and nonnormative events and transitions has resulted in the development of a number of specialty areas within family life education, with some of these specialty areas well established (parent education, sex education, marriage education) and others emerging (parent education for adolescent parents, sexual abuse education and prevention, marriage the second time around) (Hennon & Arcus, 1993).

The Framework for Life-Span Family Life Education (see the Appendix) illustrates how the content of the field varies according to broad age categories or developmental phases (i.e., children, adolescents, adults). For example, in the content area titled "ethics," education for children focuses on taking responsibility for actions, while education for adolescents broadens to include the development of a personal ethical code. Further expansion in this content area occurs at the adult level, as at least some adults assist in the formation of ethical concepts and behavior in others. (See Hennon & Arcus, 1993, for a review of major directions, issues, and limitations in the practice of family life education relevant to each of these broad age groups.)

2. *Family life education should be based on the needs of individuals and families.* It is commonly stated in family life education that family life programs should be based on the immediate needs of individuals and families (e.g., Avery & Lee, 1964). It has also been claimed that family life programs make their "maximum contribution to the enrichment of family life when they are directly related to immediate personal, family, and community needs" (National Commission on Family Life Education, 1968, p. 211).

These needs may be identified in several ways (Hennon & Arcus, 1993). Some needs may be "felt needs," that is, they are needs expressed by individuals and families themselves, such as "I need to be more assertive in my relationships" or "We need help in dealing with a family problem." Felt needs are commonly reflected in family life education through program objectives, rationales, and activities, possibly because many of these programs have been developed on the basis of a needs assessment of actual and/or potential clients.

Needs may also refer to "developmental needs," that is, needs that are common to most individuals and families (e.g., dealing with one's changing sexuality at puberty, preparing for retirement). These needs are generally identified through reference to the empirical literature of the field and to the collective wisdom and experience of family life educators. Many documents, such as the Framework for Life-Span Family Life Education (National Council on Family Life Education, 1984), are based on such developmental needs.

In many cases, there is an overlap between these two kinds of needs (Hennon & Arcus, 1993). The educational needs of new parents, for example, may be both a felt need expressed by the parents themselves and a developmental need emerging from their new roles and responsibilities. Practitioners, however, should not always assume a good match between felt needs and developmental needs. For example, although marriage educators may believe that preparation for marriage is an important developmental need, at least some participants in these programs have claimed that they "do not need it" (that is, for them, it is *not* a felt need; Fournier, 1980).

Hennon and Arcus identified another kind of need that deserves greater attention in family life education and that might best be called "societal needs." These are needs that emerge from both current and anticipated social, economic, and political conditions and that impinge in important ways on the lives of all individuals and families. Examples of these needs include the need to combat prejudice and to manage the finite resources of the world with greater care and with greater attention to social justice. If family life education is to attain the goal of meeting the needs of all individuals and families, then family life education must also address these societal needs.

Because of the importance of meeting needs in family life education, needs assessment has been seen as an important tool of the field (e.g., Hennon & Arcus, 1993; National Commission on Family Life Education, 1968). Sork (1988), however, has raised several important issues regarding needs assessment that deserve thoughtful consideration by family life education practitioners. According to Sork, conducting a needs assessment may be interpreted by some potential clients to mean that all of the needs that are identified in this way will be met by the family life program. But what if (for some reason) all of the identified needs cannot be met? If some of the needs will be addressed and others will not, how is an educator to decide and to justify which needs to address and which to ignore? What are the values reflected by the educator who makes such decisions and whose ideology will prevail if there is disagreement over the allocation of resources to meet these needs? As Sork has pointed out, any effort by educators to pass judgment on the appropriateness of identified needs may be unethical because it infringes upon the autonomy of the learner. Sork has challenged all educators (including family life educators) to ensure that their judgments regarding the needs of the audience are "made consciously, with full recognition of their philosophical basis and moral consequences" (Sork, 1988, p. 35).

The emphasis in family life education on meeting needs also raises important questions regarding the timing of family life education efforts. According to Duvall (in Avery & Lee, 1964, p. 34), some programs may "come so late it is ludicrous, or too soon to be effective." Examples of family life education programs that may come too late include *some* efforts in premarital education and in sexuality education, while those that may come too soon include some education for parenthood programs in the secondary schools. For example, de Lissovoy (1978) suggested that it is premature to focus on the specific tasks of parenthood during adolescence and that, instead, attention should be directed toward the *precursors* of parenthood—"the issues of self, interpersonal relationships and skills, and values within a democratic milieu" (p. 331).

3. *Family life education is a multidisciplinary area of study and is multiprofessional in its practice.* This operational principle recognizes that the important concepts, principles, and perspectives used in family life education come from diverse disciplines and fields of study that focus on individuals and families in particular ways. Those identified most often include (in alphabetical order) anthropology, biology, economics, home economics, law, medicine, philosophy, physiology, psychology, social work, and sociology (e.g., National Commission on Family Life Education, 1968). Fisher and Kerckhoff, however, have suggested that family life education is not really as multidisciplinary as is often claimed. In their view, family life education at the current time is best characterized as "sociology and psychology as it applies to the family," and they urge that family life education "be expanded from the narrow data base from which it now operates" (1981, p. 508).

The use of the term *interdisciplinary* in relation to family life education implies that there is some collaboration among the various disciplines. Such collaboration may be both desired and desirable, but at the current time competition and rivalry among disciplines appear to be more characteristic of family life education than cooperation. Somerville (1971) noted that competition among disciplines was one of the obstacles facing family life education in the 1960s, and there is some suggestion that this competition still exists (see Chapters 2 and 3 in Volume 1 of the *Handbook of Family Life Education*).

4. *Family life education programs are offered in many different settings.* Family life education is typically offered by many different institutions and agencies such as schools, churches, business and industry, and community, governmental, and private agencies. This diversity of settings has been seen as appropriate for providing services across the life span and to provide for a variety of perspectives in meeting the needs of as many individuals and families as possible (Chapter 1, by Arcus et al., in Volume 1). Some of these settings (schools, churches, community agencies) are well established as providers of family life education, but others such as the workplace have just begun their involvement in family life education.

Some have recommended that the family, the church, schools, and all family-serving agencies become partners in providing family life education (National Commission on Family Life Education, 1968). It is presumed that this might encourage communities to assess their needs and to avoid duplication in using resources to meet these needs. Because the roles of home, school, and church in educating children and youth for family life have not been clearly delineated (Somerville, 1971), however, concerns have been expressed about the potential for family life education to usurp parental prerogatives in this area (Arcus, 1986). These kinds of concerns may generate political problems that make it difficult to implement some family life education programs. Rivalry among institutions and agencies and concerns about infringing on "territory" may also make it difficult for family life education to become a cooperative community effort.

5. *Family life education takes an educational rather than a therapeutic approach.* Most family life educators have claimed that the purpose of action and activity in family life education is to educate or equip rather than to repair. Although there is general agreement on this statement, there are at least two difficulties in maintaining this claim. First, the conceptual distinctions between "education" and "therapy" are not clear, so that it is difficult to determine when something is educational rather than therapeutic and vice versa. Second, there is considerable confusion around the concept of education itself. At least some educators appear to equate the term *education* with a narrow view of cognition and thus place an emphasis in family life education on "imparting knowledge" (e.g., Wright & L'Abate, 1977).

According to Peters (1967), however, various analyses of the concept of education have indicated that, rather than the simple accumulation of knowledge, the purpose of education is to empower the learner to *use* knowledge in making informed, responsible choices and in acting on the basis of reason. This conception of education suggests that it is inappropriate to equate family life education only with information delivery, with the passive acquisition of facts, or with narrow training in skill development (Thomas & Arcus, 1992). Thus, if family life education is to count as *education,* then it must be centrally concerned with the development of justified beliefs and the capacities required to arrive at these beliefs.

Many family life educators have differentiated between cognitive (intellectual) development and affective (feelings and attitudes) development (e.g., Moss & Elbert, 1987), and there has been some disagreement about which of these should be emphasized (Fisher, 1986). According to Peters (1967), however, affective development occurs concurrently with cognitive development and the two cannot be separated. Attitudes and emotions necessarily have some cognitive core; that is, one cannot have feelings or attitudes without having them directed toward something that one knows about (Coombs, 1989). Coming to recognize that these two dimensions of education occur concurrently may help to reduce some of the conflict and confusion that have arisen in family life education regarding educational aims.

6. *Family life education should present and respect differing family values.* Values have long been both a theme and a problem in family life education (see Chapter 4, by Arcus & Daniels, in Volume 1). What should be the role of values in family life education? Which values should (or should not) be included in family life education programs? Should family life educators share their personal values with program participants? What is the best way to handle controversial values questions? Which values education approaches are most appropriate and most effective? How can family life educators respect differing family and cultural values? Over time, these and other related values questions have been the focus of considerable discussion and debate in the field. It is not possible to comment on all of these questions here, but a few examples may highlight the importance of giving serious attention to values questions in family life education.

What is the role of values in family life education? Although many early family life educators were unclear about whether or not values "belonged" in family life education (see Kerckhoff, 1964), at the current time the importance and centrality of values in the field have been affirmed in several ways. First, many statements of the goals of family life education are in fact statements about values, for example, to strengthen and enrich individual and family well-being, to understand and accept value differences, to develop critical thinking skills. Second, the content of family life education as specified in the Framework for Life-Span Family Life Education includes ethics (and thus ethical values) as one of the major topic areas. Third, many of the learning experiences used in various programs include values-related activities such as values questionnaires and checklists or discussions and debates about values issues. Finally, one of the important roles for family life educators has been identified as that of assisting program participants in the formation of social attitudes and values. Clearly, values are pervasive in family life education, and it is essential that family life practitioners are well prepared to address this family life education theme.

At one time or another, several different approaches have been suggested for handling values questions: to ignore them, to teach a given set of values (indoctrination or inculcation), to allow students to clarify their own values, to enhance student abilities to reason about values, and so on (see Chapter 4, by Arcus & Daniels, in Volume 1). Some of these have resulted in specific programs or models designed to provide values education (although not always under the values education label). For a discussion of some of these models, see Arcus and Daniels (Chapter 4 in Volume 1) and Hersch, Miller, and Fielding (1980).

Which of these values education approaches is the most effective and the most appropriate for family life education? This is a difficult question, because more appears to be known about what *doesn't* work than what does work. It is of some concern, however, that the most commonly used values education approach in family life education is that of Values Clarification (Raths, Harmin, & Simon, 1966). Although this approach is widely used, its acceptance (in family life education and indeed in education more generally) has been for the most part unreflective and uncritical. Serious questions have been raised about both the theoretical and the pedagogical limitations of Values Clarification, however, and these limitations have important implications for family life education.

Theoretically, Values Clarification has been criticized as having an inadequate and an internally inconsistent concept of values, for its emphasis on personal preferences and tastes rather than on values, for its extreme relativism, and for its failure to confront the central questions of normative ethics (e.g., Stewart, 1976). As well, Values Clarification provides no criteria to help one to assess the merits of various value claims, and no recognition is given to the crucial role played by value principles, standards, and rules in dealing with values issues. Because of these theoretical limitations, then, Values Clarification is theoretically inadequate and an inappropriate method of *values* education.

Critiques of the approach also indicate that Values Clarification is inadequate as a strategy for values *education*. Although the techniques are relatively simple and easy to use, in and of themselves the techniques provide little or no stimulation for students to progress beyond their current level of understanding, and no tools are provided that might help students to examine values or to deal with value conflicts. As well, at the current time, evaluative studies have provided little evidence that Values Clarification "works" as values education. (For critiques of the Values Clarification approach, see Daniels & Oliver, 1977; Hamm, 1989; Lockwood, 1978; Schulte & Teal, 1975; Stewart, 1976.) Clearly, it is time for family life educators to rethink their reliance on this particular method of dealing with values in family life education.

The question of values has been particularly significant in the controversy surrounding family life education in the schools (Arcus, 1986).

Is it appropriate for schools to teach about values? Among concerns expressed by the opponents of this education are that family life education in the schools will violate family values, that family life teachers cannot adequately handle the value differences that might exist in the classroom, and that, in fact, it is not possible to teach values in the classroom.

According to Arcus (1986), it is difficult to substantiate or refute such claims, both because of semantic difficulties and because there is little empirical evidence available concerning these issues. For example, what does it mean when one claims that "family life education violates family values"?

> Does this mean that family life education fails to promote the particular values held by a particular family, or that it negatively evaluates those values which are held by families generally, or that it encourages students to think critically about family values? Unless one is clear about what counts as "violating family values," it is difficult to assess whether or not such violation has occurred. (Arcus, 1986, p. 352)

As well, because few studies have examined how teachers handle values education in the classroom, little is known about whether or not their pedagogy is appropriate or effective.

It is not possible to elaborate more fully in this chapter on the issues and questions surrounding families and their values, family life educators and their values, and the role of family life education vis-à-vis these values. For further information, see Arcus and Daniels (Chapter 4 in Volume 1), Blustein (1982), Cunningham and Scanzoni (Chapter 8 in Volume 1), and Hildreth and Sugawara (Chapter 7 in Volume 1).

Specializations in Family Life Education

Before discussing the practice of family life education, it is important to make some brief comments regarding some of the specialized areas of study that are typically included in discussions of family life education. As noted earlier in this chapter, the responses of family life educators over time to the changing nature of families and the broader society in which families live have resulted in the development of a number of specialized areas within family life education. Some of these specialized areas of study are well-established fields in their own right and are examined in later chapters in this volume (e.g., marriage education, parent education, sexuality education). Authors of the chapters in this volume have been asked to address both the broad themes of each of these specialized areas and the variations that have emerged within the specialization as educators respond to the diverse needs and experiences of their audiences.

Although for the purposes of this handbook these areas of specialization have been included within the broad umbrella of "family life education," it is recognized that there may be some important differences among them. (See Thomas & Arcus, 1992, for example, for a discussion of conceptual differences between family life education and sexuality education.) Despite these differences, each specialized area is also a theme within the broad concept of family life education, and thus developments within the specialization are of relevance and importance to any discussion of family life education.

THE PRACTICE OF FAMILY LIFE EDUCATION

There are many interpretations of the term *practice* (e.g., Diorio, 1982), but most writers agree that it is essentially concerned with those practical activities that collectively characterize a field or profession (see also Shaw, 1981). Although there has been little systematic study of family life education practice as an educational endeavor, it is likely that the most central activities of the field include program development (course design), program implementation (planning for program use, pedagogy, and interaction with program participants), and program evaluation (assessment of learning and of program effectiveness) (e.g., see National Council on Family Relations, 1984; Sheek, 1984). In this section, these practices in family life education are discussed and critiqued.

Program Development and Family Life Education Practice

In the educational literature, the term *program development* tends to be used in two ways (Zais, 1976). The broader use of the term refers to the forces that influence the origin of programs and that shape their evolution over time (e.g., social, political, and economic movements, the implementation of laws and policies; Fullan, 1991). The more narrow use of the term is concerned with the practical tasks and questions associated with designing a curriculum or producing a program plan. In program design, one specifies and justifies what should be taught to whom and under what circumstances, determines the ends or goals of the program, and prescribes the means for achieving these ends (see Chapter 5, by Thomas, Schvaneveldt, & Young, in Volume 1). Emphasis in this chapter will be placed on issues and questions related to program design.

According to Thomas et al. (Chapter 5 in Volume 1), program design in family life education tends to emanate from a "Tylerian" model of program design. This model is based on four sequential steps, each of which is concerned with a central program design question: (a) state aims and objectives (what educational purposes should be sought?); (b) identify content and learning experiences (what educational experiences might attain the stated purposes?); (c) outline plans for instruction (how can these experiences be effectively organized?); (d) specify evaluation strategies (how can the achievement of the purposes be determined?). According to Tyler (1949), educational aims and objectives are ultimately intended to bring about changes in behavior and are to be determined by considering both the characteristics of the learners and the subject matter in relation to the educational philosophy of the program developer. These considerations collectively constitute what he termed the *rationale* for the program.

Tyler's model has been influential in family life education in several ways (Chapter 5, by Thomas et al., in Volume 1). First, most family life education programs appear to have been designed using the steps of this model and many family life education writers have advocated its use (for specific examples, see Hoopes, Fisher, & Barlow, 1984; Sheek, 1984; Wagman & Cooper, 1981). Second, considerable attention has been given to the development of program rationales, based primarily on either formal or informal needs assessments (e.g., National Commission on Family Life Education, 1968). Third, the acceptance of Tyler's notion of behavior change as the essence of education is apparent in many family life programs (e.g., Guerney & Guerney, 1981; Mace, 1981). Finally, many family life programs make extensive use of behavioral objectives to specify precisely what it is that learners must be able to do to demonstrate their attainment of the educational objectives.

Despite its widespread use, the Tyler model has been the focus of considerable criticism. For example, questions have been raised about whether it is, in fact, appropriate to equate "behavior change" with education. Behavior may be deceptive as a criterion of learning because individuals may act in the expected manner although they have not learned and, conversely, they may *not* act in the expected manner even though they have learned. As well, the emphasis on behavior change as evidence of learning does not account for the unintended learning that might occur as a result of educational experiences. Moreover, the use of the Tyler model has perpetuated the mistaken belief discussed earlier that cognitive and affective learning occur separately. Based on these criticisms, it may be time to rethink the extensive use of this model in family life education practice and to look at strategies for strengthening program development.

During the past two decades, some scholars have begun to examine the assumptions underlying the decision making associated with program design (i.e., assumptions about teaching and learning, about the nature of knowledge, and about the role of the educator). Such underlying assumptions are important because they ultimately give rise to differing perspectives on the purpose of educational programs. Miller and Seller (1990), for example, identified three differing program perspectives that they called the transmission, the transaction, and the transformation perspectives. In the transmission perspective, knowledge is equated with the subject matter or content to be learned; knowing is equated with the mastery of facts and skills; and learners are viewed as the passive consumers of this knowledge. From this perspective, the purpose of family life education would be to transmit the facts, skills, and values that prepare one to fit into society. According to the transaction perspective, knowledge is produced through inquiry, and learners are viewed as active and autonomous beings capable of rational thought and problem solving. The purpose of family life education from this perspective would be the development of cognitive skills and abilities and the use of knowledge in problem solving. In the transformation perspective, knowledge has a personal element and is developed through social interaction. Although learners are characterized by diversity and uniqueness, they are also viewed as sharing some common social needs and concerns. The purpose of family life education in this perspective would be to facilitate personal and social change.

Despite their potential importance, underlying assumptions have received little attention in family life education until recently. The work that has been done, however, underscores the significance of examining these assumptions. In a review of the stated aims and objectives of family life education, Thomas (1988) found that, although there was some evidence of the transaction and transformation perspectives, most descriptions of family life programs reflected the transmission perspective. She suggested that there was some dissonance between a conception of family life education for purposes of personal and social transformation and the perception that family life education is centrally concerned with information giving and skill development. Similarly, based on her critical analysis of the assumptions of family life education, Morgaine (1992) has suggested that the practices of the field must be reconceptualized if family life education is to achieve its stated mission.

Program Implementation and Family Life Education Practice

Program implementation is actually one of several stages associated with the introduction of an educational program (Thomas et al., Chapter 5 in Volume 1). These stages include the plans for program use (program adoption), the actual use of the program (implementation), and the stabilization of the program over time (institutionalization). Family life educators must consider important issues at each stage.

Program Adoption

In family life education, attention has focused primarily on the first stage of implementation, with relatively little attention to the latter two stages. For example, family life educators have historically engaged in considerable activity related to introducing and advocating the adoption of family life programs. Much of this activity has been concerned with overcoming public opposition to family life education and has focussed on strategies for conducting needs assessments and for gaining financial, philosophical, and administrative support for programs (e.g., Bruess & Greenberg, 1988; S. N. Wilson & Muraskin, 1985). The nature of these activities suggests that program implementation in family life education has been primarily a political endeavor. According to Fullan (1991), seeking political allies and creating an advocacy network are important first steps in undertaking to put a program into practice, and careful planning at this stage may have a significant influence on whether a program gets started.

Program Implementation

As Thomas et al. (Chapter 5, Volume 1) pointed out, the concern for the adoption of a program represents a very limited understanding of the central issues related to program implementation. In particular, they suggested that assumptions about how programs will actually be used have important implications for both program development and program evaluation. If, for example, fidelity of use is assumed (i.e., programs are used as intended by the program developers), then concerns about the extent to which the actual use of a program corresponds to the planned use become paramount during implementation and in program evaluations. "Scripted" programs, requiring specific training for the educators using them, reflect an assumption of fidelity in implementation, as do programs that outline a series of sequential classes or sessions with accompanying resource materials, specific discussion questions, and detailed guidelines for teaching. Many family life education programs (particularly sexual abuse, parent education, and some couples communication programs) reflect this concern for fidelity. In such cases, the program may be likened to an intervention or a treatment that, when used as intended, is considered to produce some predictable and measurable outcomes.

An alternative assumption about implementation is that programs are altered or adapted in practice by their users to meet the unique characteristics of their educational settings. During implementation, issues related to the situational factors associated with introducing a program and the ways in which the program is altered as it is used become paramount. There is little research on family life programs in use, but some evidence does suggest that adaptation does occur (Thomas et al., Chapter 5 in Volume 1). Program developers and evaluators may therefore need to take into account the potential alteration of programs in use and the impact of adaptation on the intended program outcomes.

At the same time, greater attention might be devoted to the central role of the educator, whose values and beliefs in part shape the program as it is implemented (e.g., Ben-Peretz, 1990). Educators must be able to justify their educational decision making as they adapt or alter programs, for decisions that "simply reflect . . . personal likes and dislikes . . . are [potentially] problematic" (Schmidt & Buchmann, 1983, p. 170).

Family Life Education Pedagogy

When considering program implementation or the actual use of a program, the teaching methodology, or pedagogy, is also relevant. There has been little systematic study of methodology, but many beliefs and preferences about what should constitute family life education pedagogy are evident in the literature. Some beliefs about family life education pedagogy reflect concern for cognitive and affective learning. For example, Klemer and Smith (1974) proposed an "empathic approach" to teaching family life education. This approach was based on their perception that, although the content of family life education can be taught "on an objective, intellectual level," students tend to "become subjective as they apply this knowledge" (p. i). They indicated that the empathic approach was "designed to encourage both subjective and objective teaching and learning" in family life education (p. 1). Similarly, Sheek (1984) referred to an "experiential methodology" in family life education, in which family life educators blend "cognitive and affective approaches to education" (p. 32). In contrast, Dixon (1977) outlined a "propositional testing approach," which involved developing "an atmosphere of empirical truth seeking" (p. 29). According to her, this approach could eliminate or reduce subjectivity in family life education by focusing on "the facts."

Other approaches to family life education pedagogy emphasize an interactive dimension, particularly small group activities. Somerville (1972), for example, identified "small group interaction in response to diverse stimuli" (p. 172) as the key approach in family life education. According to her, this approach was for "the sharing of information and questions among peers." Diverse stimuli included activities such as role-playing, debates, and data gathering. Gross (1985) also indicated that "the essence of all family life education is small group discussion." At the same time, she suggested that family life education is characterized by "two-way learning . . . [in which] . . . both the educator and participants have something to contribute to the group and . . . each can learn something from the other" (p. 22).

Moss and King (1970) described three general approaches to family life education that encompass aspects of all of the pedagogies described above. These approaches varied in terms of their attention to group processes in problem solving and decision making (the group-oriented approach), to the development of individual awareness (the sensitivity approach), or to intellectual development (the thinking-oriented approach). Moss and King stated that most family life educators are "biased toward one or more" of these approaches (p. 79), although they provided no empirical data to substantiate their claim.

An informal review of family life education journals revealed that many of the methodologies or teaching approaches just noted are prevalent in family life education. Most emphasize small group interaction as a means of learning content, and case studies, simulations, role-playing, and other interactive techniques appear frequently in the literature (e.g., Bahr, 1990; Bardour, 1989; Kaplan & Hennon, 1992; Kennedy, 1989; Moore, 1989). It is interesting to note, however, that relatively few articles address strategies for teaching the key family life education processes (i.e., communicating, problem solving, and decision making), and even fewer refer to the development of skills for critical thinking. Some exceptions include Scales (1990), Morgaine (1992), and Allen (1988).

One noteworthy trend in the field is the application of feminist pedagogy. Walker, Kees Martin, and Thompson (1988) discussed feminist principles and assumptions and identified family programs in which these were operationalized or apparent. Allen (1988) developed a framework for integrating a feminist perspective into family studies courses. These writers suggested that feminist theory brings an important perspective to family life education, as it links the personal experiences of individuals and families with the sociopolitical domain, thereby illuminating the inequities that contribute to family problems. In particular, feminist perspectives seek to uncover the power imbalances inherent in gender relations and to transform the social inequities that they create. The recognition in feminism that the "relationships and values of [women's] private, everyday world are shaped by larger social and economic forces" (Weiler, 1988, p. 61) has important implications for creating truly transformative family life education programs.

Program Evaluation

Program evaluation in family life education has generally been quite limited (e.g., Darling, 1987; Small, 1990). Most program evaluations to date reflect a concern with summative evaluation or the measurement and assessment of program outcomes, and most have employed quantitative methods, particularly surveys and experiments (see, for example, Small, 1990; Weiss & Jacobs, 1988). This emphasis in program evaluation appears to be based on the assumption that family life education has a positive influence on program participants, and most evaluation efforts have focused on determining whether changes in knowledge, attitudes, and behavior have occurred (Arcus, 1986). Because each chapter in this volume of the handbook will examine program evaluation related to specific content areas, this section will be limited to a brief discussion of some of the major issues associated with program evaluation in family life education.

As just suggested, most program evaluations in family life education are narrow in scope, limited in methodology, and confined to summative concerns, that is, with measuring program outcomes in relation to program objectives. Few evaluations in family life education have been conducted for formative purposes, that is, to understand how participants understand and respond to a program, how such perceptions and experiences might be related to potential outcomes, or how the program might be improved or revised. The focus on summative purposes in evaluation ignores the actual educational experiences of learners and fails to identify variables apart from the program itself that might influence behavior. Jacobs's (1988) five-tiered approach to evaluating family programs is one recent model that does include both formative and summative components. The model implicitly reflects a concern for fidelity of program implementation, however (i.e., the extent to which the program was implemented as intended by program developers), and formative evaluation strategies are designed with this in mind.

According to some educational writers (e.g., Aoki, 1986), this emphasis on the measurement of program outcomes and the concern for the achievement of program objectives reflect a technical view of evaluation. While such concerns are important with respect to cost-effectiveness, accountability, and funding, important insights for both program design and program impact might be gained if other evaluation perspectives were adopted. For example, if a critical perspective were to be employed in evaluation, the appropriateness of program goals, whether they are educationally justifiable and whether it is reasonable to expect that they might be achieved, could be assessed. As Bruess and Greenberg pointed out, if a program is evaluated in terms of poor or inappropriate objectives, evaluators might come to the conclusion that the program is ineffective, when in fact "the problem would be the objectives and the evaluation, not the program" (p. 302).

Perhaps the limited attention to program evaluation in family life education stems from political issues. Small (1990) suggested, for example, that, in family life education, funding and program evaluation are closely linked, as policymakers demand not only financial accountability but also verification of program effectiveness. If this is indeed the case, it is perhaps not surprising that researchers have learned relatively little about the effectiveness of family life education.

SPECIAL CONSIDERATIONS IN FAMILY LIFE EDUCATION: GENDER, ETHNICITY, AND CLASS

Although the relevance of a life span approach to program development in family life education has been well established (e.g., Arcus, 1987; Hennon & Arcus, 1993), there has been little consideration of the specific characteristics of the audiences for which such programs are planned. In particular, gender, class, and ethnicity have received little attention as factors that might affect family life education programs. This section will review and discuss these factors as they relate to the practice of family life education. It should be noted that, although each will be discussed separately, in reality they are interrelated (e.g., see Weiler, 1988).

To some extent, gender has historically been an issue in family life education. As Lewis-Rowley et al. (Chapter 2, Volume 1) and Somerville (1971) indicated, family life education has long been perceived as female education. Indeed, much of the early education for family living suggested that to become a wife and mother was a female's "God-given right" (Stamp, 1977).

This perception appears to have persisted. Kostash (1987), for example, indicated that in public schools more females continue to enroll in this "classically feminine" subject. A recent national survey of high school family relations courses (King, Simerly, & Packard, 1991) revealed that, although more boys enroll in these courses today than 20 years ago, classes still contain proportionately more girls than boys. Similarly, Scott-Jones and Peebles-Wilson (1986) noted the tendency for more females than males to participate in parent education courses. They also pointed out that many contemporary parent education programs focus on mothers and either trivialize or ignore the changing roles of fathers in child rearing.

The perception of family life education as female education has been also reinforced by some recent research in classrooms. The findings of one study suggested that, even when family life education classes were coeducational (i.e., both females and males were enrolled), the classroom discourse and interaction reflected the predominance of a "female orientation" (Thomas, 1992). This may have been due in part to the fact that all of the family life educators in this study were female. Indeed, as Sheek (1984) pointed out, there is a need for both female and male role models in family life education. S. M. Wilson's (1990) informal study of male and female team teaching in human sexuality underscored Sheek's observation and suggested that role models of both genders may be significant factors in students' comfort level and in their classroom learning.

Paradoxically, while family life education has been described as education for females, some have argued that the implicit conception of females in this education reflects a male perspective. For example, Bubolz and McKenry (Chapter 6 in Volume 1) discussed gender bias in family life education content. Their review revealed that much of the traditional family science content has overlooked the concerns of women and has possibly misrepresented and trivialized female experiences. They concluded that the content of family life education is based on traditional models of male and female role behaviors that inherently reflect an imbalance of power.

The portrayals of males and females in many family life and sexuality education programs and materials also convey a male or patriarchal perspective and reinforce gender stereotypes. Some research in sexuality education suggested that these courses tend to ignore female sexual response, to characterize females as passive victims of male sexuality, and to sanction female sexuality within the context of heterosexual relationships for the purpose of reproduction (e.g., Diorio, 1982; Fine, 1988). Thus females are generally encouraged to repress their sexuality, while males are encouraged to express it (Rury, 1987), and behaviors and attitudes associated with the social conditioning of males and females in a patriarchal society are reinforced and gender inequity is perpetuated (Szirom, 1988).

As suggested earlier, issues of gender are also related to class and ethnicity. A number of writers have criticized family life education for reflecting a particularly narrow orientation to class and ethnicity. For example, in his evaluation of textbooks for family living courses, Rodman (1970) identified a bias toward "white, middle-class" values in family life education materials. Similarly, Scott-Jones and Peebles-Wilson (1986) reported that many parent education programs reflected a bias toward middle-class white female parents. Such programs are generally voluntary, charge a fee, and sometimes require a certain level of competency in the English language, thus potentially excluding parents of a certain socioeconomic status. Moreover, Scott-Jones and Peebles-Wilson stated that many parent education programs give little attention to cultural differences in child-rearing practices or to the differing needs of poor and middle-income parents.

Other writers have examined the portrayal of various ethnic groups in family life and sexuality education materials. Bryant and Coleman's (1988) study revealed that few marriage and family textbooks employed the "cultural variant" perspective in their portrayal of black families. The authors indicated that this perspective more accurately depicts the cultural realities of black families, as they are viewed "within the context of [their] own history and sociopolitical milieu" (p. 259). M. H. Whatley's (1988) report on photographic images of blacks in sexuality texts indicated that blacks were portrayed as "exotic," "sexually dangerous," "asexual," or in terms of "paternal responsibility" (i.e., as members of intact nuclear families). She argued that such portrayals act to reinforce ethnic stereotypes rather than to dispel them.

The preceding examples illustrate the pervasiveness and complexity of issues related to gender, class, and ethnicity in family life education. To date, relatively little has been written that either clarifies the issues or provides specific approaches to creating a more equitable, culturally relevant education for family life. Obviously, this is an area in need of considerable attention by family life educators.

THE FAMILY LIFE EDUCATOR

One of the ongoing concerns in family life education has been that of the preparation of family life educators. Any literature review indicates clearly that competent family life educators are crucial to the successful realization of the goals of the field (e.g., Fohlin, 1971; National Commission on Family Life Education, 1968; National Council on Family Relations, 1984; Somerville, 1971; A. E. Whatley, 1973). Most authors have acknowledged that in many ways the family life educator *is* the program, as it is the educator who selects, designs, and implements the program; selects and uses resources, materials, and activities; and responds to or ignores the interests and needs of the audience. Thus in all ways it is the family life educator who bears responsibility for the shaping of a program and for the nature of the educational experience for the participants. Previous sections of this chapter have referred to specific ways in which the decisions made by family life educators influence the practice of family life education.

Historically, some attention in the field has been directed toward identifying the qualities and characteristics believed to be important in family life educators. To summarize this literature, the following seem to be among the most important: (a) sound knowledge in the content areas of family life education, plus the ability to integrate findings from different disciplines and to apply these to family concepts and issues; (b) knowledge of and identification with the field of family life education itself; (c) skill in using a variety of educational methods and in using and evaluating family life education materials and resources; (d) the ability to work effectively with family life education participants, both individually and in groups; (e) insight into one's own feelings and attitudes concerning family life topics and acceptance of one's own life experiences; and (f) awareness of and the ability to work within the current local situation (Arcus, 1979). Although these are believed to be important characteristics of family life educators, few studies have attempted to examine the relationship between these characteristics and one's success as a family life educator.

While it is an important first step to identify the necessary characteristics of family life educators, major efforts must be directed toward ensuring that educators with the appropriate qualifications are prepared for their role in family life education. Ideally, family life educators would be selected and trained during formal preservice education, with some kind of certification granted at the conclusion of this preparation or at the conclusion of some specific apprenticeship or practice period.

Continuing certification would then be dependent upon evidence of ongoing in-service education in the field.

This ideal preparation process has seldom been met in family life education, however. Few family life educators have gone through any formal selection procedure, and there is little evidence that educational institutions are attempting such selection. Thus, for good or for ill, many family life educators are self-selected. Some family life educators have had some preparation in some of the content areas of family life education, but several surveys have indicated that both the kinds and the amounts of preparation vary considerably (see Arcus, 1986). It is clear that many efforts in recent years have been directed toward the provision of in-service educational experiences for family life educators (e.g., special workshops and training programs), but it is unclear whether this education has had an impact on family life education, and, if so, what kind.

One of the major new developments in recent years has been the establishment of the Family Life Education Certificate program, developed under the auspices of the National Council on Family Relations (1984). This certificate program was designed to recognize those individuals who have met minimum academic criteria in the field of family life education. Because it is a relatively new program, there have been no studies that have examined the influence of this program on the qualifications of family life educators.

CONCLUSIONS

The purpose of this chapter has been to provide an overview of the current status of family life education study and practice. From its beginnings as "mother education" around the turn of this century, the movement called "family life education" is now fairly well established, with many activities taking place under its name. Programs in response to individual and family needs have proliferated, and some progress has been made in clarifying the scholarly foundations of the field.

Despite these signs of the health of the field, considerable work still needs to be done to further the ability of family life education to accomplish its goals. Among those that appear to be the most critical are the following:

1. *Continue the scholarly clarification of the concept of family life education to bring some needed cohesion to the field and to advance its work theoretically, empirically, practically, and politically.* In particular, attention needs to be

given to an examination of the assumptions underlying family life education practice and to the identification of the normative beliefs that characterize the field. Some critical reflection on the operational principles of family life education also appears to be warranted.

2. Become as multidisciplinary as is often claimed, both through the use of knowledge from a broader range of disciplines and through greater cooperation among the contributing disciplines on behalf of individuals and families. As one example, the discussion in this chapter has highlighted the importance of giving attention to concepts and insights from the discipline of education. It is of major concern to note that many family life educators continue to use educational approaches (e.g., the Tylerian approach to program planning, the Values Clarification approach to values education) that have been the subject of considerable scholarly criticism in the educational literature.

3. Give greater attention to issues of diversity (e.g., gender, class, ethnicity) among the participants and the potential participants in family life education programs. Given the field's expressed concerns for valuing and respecting differences, attention to diversity is a critical undertaking and one that is long overdue.

4. Continue efforts toward the professionalization of family life educators. In particular, serious attention needs to be directed toward developing more comprehensive strategies and approaches for preparing family life educators. If indeed the family life educator *is* the program, then programs of preparation need to go beyond the development of technical skills and focus on the assumptions and beliefs that underlie decision making at all stages of family life education program development and delivery.

These critical issues indicate that family life education is still developing as a field of study and practice and that there is no shortage of scholarly and practical questions to be addressed. Within this emergent nature of the field rests both the promise and the challenge of family life education. It is hoped that all family life educators will respond to the challenges to fulfill the promise of family life education to strengthen and enrich individual and family living.

NOTE

1. Although many family life educators have used the term *quality of life* with respect to the goals of family life education, analyses of the concept of quality of life have indicated

that this term does not refer to individual and family well-being but to ensuring that basic needs are met for all who live within a given region (a village, a city, a country). The greater the percentage of those in a given region for whom basic needs are met, the higher the quality of life in that region. (See Arcus, 1985.) Because ensuring that basic human needs are met does not seem to describe what is typically done in family life education, Thomas and Arcus concluded that it was inappropriate to claim improved quality of life as the intended outcome of family life education.

REFERENCES

Allen, K. R. (1988). Integrating a feminist perspective into family studies courses. *Family Relations, 37*, 29-35.

Aoki, T. (1986). Interests, knowledge and evaluation: Alternative approaches to curriculum evaluation. *Journal of Curriculum Theorizing, 6*(4), 27-44.

Arcus, M. E. (1979). In-service education in family life education. *Canadian Journal of Education, 4*(3), 42-52.

Arcus, M. E. (1985, July). Quality of life: Toward conceptual clarification. Paper presented at the Beatrice Paolucci Symposium, Michigan State University, East Lansing, Michigan.

Arcus, M. E. (1986). Should family life education be required for high school students? An examination of the issues. *Family Relations, 35*, 347-356.

Arcus, M. (1987). A framework for life-span family life education. *Family Relations, 36*, 5-10.

Avery, C. E., & Lee, M. R. (1964). Family life education: Its philosophy and purpose. *The Family Life Coordinator, 13*(2), 27-37.

Bahr, K. S. (1990). Student responses to genogram and family chronology. *Family Relations, 39*, 243-249.

Bardour, J. R. (1989). Teaching a course in human relationships and sexuality: A model for personalizing large group instruction. *Family Relations, 38*, 142-148.

Barozzi, R. L., & Engel, J. W. (1985). A survey of attitudes about family life education. *Social Casework, 66*, 106-110.

Ben-Peretz, M. (1990). *The teacher-curriculum encounter: Freeing teachers from the tyranny of facts.* Albany, NY: State University of New York Press.

Blustein, J. (1982). *Parents and children: The ethics of the family.* New York: Oxford University Press.

Bruess, C. C., & Greenberg, J. S. (1988). *Sexuality education: Theory and practice* (2nd ed.). New York: Macmillan.

Bryant, Z. L., & Coleman, M. (1988). The black family as portrayed in marriage and family textbooks. *Family Relations, 37*, 255-259.

Coombs, J. R. (1989). Attitudes as educational goals. In R. W. Marx (Ed.), *Curriculum: Towards developing a common understanding* (pp. 75-93). Victoria: British Columbia Ministry of Education.

Cromwell, R. E., & Thomas, V. L. (1976). Developing resources for family potential: A family action model. *The Family Coordinator, 25*, 13-20.

Daniels, L. B., & Oliver, C. (1977). Values education in Canada: An introduction and current assessment. In H. A. Stevenson & J. D. Wilson (Eds.), *Precepts, policy and process: Perspectives on contemporary Canadian education.* London, Ontario: Alexander, Blake Associates.

Darling, C. A. (1987). Family life education. In M. B. Sussman & S. K. Steinmetz (Eds.), *Handbook of marriage and the family* (pp. 815-833). New York: Plenum.

de Lissovoy, V. (1978). Parent education: White elephant in the classroom? *Youth & Society,* *9,* 315-338.

Diorio, J. A. (1982). Knowledge, autonomy, and the practice of teaching. *Curriculum* *Inquiry, 12*(3), 257-281.

Dixon, B. P. (1977). A tool for teaching family life education. *Canadian Home Economics* *Journal, 27*(3), 28-37.

Fine, M. (1988). Sexuality, schooling, and adolescent females: The missing discourse of desire. *Harvard Educational Review, 58*(1), 29-53.

Fisher, B. L. (1986, February). *Theory building: Delayed development in family life education.* Paper presented at the Symposium on Family Life Education, Brigham Young University, Provo, UT.

Fisher, B. L., & Kerckhoff, R. K. (1981). Family life education: Generating cohesion out of chaos. *Family Relations, 30,* 505-509.

Fohlin, M. B. (1971). Selection and training of teachers for life education programs. *The* *Family Coordinator, 20,* 231-240.

Fournier, D. (1980, May). *Strengthening the premarital dyad: Some effective strategies in* *marriage preparation.* Paper presented at the National Symposium on Building Family Strengths, Lincoln, NE.

Fullan, M. (1991). *The new meaning of educational change.* Toronto, Ontario: OISE Press.

Gaylin, N. L. (1981). Family life education: Behavioral sciences Wonderbread? *Family* *Relations, 30,* 511-516.

Gross, P. (1985). *On family life education: For family life educators* (2nd ed., rev.). Montreal: Centre for Human Relations and Community Studies.

Guerney, B., Jr., & Guerney, L. F. (1981). Family life education as intervention. *Family* *Relations, 30,* 591-598.

Hamm, C. M. (1989). *Philosophical issues in education: An introduction.* Philadelphia: Falmer.

Hennon, C. B., & Arcus, M. (1993). Life-span family life education. In T. H. Brubaker (Ed.), *Current issues in the family: Vol. 1. Family relations: Challenges for the future.* Newbury Park, CA: Sage.

Herold, E. S., Kopf, K. E., & deCarlo, M. (1974). Family life education: Student perspectives. *Canadian Journal of Public Health, 65,* 365-368.

Hersch, R. H., Miller, J. P., & Fielding, G. D. (1980). *Models of moral education: An appraisal.* New York: Longman.

Hill, R., & Aldous, J. (1969). Socialization for marriage and parenthood. In D. A. Goslin (Ed.), *Handbook of socialization theory and research* (pp. 885-950). Chicago: Rand McNally.

Hoopes, M. H., Fisher, B. L., & Barlow, S. H. (1984). *Structured family facilitation programs:* *Enrichment, education, and treatment.* Rockville, MD: Royal Tunbridge Wells.

Jacobs, F. H. (1988). The five-tiered approach to evaluation: Context and implementation. In H. B. Weiss & F. H. Jacobs (Eds.), *Evaluating family programs* (pp. 37-68). New York: Aldine De Gruyter.

Kaplan, L., & Hennon, C. B. (1992). Remarriage education: The personal reflections program. *Family Relations, 41,* 127-134.

Kennedy, G. E. (1989). Involving students in participation research on fatherhood: A case study. *Family Relations, 38,* 3-7.

Kerckhoff, R. K. (1964). Family life education in America. In H. T. Christensen (Ed.), *Handbook of marriage and the family.* Chicago: Rand McNally.

King, K. F., Simerly, C. B., & Packard, M. (1991, November). *Family relations courses taught* *in high schools in the United States 1970-1991.* Paper presented at the annual conference of the National Council on Family Relations, Denver, CO.

Kirkendall, L. A. (1973). Marriage and family living, education for. In A. Ellis & A. Abarbanel (Eds.), *The encyclopedia of sexual behavior* (2nd ed.). New York: Hawthorne.

Klemer, R. H., & Smith, R. M. (1974). *Teaching about family relationships*. Minneapolis, MN: Burgess.

Kostash, M. (1987). *No kidding: Inside the world of teenage girls*. Toronto, Ontario: McClelland and Stewart.

Litke, R. (1976). Who is to say what should be taught in values education. In J. R. Meyer (Ed.), *Reflections on values education* (pp. 89-110). Waterloo, Ontario: Wilfred Laurier University Press.

Lockwood, A. (1978). The effects of Values Clarification and moral development curricula on school age subjects: A critical review of recent research. *Review of Educational Research, 48,* 325-364.

Mace, D. (1981). The long, long trail from information-giving to behavioral change. *Family Relations, 30,* 599-606.

Miller, J. P., & Seller, W. (1990). Curriculum perspectives and practices. New York: Longman.

Moore, C. M. (1989). Teaching about loss and death to junior high school students. *Family Relations, 30,* 3-7.

Morgaine, C. A. (1992). Alternative paradigms for helping families help themselves. *Family Relations, 41,* 12-17.

Moss, J. J., & Elbert, M. (1987, November). *The affective domain in family life education.* Paper presented at the annual meeting of the National Council on Family Relations, Atlanta, GA.

Moss, J. J., & King, K. F. (1970). Involving students for productive learning in marriage and family living classes. *The Family Coordinator, 19,* 78-82.

National Commission on Family Life Education (Task Force of the National Council on Family Relations). (1968). Family life education programs: Principles, plans, procedures. *The Family Coordinator, 17,* 211-214.

National Council on Family Relations. (1970). Position paper on family life education. *The Family Coordinator, 19,* 186.

National Council on Family Relations. (1984). *Standards and criteria for the certification of family life educators, college/university curriculum guidelines, and content guidelines for family life education: A framework for planning programs over the life span.* Minneapolis, MN: Author.

Peters, R. S. (1967). *The concept of education.* London: Routledge & Kegan Paul.

Raths, L. E., Harmin, M., & Simon, S. (1966). *Values and teaching.* Columbus, OH: Charles E. Merrill.

Rodman, H. (1970). *Teaching about families: Textbook evaluations and recommendations for secondary schools.* Cambridge, MA: Howard A. Doyle.

Rury, J. (1987). "We teach the girl repression; the boy expression": Sexuality, sex equity and education in historical perspective. *Peabody Journal of Education, 64*(4), 44-58.

Scales, P. (1990). Prevention and early adolescence: Why we must be filled with wishful thinking. *Family Life Educator, 8*(4), 10-16.

Schmidt, W. H., & Buchmann, M. (1983). Six teachers' beliefs and attitudes and their curricular time allocation. *The Elementary School Journal, 84*(2), 162-171.

Schulte, J. M., & Teal, S. M. (1975). The moral person. *Theory into Practice, 14*(4), 224-235.

Scott-Jones, D., & Peebles-Wilson, W. (1986). Sex equity in parenting and parent education. *Theory into Practice, 25*(4), 235-242.

Shaw, B. (1981). Is there any relationship between educational theory and practice? *British Journal of Educational Studies, 24*(1), 19-28.

Sheek, G. W. (1984). *A nation for families.* Washington, DC: American Home Economics Association.

Small, S. A. (1990). Some issues regarding the evaluation of family life education programs. *Family Relations, 39,* 132-135.

Smith, W. M., Jr. (1968). Family life education—Who needs it? *The Family Coordinator, 17,* 55-61.

Somerville, R. M. (1971). Family life and sex education in the turbulent sixties. *Journal of Marriage and the Family, 33,* 11-35.

Somerville, R. M. (1972). *Introduction to family life and sex education.* Englewood Cliffs, NJ: Prentice-Hall.

Sork, T. J. (1988). Ethical issues in program planning. In R. G. Brockett (Ed.), *Ethical issues in adult education* (pp. 34-50). New York: Columbia University, Teachers College Press.

Stamp, R. (1977). Teaching girls their "God-given place in life." *Atlantis, 2,* 18-34.

Stern, E. E. (1969). Family life education: Some rationales and contents. *The Family Coordinator, 18,* 39-43.

Stewart, J. S. (1976). Problems and contradictions of Values Clarification. In D. Purpel & K. Ryan (Eds.), *Moral education . . . it comes with the territory* (pp. 136-151). Berkeley, CA: McCutchan.

Szirom, T. (1988). *Teaching gender? Sex education and sexual stereotypes.* London: Allen & Unwin.

Thomas, J. (1988, November). *Theoretical perspectives of curriculum in family life education: Implications for practice.* Paper presented at the annual meeting of the National Council on Family Relations, Philadelphia.

Thomas, J. (1992). Two worlds of curriculum: The case of family life education. In L. B. Peterat & E. Vaines (Eds.), *Lives and plans: Signs for transforming practice* (Yearbook 12, pp. 69-88). Mission Hills, CA: Macmillan/McGraw-Hill.

Thomas, J., & Arcus, M. (1992). Family life education: An analysis of the concept. *Family Relations, 41,* 3-8.

Tyler, R. W. (1949). *Basic principles of curriculum and instruction.* Chicago: University of Chicago Press.

Wagman, E., & Cooper, L. (1981). *Family life education: Teacher training manual.* Santa Cruz, CA: Network.

Walker, A. J., Kees Martin, S. S., & Thompson, L. (1988). Feminist programs for families. *Family Relations, 37,* 17-22.

Weiler, K. (1988). *Women teaching for change: Gender, class and power.* South Hadley, MA: Bergin & Garvey.

Weiss, H. B., & Jacobs, F. H. (1988). *Evaluating family programs.* New York: Aldine De Gruyter.

Whatley, A. E. (1973). Graduate students' perceptions of needed personal characteristics for family life educators. *The Family Coordinator, 22,* 193-198.

Whatley, M. H. (1988). Photographic images of blacks in sexuality texts. *Curriculum Inquiry, 18*(2), 137-155.

Wilson, S. M. (1990). Male/female co-teaching of human sexuality: Addressing a gender-linked gap. *Family Life Educator, 8*(2), 4-8.

Wilson, S. N., & Muraskin, L. D. (1985). *Creating family life education programs in the public schools: A guide for state policy makers.* Alexandria, VA: National Association of State Boards of Education.

Wright, L., & L'Abate, L. (1977). Four approaches to family facilitation: Some issues and implications. *The Family Coordinator, 26,* 176-181.

Zais, R. S. (1976). *Curriculum: Principles and foundations.* New York: Crowell.

2

Educating for Marriage and Intimate Relationships

Robert F. Stahmann
Connie J. Salts

BECOMING A COUPLE has been termed one of the most complex and difficult transitions of the family life cycle. It involves negotiation of an enormous number of individual and family of origin issues (McGoldrick, 1989). The interpersonal patterns that are developed during premarital courtship have been found to have an impact on the success of the marriage (Cate & Lloyd, 1988). Thus, to help couples evaluate their relationship and to learn ways to be more successful in their marriage, formal programs in premarital counseling and premarital education programs have been developed (Bagarozzi & Rauen, 1981). Formal marital education was first instituted in the early 1930s when the Merrill-Palmer Institute established a premarital educational program (Rutledge, 1968). One of the earliest premarital counseling programs, established at the Philadelphia Marriage Council (Mudd, Freeman, & Rose, 1941), was designed to provide education and information about married life to couples contemplating marriage and to help prospective spouses work out interpersonal difficulties they might be encountering.

Since that time, a number of factors have probably added to the difficulty of adjusting to marriage. McGoldrick (1989) suggested that the changing role of women, the frequent marriage of partners from widely different cultural backgrounds, and the increasing physical distance from families of origin were placing a much greater burden on couples than was present in traditional family structures. With a lifetime divorce probability now over 50% in the United States (White, 1990), the major task of family life educators could very well be the education and preparation of individuals and couples for marriage and remarriage.

The purpose of this chapter is to provide a critical overview of the literature related to educating for marriage. Theoretical and empirical literature on forming, maintaining, and ending relationships will be reviewed and critiqued for relevance to family life education. Three approaches to education for marriage will be addressed: a general educational model, premarital counseling, and marital enrichment. Issues of divorce and remarriage for family life educators will also be addressed. Finally, future directions for research and program development in this area of family life education will be discussed.

THEORETICAL AND EMPIRICAL FOUNDATIONS

A major tenet in family life education is that programs should be based on a strong scholarly foundation. Thus educating for marriage and intimate relationships requires current theoretical and empirical knowledge about forming, maintaining, and ending relationships. In this section, theories and research on mate selection and premarital relationship development will be reviewed, followed by a review of theory and research related to maintaining relationships and to the process of relationship dissolution. A brief discussion of the relevance of the various theories and research to educational practice will be provided at the end of each section.

Forming Relationships

Many elements involved in the process of mate selection and relationship development have an impact on the potential for success of the marital relationship (Cate & Lloyd, 1988; Surra, 1990). In general, research has indicated that "maritally adjusted and satisfied couples are characterized premaritally by positive communication patterns which are relatively low in anger and resentment, as well as by relatively low rates of arguing and communication of negative feelings" (Cate & Lloyd, 1988, p. 411; Kelly, Huston, & Cate, 1985; Markman, 1979, 1981).

Several theories of mate selection and relationship development have been postulated over the past 40 years in an effort to determine what variables influence premarital and marital relationships. Cate and

Lloyd (1988) categorized these theoretical frameworks for establishing premarital relationship into three types: compatibility, social exchange, and interpersonal process models.

Compatibility Models

Compatibility models of premarital relationships have focused on the importance of matching in such areas as personality, values, roles, and demographic aspects such as age, race, and religion. Three different kinds of compatibility models have been proposed: complementarity, similarity, and sequential filter models.

Winch (1954) held the opinion that the sociocultural environment encouraged homogamy by limiting an individual's choice to a "field of eligibles" who were similar in education, socioeconomic status, culture, religion, race, and age. From this field, the individual then selected a mate based on the psychological factors of complementary needs. A typical example would be a male who is high in dominance selecting a female who is low in dominance, or a woman with a high nurturance need being attracted to a man having a need for succoring (Murstein, 1976a). One major criticism of Winch's theory indicated that efforts to replicate the findings supporting the theory have been unsuccessful (Cate & Lloyd, 1988). As the Cate and Lloyd review indicated, complementarity may be facilitative only in certain role relationships. (For further explanation of the complementary needs model, see Kerckhoff & Davis, 1962; Winch, 1967.)

The second compatibility model states that individuals select marital partners on the basis of similarity rather than complementarity. Similarity between premarital and marital partners has been found on such characteristics as family background, religion, ethnic background, intelligence, personality, attitudes, values, and physical attractiveness (Antill, 1983; Hendrick, 1981; Murstein & Christy, 1976; Schellenberg, 1960). Several criticisms have been raised regarding the similarity model, however (Cate & Lloyd, 1988). For example, one question concerns whether people actually use similarity as an explicit choice factor in mate selection. It has been noted that, as the influence of one's social network declines, people are less likely to select similar partners. Perhaps the main weakness in the similarity theories is that they do not offer an explanation for the many successful marriages that occur between partners who do not have similar characteristics.

Limitations in the similarity and complementarity models have led to the development of various sequential filter models of mate selection

(Kerckhoff & Davis, 1962; Lewis, 1973; Murstein, 1976b). Basically, these models have suggested that individuals evaluate marital compatibility by using different criteria at various stages in the courtship. Kerckhoff and Davis (1962) proposed that individuals first "filter" partners on the basis of social similarity, then by value similarity, and finally on the basis of personality complementarity. Murstein's (1980) filter system included first the stimulus (e.g., physical attractiveness), then values compatibility, followed by role compatibility. In addition to methodological, statistical, and conceptual weaknesses, research findings supporting the sequential filter models have not been replicated and the assumption that dating partners are aware of their partners' attitudes, values, and personalities may not be valid (Cate & Lloyd, 1988).

Social Exchange Models

Social exchange models of relationship development have assumed that the development of a relationship is based on the satisfactory exchange of rewards between partners (Huston & Cate, 1979). There are two different social exchange models: the equity model and the investment model. According to Cate and Lloyd (1988), the equity model of social exchange postulates that initial attraction to a partner, plus the likelihood that the other person will reciprocate one's attraction, are necessary to begin relationship development. This is followed by the partner's provision of rewards not easily available elsewhere, the added dimension that these rewards are at a level high enough to motivate the partners to intensify the involvement, and the expectation that these rewards are likely to be available in the future (Altman & Taylor, 1973; Huesmann & Levinger, 1976; Huston & Cate, 1979; Shanteau & Nagy, 1976). Although the equity model of social exchange has been shown to predict satisfaction with premarital relationships, it has not been found to successfully predict commitment to marriage. In addition, proponents of equity theory have not recognized that equity may play different roles at different times in a relationship (Cate & Lloyd, 1988).

Viewed from the investment model of social exchange, additional aspects that motivate individuals to continue relationships include the steady increase of rewards over time, social network support of the relationship, and the desire not to lose one's previous investment (Rusbult, 1980, 1983). The framework proposes that commitment to a partner is developed when satisfaction with the partner is high, costs in terms of the exchange theory are low, alternatives are low, and investments in the relationship are high. Further information on these models may be found in Huston and Cate (1979) and Rusbult (1980).

Interpersonal Process Model

Recent theoretical work and research in premarital relationships have focused on the development of the interpersonal process framework of mate selection (Cate, Huston, & Nessebroade, 1986; Surra, 1985, 1987). This framework has acknowledged the importance of factors associated with both the compatibility and the social exchange frameworks. The proponents of the interpersonal process model, however, have assumed that the interactions between individuals in the relationship help to shape the development of the relationship and the choice of a mate (Cate & Lloyd, 1988). Compatibility of background, values, personality, and demographic features are less salient issues for this model than is a couple's ability to functionally interact regarding incompatibility in these and other areas (Levinger & Rands, 1985). Cate and Lloyd (1988, p. 422) concluded that courtships differ in their progression to marriage due to "(a) the interpersonal processes that occur between partners, (b) interaction between partners and their networks, (c) intrapsychic factors, and (d) circumstantial or environmental factors." As the interpersonal process model has been proposed rather recently, further research is needed to test the concept. Because this model incorporates the important aspects of the compatibility models and the social exchange models, however, family life educators should include a focus on the interpersonal process model when teaching about relationship development. Further information on the interpersonal process model may be found in Cate, Huston, and Nessebroade (1986), Duck and Sans (1983), and Surra (1985, 1987).

Maintaining Relationships

For the purposes of this chapter, maintaining relationships will address the issues of both marital stability and marital quality. A review of research on divorce and research on marital quality has identified situational factors and interpersonal processes important in the maintenance of marital relationships. The literature relating divorce to various demographic and life course factors, for example, has revealed that persons who have experienced the following are less likely to maintain their marriage: (a) previous marriage, (b) divorced parents, (c) premarital cohabitation, (d) marriage at an early age (in the teens), (e) or premarital bearing of children (White, 1990). This information from high-quality empirical work provides family life educators with information useful in helping couples to identify potential at-risk marriages.

Literature that has related the interpersonal process of couples and families to marital satisfaction and stability provides a basis for the development of educational materials and skill training programs designed to help couples maintain their relationships. Research on relationship quality has indicated that the areas of highest conflict for marital couples are communication, sexuality, and the dispositional characteristics of the partner (Schaap, Buunk, & Kerkstra, 1988). Of these, the communication variable was the best predictor of daily marital satisfaction (Jacobson & Moore, 1981). Three studies have indicated that shared time together is associated with lower divorce rates (Booth, Johnson, White, & Edwards, 1985, 1986; Hill, 1988). Couples in happy marriages were found to spend more time talking, discussing personal topics, and less time in conflict than couples in unhappy marriages (Kirchler, 1989). Nondistressed couples exchanged more rewards (agreement, approval, assent, humor, and laughter) and fewer punishments (criticism, complaints, and sarcastic remarks) than did distressed couples (Noller & Fitzpatrick, 1990).

Research by Gottman and Levenson (1984) indicated that high levels of negative affect produced emotional withdrawal and bursts of negative affect reciprocity in couples. Gottman and Levenson proposed that the "underlying mechanism that maintains closeness in marriages is symmetry in emotional responsiveness, particularly in the kind of low-intensity affective interactions captured by sharing the events of the day" (p. 101). They believed these measures tapped the quality of friendship in marriage. Similar aspects of the interpersonal process have been defined by Reis and Shaver (1988) as intimacy; that is, intimacy is a process of two partners experiencing and expressing feelings, communicating verbally and nonverbally, satisfying social motives, augmenting or reducing social fears, talking and learning about themselves and their unique characteristics, and becoming psychologically and physically close.

From this overview of research and theory on relationships, it can be surmised that education for maintaining successful marriages and intimate relationships should focus on the development of interpersonal processes. The most salient aspects for satisfactory interpersonal relationships appear to be effective communication, time together for talking, and positive affect. Therefore programs for maintaining relationships should include communication training with a focus on the use of positive exchanges and a commitment to spending time together on a daily basis.

In a critique of research on relationship quality and the determinants of divorce, White (1990) discovered that individuals reported their divorces were caused by factors that have not been explored extensively by empirical research on relationship quality. These factors included alcoholism and drug abuse, infidelity, incompatibility, physical and emotional abuse, disagreements about gender roles, sexual incompatibility, and financial problems (Albrecht, Bahr, & Goodman, 1983; Bloom, Niles, & Thatcher, 1985; Cleek & Pearson, 1985; Kitson & Sussman, 1982). This suggests that family life educators need to provide education that will help couples to identify particular problem areas within their relationship that may interfere with satisfying interactions and to include in the educational programs resources and referrals for addressing these specific problems.

Ending Relationships

Understanding the process of ending relationships can improve one's ability to identify relationships that would be best dissolved. As well, it may provide useful input for the prevention of dissolution and for the repair of those relationships where this is desirable (Duck, 1982). In the case of remarriage, preparation for the remarriage begins with the quality of the dissolution that each partner has had from his or her previous spouse (Sager, 1989).

A four-stage conceptual model of the process of relationship dissolution has been proposed by Duck (1982): (a) the intrapsychic stage, which involves internal turmoil caused by an individual's dissatisfaction with the relationship; (b) the dyadic stage, which encompasses mutual negotiation of the breakup with the partner; (c) the social stage, which represents the presentation of the breakup to family and friends; and (d) the grave-dressing stage, which focuses on "getting over" the breakup and coming to terms with past memories. Duck's model offers a global theory of dissolution of intimate relationships, thus it can be used in family life education for dating as well as marital couples.

Many different authors have theorized various stages regarding the process of divorce. Textor (1989) appears to have captured the essence of these different models in his description of divorce as a three-phase transition. First is the predivorce phase in which individuals recognize a sense of relational disenchantment, either with the marriage itself or with their partner. This results in decisional conflict within the individual and/or between the marital partners regarding the move toward separation. Once the decision for separation is made, the divorce phase begins. The actual separation involves issues of change in the financial situation, child rearing, and children's reactions as well as everyday changes in household management, personal habits, and life-style. The divorce phase also involves legal aspects. According to Textor, the postdivorce phase involves network changes, dating, relationship issues with the former spouse, and continued issues of child rearing and the reactions of the children. Many adults continue this transition into the remarriage phase with new courtship issues and stepfamily concerns.

The level of stress and emotional intensity experienced during the divorce process can be extremely high. Whitaker and Keith (1984) have pointed out that marriage is a model of intimacy. While most other intimate relationships involve only parts of the person, marriage is unique in its lifetime commitment, the physical sexuality, and the whole-person to whole-person quality of the relationship. Thus the dissolution of the encompassing aspects of marital intimacy often results in depression about divorce on both an individual and a societal level.

Peck and Manocherian (1988) have suggested that, because divorce is a transitional crisis, the family is required to interrupt its developmental tasks and to negotiate new adjustments and life-cycle phases. The ending of a relationship thus creates major hurdles for the spouses to transcend, with the resolution of the problems taking from 1 to 3 years. Family life education programs that provide support and the provision of educational information may contribute to a speedier divorce adjustment period for some families. Other families, however, may need services such as family therapy that lie outside the family life educator's realm.

APPROACHES TO EDUCATION FOR MARRIAGE

The typical goals of education for marriage and intimate relationships are to increase couple and family stability and satisfaction and to improve the quality of couple and family relationships. Historically, four approaches have been developed to educate for marital preparation, enhancement, and relationship maintenance: generalized educational programs, premarital counseling, enrichment programs, and marital and premarital therapy (Schumm & Denton, 1979).

Marital and premarital therapy are designed for the purpose of assisting a couple with specific problems or concerns that they believe need remediation. Because the problems dealt with in marital and premarital therapy are often complex and severe, they are most appropriately dealt with by a trained marriage and family therapist. In general, therapy is not the province of family life educators, nor do most family life educators have the skills relevant for providing therapy. Therefore the therapy approach will not be further discussed in this chapter.

TABLE 2.1. Content and Goals for Marriage Preparation Programs

---

1. Enhance the communication skills of the couple:

   foster verbal and nonverbal communication (Kelly, Huston, & Cate, 1985;
      Markman, 1979, 1981)
   increase their ability to discuss personal topics (Kirchler, 1989)
   discuss and share events of the day (Gottman & Levenson, 1984)

2. Develop friendship and commitment to the relationship:

   take time together for talking (Kirchler, 1989)
   have fun together (Noller & Fitzpatrick, 1990)

3. Develop couple intimacy:

   share feelings (Gottman & Levenson, 1984)
   share personal experiences (Reis & Shaver, 1988)
   become psychologically close (Reis & Shaver, 1988)

4. Develop problem-solving skills and apply them to the areas of

   marital roles (White, 1990)
   finances (White, 1990)
   affective behavior (Schaap, Buunk, & Kerkstra, 1988)

5. Focus on developing positive, rather than negative, communication (Noller &
   Fitzpatrick, 1990)

This section of the chapter, however, will examine specific goals, methods, strengths, weaknesses, and related issues of generalized educational programs, premarital counseling programs, and marital and premarital enrichment programs. As divorce and remarriage are prominent components of many relationships, specific educational issues for these stages of family life will be addressed. To more effectively use information from the previous section, Table 2.1 provides a summary of the theoretical and empirical basis for selecting content and goals for family life educators and for evaluating and developing approaches to educating for marriage.

General Marriage Preparation Programs

General marriage preparation programs have been offered through family life education classes in high schools and colleges (Cox, 1990; Rice, 1990) and, more recently, through community adult education courses and extension programs (Fitzpatrick, Smith, & Williamson, 1992). The courses are usually structured so that the participant gains knowledge about marriage and relationships and can learn to apply it in practical ways. Therefore goals may include obtaining information (e.g., marriage rates, homogamy, marital satisfaction factors), developing skills (e.g., communication, problem solving, decision making), and exploring values and attitudes (e.g., marital expectations, roles). The goals of marriage preparation in family life education classes differ, however, due to the varying developmental age levels of the participants. At the high school level, because most students have not yet selected a partner, nor are they ready to enter marriage, the focus would be less on the nature of specific relationships and relationship issues and more on the development of knowledge about marriage, gaining general interpersonal skills, exploring attitudes and values regarding marriage, selecting a marriage partner, and other such developmentally appropriate material. Although considerable education for marriage occurs at the high school level, little is known about it beyond various curriculum guidelines such as in Thomas and Farnden (1991), which provides specific resources and activities for teachers to use. Research regarding the effectiveness of various teaching techniques for marriage preparation at the high school level has been limited.

Although there is little specific information available, the marriage preparation programs offered in college/university settings typically use a specific textbook and follow a structured classroom educational format (see Cox, 1990; Rice, 1990). Both instructors and students may find a student study guide to be useful (Kohl, 1990). Kohl's guide contains learning objectives, a summary/outline of the text, and review questions based on the text. Kohl's guide also provides an opportunity for the student to address personally specific topics relating to intimacy, marriage, and the family, as it includes questions and applications on specific topics to assist the student in articulating values and sensitive topics. The technique used by Kohl asks the student to respond by writing personal beliefs, feelings, and attitudes in regard to specific topics. The instructor may or may not review this information with the student.

Research conducted by Avery, Ridley, Leslie, and Handis (1979) indicated that students who participated in a family life education class composed of dating couples (a) studied more, (b) were more motivated to learn, (c) were more interested in the course, and (d) indicated the course material was more relevant than students in a similar class composed of noncouples. Thus more positive outcomes may be obtained from family life education programs when these programs are structured to meet specific current needs and concerns of the participants.

In community education and extension marriage education programs, the experience is often less structured and academic because the
outcome of offering academic credit for the class is not present. Thus
instructors may obtain materials from many sources beyond textbooks,
including popular magazines and lay audience books (Fitzpatrick et al.,
1992). Discussion of topics and experiential exercises would be more
common in these classes, along with structured skill training for couples.

Ulrici, L'Abate, and Wagner (1981) offer a model for categorizing
marital and family skill training programs according to whether the
theoretical orientation of the program is an emotional, reasoning, or
action approach. When offering skill training, family life educators need
to be alert to the psychological dimensions operating within various
programs and to the effect these variables have on program participants.
Ulrici et al. also indicate that family life educators need to use theoretical
frameworks for more explicit investigation of skill training program
outcomes.

Premarital Counseling Programs

Premarital counseling programs are intended to help couples learn
about themselves and to provide them with specific information through a
couple format. This approach is often carried out in the church setting
by trained clergy or laypeople. Clinebell (1984) has argued that in most
cases what has been ordinarily described as premarital counseling actually is not counseling in the sense of dealing mainly with problems.
Rather, it is personalized training, the aim of which is to enhance the
couple's relationship-building insights and communication skills. That
is, it is a type of "educative counseling." Stahmann and Hiebert (1984)
stated that the goal of premarital counseling was to enhance the premarital relationship so that it might develop into a more satisfactory and
stable marital companionship. With this goal, premarital counseling not
only aids in the premarital preparation process but also in the establishment of skills to maintain the quality of the relationship over the life
span. According to Buckner and Salts (1985), a premarital program also
offers the couple an opportunity to assess their strengths and weaknesses
as a couple and, as individuals, to reevaluate and confirm that the
partner is the person that he or she wants to marry.

It has been suggested that there are three key ingredients to a successful marriage: (a) commitment to growth as individuals and as marital partners, (b) an effectively functioning communication system, and
(c) the ability to resolve conflict creatively (Mace, 1986). These ingredi-

TABLE 2.2. Topical Areas for Marriage Preparation Programs

---

1. Marriage as a commitment

2. Family of origin and individual backgrounds

3. Temperaments and personalities of partners (e.g., adaptability, humor)

4. Communication skills

5. Each person's roles in marriage

6. Couple interaction patterns

7. Conflict resolution skills

8. Decision-making skills

9. Financial resources and resource management skills

10. Leisure and recreational interests

11. Educational, work and career goals and expectations

12. Information on sexuality and affection

13. Expectations in regard to children and parenting

14. Religious or spiritual values and expectations

15. Perceived strengths in the relationship

16. Plans for the wedding

---

ents are congruent with the theoretical and empirical findings listed in Table 2.1 and thus can be useful to family life educators in developing programs for the preparation and achievement of successful marriage. A review of selected premarital programs indicates some consistency in the topics covered in these programs.[1] Table 2.2 presents a summary of topic areas that have been included in marital preparation programs and that are consistent with the research recommendations listed in Table 2.1.

In addition to determining goals and specific content for premarital programs, educators must also give attention to format. Several premarital preparation programs have been designed to educate and counsel groups of couples (Bader, Microys, Sinclair, Willett, & Conway, 1980; Bader, Riddle, & Sinclair, 1980; Eichelberg & Wilson, 1972; Freeman, 1965; Gangsei, 1971; Gleason & Prescott, 1977; Meadows & Taplin, 1970; Nickols, Fournier, & Nickols, 1986; Rolfe, 1975, 1977; Rutledge, 1968; Stahmann & Hiebert, 1987). Other programs are designed to educate, counsel, and assess each couple separately (Ball & Henning, 1981; Buckner

& Salts, 1985; Elkin, 1977; Oates & Rowatt, 1975; Olson, Fournier, & Druckman, 1979/1982; Rolfe, 1976; Shonick, 1975; Stahmann & Hiebert, 1980, 1987; Trainer, 1979; Wright, 1977).

According to Gleason and Prescott (1977), there are several advantages to group counseling. It may be more economical than individual counseling because each client pays a lower fee and the group leader can work with more people within a given time period. A group experience may help a couple be more realistic about their relationship by providing them with the opportunity to compare their relationship with others'. Groups also provide feedback from others, and partners can observe how their future spouse interacts with others.

There are limitations to the group format as well. One couple may dominate the group with their needs, especially if they are having a problem in a particular area. All of the issues that are raised by couples in the group may not be addressed due to time constraints of the group, or a couple may identify with another couple in the group and work on that couple's problems rather than their own. As well, some people do not disclose as freely in a group setting, either because they are afraid of a group situation or because they are not able to talk in a group setting (Gleason & Prescott, 1977).

There are a number of advantages to counseling couples individually. The counselor can focus energy and thoughts on one couple instead of dealing with group process issues; topics can be personalized to meet the couple's needs; and a closer relationship may be formed between the educator and the couple, thus allowing for greater sharing. In individual counseling, the couple must focus on their own issues and cannot be sidetracked by issues of other couples. There are also limitations to counseling individual couples, however. In particular, the couple does not have the opportunity to observe how other couple relationships function and to learn from the group experience. As well, some couples may view groups more positively than they do individual counseling (Gleason & Prescott, 1977).

When working with individual couples, some family life educators have suggested that each member should be seen alone at least once to discuss issues that one partner may feel uncomfortable bringing up when the other partner is present (Elkin, 1977; Meadows & Taplin, 1970; Rolfe, 1977; Shonick, 1975). During the individual session, strengths and weaknesses can be discussed, and these can later be shared with the partner during a conjoint session (Shonick, 1975). Stahmann and Hiebert (1987) have indicated a preference for working with the couple together. They gave four reasons for this: (a) It implies that the counselor values the individuals and also the couple's relationship; (b) it gives the counselor a chance to see how the couple interacts, to observe the relationship in action; (c) it can heighten the bilateralism (meaning that marriage is a two-way street, a quid pro quo experience); and (d) it underscores the idea that the counselor does not want to be the keeper of secrets.

The format one chooses for premarital counseling depends on the goals of the program, the couples participating, and the training of the premarital counselor. As yet, the limited research on premarital counseling has not addressed the issue of comparing group and individual couple programs. Nickols, Fournier, and Nickols (1986), however, reviewed factors associated with the success or failure of premarital programs. This review indicated that programs containing relationship skill development or process-oriented activities for the couples were more effective than were lecture/discussion programs. Based on the experience of both researchers and practitioners, they proposed the following process principles for developing or revising existing premarital counseling programs:

(1) that facilitators provide couples with specific information about relationship strengths and weaknesses as early as possible in the program;

(2) that small group discussions be used whenever feasible and over dependence on lecture be avoided;

(3) that programs last long enough to have an impact on couples (avoid one day programs);

(4) that programs occur at least 3 to 6 months before the wedding since couples are less open and distracted as the wedding date nears;

(5) that programs provide pertinent content relevant to marriage and ways to help couples assess their own progress during the program. (Nickols, Fournier, & Nickols, 1986, p. 564)

Using these principles, Nickols, Fournier, and Nickols (1986) developed the Preparation for Marriage Workshop, a program designed for groups of couples. This program was evaluated using PREPARE, an instrument for premarital personal and relationship assessment, in a pretest-posttest research design (Fournier, 1979; Fournier, Olson, & Druckman, 1983; Olson et al., 1979/1982). The findings indicated that couples perceived improvement in their relationship in several categories, with particular satisfaction in the areas of sexual understanding and communication skills. It was noted that teaching communication skills, which enhanced the quality of couple interaction, was basic to the entire workshop.

In an evaluation study designed to assess the potential of the Buckner and Salts (1985) Premarital Assessment Program (PAP), Parish (1990) found that combining the PAP with segments of the Couples Communication Program (Miller, Nunnally, & Wackman, 1975) resulted in the couples making significant gains in dyadic adjustment and commitment to the continuance of the relationship. Use of the PAP alone was not sufficient to obtain these significant gains. These findings indicate that, in addition to a general interactive program such as the PAP, specific communication skill development should be included in premarital programming.

It has been estimated that clergy provide more than 50% of premarital preparation services in the country (Elkin, 1977; Rolfe, 1975; Stahmann & Hiebert, 1987). Overall, little research is available as to the long-term effectiveness of clergy-provided experiences for the couple, but some information is available. At a 6-month follow-up, one study reported little or no benefit to the couples from the general premarital interviews with their clergy members (Guldner, 1971). This study found, however, that postmarital counseling or education was more effective than premarital counseling.

Further investigation of the evaluation of premarital counseling programs has indicated two major methodological problems to overcome in evaluating the effectiveness of a marriage preparation program: self-selection of the participants and defining what is meant by the success of a program (Bader, Microys, et al., 1980). Most program evaluations have relied exclusively upon couple self-report of the benefits derived immediately following the program or their self-report of their marital satisfaction shortly after the wedding, thus providing no information on the long-term effect of premarital counseling (Schumm & Denton, 1979).

One exception was the research conducted by Bader, Microys, et al. (1980). Their pretest-posttest research design included random assignment to a control and to an experimental group. The experimental group participated in a program that used a five-session traditional prewedding approach plus a three-session postwedding component. The first five sessions were held about 3 months before the wedding and the final three sessions were held about 6 months after the wedding.

Evaluation consisted of a self-report questionnaire about family relationships, attitudes, disagreements, and help-seeking behavior, plus two interactive couple tasks. Evaluation was obtained three times: 1

month prior to the program, 1 month prior to the postwedding sessions, and a week or two after the couple's first anniversary.

The couples who participated in the marriage preparation program showed a decrease in reporting conflict about interpersonal topics over the three interviews. In day-to-day living situations, conflict more often had a negative effect on the marriage for those couples who had not participated in the marriage preparation program. Marriage preparation couples showed a steady, significant increase in their ability to resolve hypothetical conflict situations whereas the control couples stayed the same. While help seeking behaviors decreased in both the control group and the experimental groups, it decreased more for the control group after marriage.

It was also found that the experimental couple's ability to resolve hypothetical conflict constructively did not increase significantly from the premarriage sessions to the 6-month interview but did increase significantly from the 6-month to the 1-year interview. The authors implied that sessions after marriage might be more effective than premarital sessions.

In a follow-up study, all of these differences continued to be evident 5 years later. Even though the sample was small at this time, 10% of the control group couples compared with 5% of the experimental group couples were either separated or divorced (Bader, Riddle, et al., 1980). Other differences were also found between the groups; that is, a greater number of experimental couples reported sharing things with their partners and the number of hostile comments used in resolving conflict decreased in the experimental couples but increased in the control couples.

These findings indicate that couples may be ready to address certain issues more effectively following marriage than they are premaritally. Although additional outcome research is needed regarding premarital counseling, these results suggest that education for marriage should extend beyond the premarital stage.

Enrichment Programs

The newest of the approaches to educating for marriage are marital enrichment programs.[2] These programs emerged around the early 1960s, and many were connected to religious institutions (e.g., the Roman Catholic Marriage Encounter program, first established in Spain by Father Gabriel Calvo; the marriage enrichment retreats for Quakers led by David and Vera Mace; the United Methodist Church leadership training programs for couples, developed by Leon and Antoinette Smith; see Mace & Mace, 1986). Several secular programs for marriage enrichment have also been developed, including Otto's *More Joy in Your*

Marriage (1969), the Minnesota Couples Communication Program (Miller et al., 1975), and Relationship Enhancement (Guerney, 1977).

A useful overview of marriage enrichment has been provided by Hof and Miller (1980). These authors noted that marriage enrichment is a philosophy and a process as well as a variety of programs. As a philosophy, marriage enrichment is based on "a philosophy of growth and the human-potential hypothesis that all persons and relationships have a great number of strengths and resources and a tremendous amount of unused potential which can be tapped and developed" (Hof & Miller, 1980, p. 4). Proponents of marriage enrichment believe that all relationships have a need for growth and that, given appropriate conditions, all persons can learn to maintain significant interpersonal relationships. Thus at the core of marriage enrichment is a "positive, growth-oriented, and dynamic view of marriage" (Hof & Miller, 1980, p. 4).

Despite considerable diversity in programs, Hof and Miller (1980) suggested that marriage enrichment as a process typically has the following features: (a) It is dynamic, experiential, educational, and preventive in nature; (b) it typically promotes a balance between relational and individual growth; (c) it is ongoing, that is, the marriage enrichment experience is intended to be a beginning for marital growth, not an end; (d) it focuses on identifying, sharing, and developing the positive aspects of the relationship; and (e) it emphasizes the ability to communicate effectively. It is also important to the process of marriage enrichment that the leaders of the program model the skills and the growth-oriented relationships being promoted (e.g., Mace & Mace, 1976; Regula, 1975).

Numerous programs in marriage enrichment have been developed, including those by Bosco (1973), Clinebell (1975), Dinkmeyer and Carlson (1984), Guerney (1977), L'Abate (1975, 1977), Mace (1982), Miller (1975), Otto (1969, 1976), Regula (1975), and Sherwood and Scherer (1975). More recently, the scope of marital enrichment programs has expanded to include work with specific target groups: alcoholics (Matter, McAllister, & Guerney, 1984), wife batterers (Waldo, 1986), dual-career couples (Avis, 1986b), remarried couples (Ellis, 1984), dating couples (Heitland, 1986), and singles (Preston & Guerney, 1982). Regardless of the specific program, however, the major goals of marriage enrichment are to increase self- and other awareness to explore and express thoughts and feelings with honesty and empathy and to develop and use skills important in relationships, such as communication, problem solving, and conflict resolution (Hof & Miller, 1980). Mace's 1982 book, *Close Companions: The Marriage Enrichment Handbook*, provides an excellent overview of the typical content and process of marriage enrichment programs.

Hof and Miller (1980) identified several differences in the delivery of marriage enrichment programs. Some programs are offered as intensive weekend retreats while others are delivered through a series of weekly meetings. Some programs are highly structured with little opportunity for leader or participant input, while others are relatively nonstructured to meet the emerging needs of a particular group. Programs also differ in the amount of attention given to dyadic interaction, small group or total group interaction, and individual reflection. At the current time, marriage enrichment programs are led by a variety of people (married couples, nonmarried couples, individuals) who have varying professional and nonprofessional backgrounds, degrees of training, and leadership types. This diversity has raised important questions regarding the selection, training, and certification of marriage enrichment leaders. (See Dyer & Dyer, 1986, for a discussion of these issues and for an overview of different leadership training models.)

There have been several major reviews of evaluation research on marriage enrichment programs (e.g., Giblin, 1986; Giblin, Sprenkle, & Sheehan, 1985; Guerney & Maxson, 1990; Zimpfer, 1988). In general, these reviews have indicated that marriage enrichment programs do make a difference. Greater change has been found when programs are longer and when they are experiential and involve behavioral rehearsal processes. The effects of marriage enrichment programs do appear to diminish over time, lending support to advocates of booster programs (Guerney & Maxson, 1990). Despite some evidence of negative effects (e.g., Doherty, Lester, & Leigh, 1986), Guerney and Maxson (1990) have claimed that the basic worth of marriage enrichment has now been established and that the major questions requiring research attention in the future have to do with which programs work best for which populations and why. Other important questions to be addressed include how programs can be made more efficient and less costly and can be better marketed.

Education for Divorce

The major focus of this chapter has been on forming and maintaining relationships, yet, with the high divorce rate, there is a need for education regarding the dynamics of ending the relationship as well. Possibly because it would seem rather paradoxical to do so, few educational efforts have spent time in preparing a couple for divorce.

There are, however, some powerful educational or enrichment programs designed to provide knowledge for those who have already separated or divorced. Several postdivorce group models have proposed that divorced persons need and desire programs that are structured (Fisher, 1974; Granvold & Welch, 1977; Hassall & Madar, 1980; Hoopes, 1978; Kessler, 1977a, 1977b). These groups have used such techniques as time-limited task-oriented sessions, leader-led discussions, and prearranged role-playing. The Fisher (1974) and Kessler (1977a, 1977b) models are examples of such programs that provide information relevant to family life educators. Short-term, structured postdivorce groups have been shown to improve adjustment for individuals who are past the shock and denial stage of divorce adjustment (Salts, 1989).

A review of outcome research on divorce adjustment education groups (Salts, 1989) has indicated that effective groups have been directed toward helping the individual adjust to the status and roles of singlehood. This adjustment involves personal growth and changes in attitudes, feelings, and behavior toward the self, the ex-spouse, children, relatives, friends, sex and dating, marriage, work, hobbies, and life as a whole. These adjustment groups have also provided the divorced adult with the opportunity to achieve autonomy, to gain increased understanding of self and others, and to acquire an enhanced ability to handle problems that may arise in the future (Salts, 1989).

Adjustment groups are not recommended for all divorced individuals. Thus care must be taken to properly screen appropriate participants (Salts, 1989). Family or individual therapy may be the most appropriate program for those divorced persons who are highly stressed and experiencing shock and crisis. To benefit from divorce educational groups, an individual must have resolved basic needs and material support such as finances, housing, food, and child care. Unless these needs have been resolved, an individual is not able to maintain the group focus on emotional and social adjustment (Salts, 1989).

Education for Remarriage

Current estimates indicate that two thirds of all recently contracted first marriages will eventually end in divorce. At the current time, over 40% of marriages in the United States are remarriages for one or for both partners. Among marriages formed between 1980 and 1985, the divorce rate is 25% higher for second than for first marriages (Glick, 1980; Martin & Bumpass, 1989). For the family life educator, these statistics indicate that the need for education for remarriage and the forming of stepfamilies is just as important as education for first marriages.

The need for family life education for remarried family members has repeatedly been mentioned in the literature (Chilman, 1983; Hutchinson

& Hutchinson, 1979; Pasley, 1985; Pasley & Ihinger-Tallman, 1982; Pill, 1981; Rolfe, 1985; Turnbull & Turnbull, 1983). In a study of 784 remarried men and women (Pasley, 1985), only 6% of the men and 9.5% of the women had used counseling services. The majority turned to more informal sources of support and education, such as lectures and workshops. Chilman (1983) suggested that low-cost, effective educational programs should confront such issues as the negative effect of comparing the remarried family with the nuclear family, the development of communication skills, and recognition that negative feelings between ex-spouses need to be eliminated. Hutchinson and Hutchinson (1979) outlined a potential six-session program that would focus on remarried family relationships, stepfamily histories, communication, decision making, and celebration.

Following an extensive review of the literature, Fitzpatrick et al. (1992) listed the most commonly cited remarried family challenges. These challenges were organized into seven categories identified as salient to remarried family development:

(a) creating a unique family style,
(b) combining two families and meeting everyone's needs,
(c) developing a solid marital relationship,
(d) defining the stepparent role,
(e) deciding on discipline,
(f) defining relationships with extended family members, and
(g) coping with economic issues.

Fitzpatrick et al. (1992) used this information to develop two versions of a remarried education program, one for use by professionals providing family life education and one for use by the general public. Two formats for presenting the material were employed: a written format and an audiotape format. The professional version of the program was evaluated for its effectiveness in increasing the understanding of county extension agents regarding remarried family issues. Results from research using a pretest-posttest design indicated that professionals using the written format had significantly greater posttest scores on the evaluation measure (Fitzpatrick et al., 1992).

One of the problems in research on remarriage and stepfamilies has been the use of the nuclear family ideology as the implicit norm for evaluation purposes, with inadequate attention given to the structural complexity and diversity of remarriages and stepfamilies (Coleman & Ganong, 1990). Because remarriage must be considered to be a process that may have begun with the previous marriage and family experiences and cannot be understood without careful consideration of the couple's experiences preceding the remarriage (Coleman & Ganong, 1990), it is important for family life educators to develop programs that acknowledge and work with the differences between first marriages and remarriages.

Issues, Needs, and New Directions in Educating for Relationships

Although the current literature about educating for marriage and intimate relationships provides important information for family life educators, there are a number of gaps and some relatively unresolved areas.

Who determines the content of family life education programs dealing with preparation for marriage? Schumm and Denton (1979) pointed out that virtually all premarital programs have been designed without input from the premarital couples themselves. A recent study echoed this same view and pointed out that the topics covered in most marriage preparation programs have been based on the ideas of clinicians and researchers rather than on those of the clients or consumers of such programs (Sillman & Schumm, 1989). Thus they surveyed young single adults (ages 18-25) at a midwestern university and found that they "are interested in both interactive skills, such as listening and conflict resolution, and specific issues, such as parenting and money management." They found that the students ranked marital roles, sexuality, and stress management lower than expected and suggested that this "may reflect some lack of an awareness of day-to-day issues in married life. In this regard, young adults may use experience with premarital relationships and role focused impressions of marriage to anticipate priority issues in married life. If this speculation is fact, one important caveat is that clients' input should be a critical, but not solitary determinant of premarital programming" (Sillman & Schumm, 1989, pp. 204-205). Thus an important message for the family life educator is to use input from all sources—theoretical, clinical, educational, and the consumer—in designing and delivering education for marriage.

Throughout the review of literature for this chapter, it was encouraging to see a focus on strengths for marriage rather than on problems or dysfunctions of marriage. Helping individuals to look at themselves, their intended spouses, their families of origin, interpersonal skills, marital expectations, and so on as a foundation for a healthy and functional marriage appears to be the most productive and justified marriage preparation model. This strength approach is the main thrust in a majority of the new literature available and is found in the most recent edition of a widely used college-level textbook in marriage preparation (Cox, 1990).

There are many so-called self-help books, magazine articles, audio- and videotapes, public speakers, and so forth that focus on marriage and are widely available to the public. As limited research is available regarding the credibility of these materials, however, the family life educator should be cautious when using them. Specifically, the materials should be critiqued as to whether the information is accurate and current and is suited to the audience and goals of the planned program. An important function of family life education is to assist people in being wise consumers of these materials and to skillfully integrate them into programs for marriage preparation.

What about life span education for marriage? What can people expect and what can be done to foster appropriate marital growth and adjustment over the years? Some textbooks (Cox, 1990; Rice, 1990) have attempted to address this question but have provided minimal information. For example, one excellent text devotes only 30 of 626 pages in a chapter titled "Family Life Stages: Middle Age to Surviving Spouse" (Cox, 1990). This is an area in need of some attention in family life education.

Thus far, the literature has not addressed the issue of educational level and ethnicity in regard to educating for marriage and intimate relationships. In most of the research on the effectiveness of marital enrichment, the level of education for participants was high (i.e., 15 years, which is well above the U.S. average; Guerney & Maxson, 1990) and most of the samples were mainly white. A future task is to determine which programs work best for what populations, including various educational levels and ethnic populations.

The issues of gender and the changing roles of both men and women must also be addressed in the programs offered by the family life educator. The family life educator's role is to help people of both sexes learn a nonsexist view regarding the meaning, the responsibilities, and the limitations of their gender. To provide nonsexist information, family life educators must become aware of their personal values regarding gender. Family life educators may or may not have stereotypical expectations of men and women, accept traditional relationship arrangements as the most functional (if not ideal) arrangements, and fail to appreciate the consequences of traditional socialization. There is the possibility that family life educators may respond differently to men and women and behave in ways that reinforce stereotyped roles and behaviors, whether or not they do so intentionally. Avis (1986a) pointed out four biases that may be particularly prevalent among family life educators: (a) assuming that moving into or remaining in a marriage would result in better adjustment for women, (b) demonstrating less interest in and sensitivity to a woman's career than a man's, (c) perpetuating the belief that a child's problems and child rearing are primarily women's responsibilities, and (d) deferring to a husband's needs over a wife's. Thus the issue of gender needs to be addressed both as content for family life education and as personal awareness issues for family life educators.

There has been some suggestion that the timing for marital preparation may not be limited only to that time before marriage! That is, perhaps the best way to prepare for marriage is to begin the process before the wedding and to continue it after the wedding. This is not to deny the evidence that the majority of the programs discussed in this chapter have had an important impact as premarital programs. Yet, at least three studies have suggested that postwedding counseling sessions are more likely to prepare couples for marriage than are premarital counseling programs. Guldner (1971) was the first to directly explore this question. He concluded that engaged couples were too "starry eyed" to be objective about their relationships. His research indicated that the effectiveness of premarital counseling was limited because "couples needed some time to experience the realities of marriage before they can respond adequately to external help with their marriage" and thus were more capable of responding to counseling after 6 months of marriage than were engaged couples (p. 118). In his study, Baum (1977) found that couples who were living together scored much better in pre- and posttests that measured improvement in their relationships than did engaged couples. Another study observed that "the sessions after marriage were more effective than those before marriage" (Bader, Microys, et al., 1980, p. 177). Thus future research needs to address the timing regarding educating for marriage and intimate relationships.

Educating for marriage and intimate relationships is a crucial role for family life educators. Although most people expect family life educators to have the knowledge and ability to educate for marriage and intimate relationships, the research base for such knowledge and application is limited and needs to be expanded.

NOTES

1. See Bader, Microys, et al. (1980); Bader, Riddle, et al. (1980); Ball and Henning (1981); Buckner and Salts (1985); Eichelberg and Wilson (1972); Elkin (1977); Freeman (1965); Gangsei (1971); Gleason and Prescott (1977); Meadows and Taplin (1970); Nickols, Fournier, and Nickols (1986); Oates and Rowatt (1975); Olson et al. (1979/1982); Rolfe

(1975, 1976, 1977); Rutledge (1968); Shonick (1975); Stahmann and Hiebert (1980, 1987); Trainer (1979); and Wright (1977).

2. Only marriage enrichment programs will be discussed in this chapter. For information on family enrichment, see Sawin (1986).

REFERENCES

Albrecht, S., Bahr, H., & Goodman, K. (1983). *Divorce and remarriage: Problems, adaptations, and adjustments.* Westport, CT: Greenwood.

Altman, I., & Taylor, D. (1973). *Social penetration: The development of interpersonal relationships.* New York: Holt, Rinehart & Winston.

Antill, J. (1983). Sex role complementarity versus similarity in married couples. *Journal of Personality and Social Psychology, 45,* 145-155.

Avery, A. W., Ridley, C. A., Leslie, L. A., & Handis, M. (1979). Teaching of family relations to dating couples versus non-couples: Who learns better? *The Family Coordinator, 28,* 41-45.

Avis, J. (1986a). Feminist issues in family therapy. In F. Piercy & D. Sprenkle (Eds.), *Family therapy sourcebook* (pp. 213-242). New York: Guilford.

Avis, J. M. (1986b). Working together: An enrichment program for dual-career couples. *Journal of Psychotherapy and the Family, 2,* 29-45.

Bader, E., Microys, G., Sinclair, C., Willett, E., & Conway, B. (1980). Do marriage preparation programs really work? A Canadian experiment. *Journal of Marital and Family Therapy, 6,* 171-179.

Bader, E., Riddle, R., & Sinclair, C. (1980). *Do marriage preparation programs help? A five year study.* Toronto: University of Toronto, Department of family and Community Medicine.

Bagarozzi, D., & Rauen, P. (1981). Premarital counseling: Appraisal and status. *American Journal of Family Therapy, 9*(3), 13-28.

Ball, J., & Henning, L. (1981). Rational suggestions for premarital counseling. *Journal of Marital and Family Therapy, 7*(1), 69-73.

Baum, M. (1977). The short term, long term, and differential effects of group vs. bibliotherapy relationship enhancement programs for couples (Doctoral dissertation, University of Texas, Austin). *Dissertation Abstracts International, 38,* 6132B-6133B.

Bloom, B., Niles, R., & Thatcher, A. (1985). Sources of marital dissatisfaction among newly separated persons. *Journal of Family Issues, 6,* 359-373.

Booth, A., Johnson, D., White, L., & Edwards, J. (1985). Predicting divorce and permanent separation. *Journal of Family Issues, 6,* 331-346.

Booth, A., Johnson, D., White, L., & Edwards, J. (1986). Divorce and marital instability over the life course. *Journal of Marriage and the Family, 49,* 549-558.

Bosco, A. (1973). *Marriage Encounter: A rediscovery of love.* St. Meinard, IN: Abbey.

Buckner, L., & Salts, C. (1985). A premarital assessment program. *Family Relations, 34,* 513-520.

Cate, R., Huston, T., & Nessebroade, J. (1986). Premarital relationships: Toward the identification of alternative pathways to marriage. *Journal of Social and Clinical Psychology, 4,* 3-22.

Cate, R., & Lloyd, S. (1988). Courtship. In S. Duck (Ed.), *Handbook of personal relationships* (pp. 409-427). London: Academic Press.

Chilman, C. (1983). Remarriage and stepfamilies: Research results and implications. In E. Macklin & R. Rubin (Eds.), *Contemporary families and alternative lifestyles* (pp. 147-163). Beverly Hills, CA: Sage.

Cleek, M., & Pearson, T. (1985). Perceived causes of divorce: An analysis of interrelationships. *Journal of Marriage and the Family, 47*, 179-183.

Clinebell, H. J. (1975). *Growth counseling for marriage enrichment*. Ann Arbor, MI: Books on Demand.

Clinebell, H. (1984). Religious and value dimensions in prewedding counseling. In R. Stahmann & W. Hiebert (Eds.), *Counseling in marital and sexual problems* (pp. 249-263). Lexington, MA: Lexington.

Coleman, M., & Ganong, L. (1990). Remarriage and stepfamily research in the 1980s: Increased interest in an old family form. *Journal of Marriage and the Family, 52*, 925-940.

Cox, F. (1990). *Human intimacy: Marriage, the family and its meaning* (5th ed.). St. Paul, MN: West.

Dinkmeyer, D., & Carlson, J. (1984). *TIME for a better marriage*. New York: Random House.

Doherty, W. J., Lester, M. E., & Leigh, G. (1986). Marriage Encounter weekends: Couples who win and couples who lose. *Journal of Marital and Family Therapy, 12*, 49-61.

Duck, S. (1982). A topography of relationship disengagement and dissolution. In S. Duck (Ed.), *Personal relationships: Vol. 4. Dissolving personal relations* (pp. 1-30). London: Academic Press.

Duck, S. W., & Sans, H. K. A. (1983). On the origins of the specious: Are interpersonal relationships really interpersonal states? *Journal of Social and Clinical Psychology, 1*, 27-41.

Dyer, P. M., & Dyer, G. H. (1986). Leadership training for marriage and family enrichment. *Journal of Psychotherapy and the Family, 2*, 97-110.

Eichelberg, S., & Wilson, A. (1972). Experiments in group premarital counseling. *Social Casework, 53*, 551-562.

Elkin, M. (1977). Premarital counseling for minors: The Los Angeles experience. *Family Coordinator, 26*, 429-443.

Ellis, A. J. (1984). Second time around: A preventive intervention for remarried couples. *Australian Journal of Sex, Marriage and Family, 5*, 139-146.

Fisher, E. (1974). *Divorce: The new freedom. A guide to divorcing and divorce counseling*. New York: Harper.

Fitzpatrick, J., Smith, T., & Williamson, S. (1992). Educating extension agents: An evaluation of method and development of a remarried family education program. *Family Relations, 41*, 70-73.

Fournier, D. (1979). 1979 validation of PREPARE: A premarital counseling inventory (Doctoral dissertation, University of Minnesota). *Dissertation Abstracts International, 40*(6), 23-85.

Fournier, D., Olson, D., & Druckman, J. (1983). Assessing marital and premarital relationships: The PREPARE-ENRICH inventories. In E. Filsinger (Ed.), *A sourcebook in marriage and family assessment* (pp. 229-250). Beverly Hills, CA: Sage.

Freeman, D. (1965). Counseling engaged couples in small groups. *Social Work, 10*, 36-42.

Gangsei, L. (1971). *Manual for group premarital counseling*. New York: Association Press.

Giblin, P. (1986). Research and assessment in marriage and family enrichment: A meta-analysis study. In W. Denton (Ed.), *Marriage and family enrichment* (pp. 79-96). New York: Haworth.

Giblin, P., Sprenkle, D., & Sheehan, R. (1985). Enrichment outcome research: A meta-analysis of premarital, marital, and family interventions. *Journal of Marital and Family Therapy, 11*, 257-271.

Gleason, J., & Prescott, M. (1977). Group techniques for premarital preparation. *Family Coordinator, 26*, 277-280.

Glick, P. (1980). Remarriage: Some recent changes and variations. *Journal of Family Issues, 1*, 455-478.

Gottman, J., & Levenson, R. (1984). Why marriages fail: Affective and physiological patterns in marital interaction. In J. Masters & K. Yarkin-Levin (Eds.), *Boundary areas in social and developmental psychology* (pp. 67-106). New York: Academic Press.

Granvold, D., & Welch, G. (1977). Intervention for postdivorce adjustment problems: The treatment seminar. *Journal of Divorce, 1,* 81-92.

Guerney, B. (1977). *Relationship enhancement: Skill-training programs for therapy, problem prevention, and enrichment.* San Francisco: Jossey-Bass.

Guerney, B., & Maxson, P. (1990). Marital and family enrichment research: A decade review and look ahead. *Journal for Marriage and the Family, 52,* 1127-1135.

Guldner, C. (1971). The post-marital: An alternate to pre-marital counseling. *The Family Coordinator, 20,* 115-119.

Hassall, E., & Madar, D. (1980). Crisis group therapy with the separated and divorced. *Family Relations, 29,* 591-197.

Heitland, W. (1986). An experimental communication program for premarital dating couples. *School Counselor, 34,* 57-61.

Hendrick, S. (1981). Self-disclosure and marital satisfaction. *Journal of Personality and Social Psychology, 40,* 1150-1159.

Hill, M. (1988). Marital stability and spouses' shared time. *Journal of Family Issues, 9,* 427-451.

Hof, L., & Miller, W. R. (1980). Marriage enrichment. *Marriage & Family Review, 3,* 1-27.

Hoopes, M. (1978). *Structured group treatment for divorced persons.* Unpublished outline, Brigham Young University, Provo, UT.

Huesmann, L., & Levinger, G. (1976). Incremental exchange theory: A formal model for progression in dyadic social interaction. In L. Berkowitz & E. Walsher (Eds.), *Advances in experimental social psychology* (pp. 193-229). New York: Academic Press.

Huston, T., & Cate, R. (1979). Social exchange in intimate relationships. In M. Cood & G. Wilson (Eds.), *Love and attractions* (pp. 263-269). London: Pergamon.

Hutchinson, I., & Hutchinson, K. (1979). Issues and conflicts in stepfamilies. *Family Perspectives, 13*(3), 111-121.

Jacobson, N., & Moore, D. (1981). Spouses as observers of events in their relationship. *Journal of Consulting and Clinical Psychology, 49,* 269-277.

Kelly, C., Huston, T., & Cate, R. (1985). Premarital relationships correlates of the erosion of satisfaction in marriage. *Journal of Social and Personal Relationships, 2,* 167-178.

Kerckhoff, A., & Davis, K. (1962). Value consensus and need complementarity in mate selection. *American Sociological Review, 27,* 295-303.

Kessler, S. (1977a). *Beyond divorce: Leader's guide.* Atlanta, GA: National Institute for Professional Training.

Kessler, S. (1977b). *Beyond divorce: Participants guide.* Atlanta, GA: National Institute for Professional Training.

Kirchler, E. (1989). Everyday life experiences at home: An interaction diary approach to assess marital relationships. *Journal of Family Psychology, 2,* 311-336.

Kitson, G., & Sussman, M. (1982). Marital complaints, demographic characteristics, and symptoms of mental distress in divorce. *Journal of Marriage and the Family, 44,* 87-101.

Kohl, J. (1990). *Study guide to accompany intimate relationships, marriages, and families.* Mountain View, CA: Mayfield.

L'Abate, L. (1975). *Manual: Enrichment programs for the family life cycle.* Atlanta, GA: Social Research Laboratories.

L'Abate, L. (1977). *Enrichment: Structural interventions with couples, families and groups.* Washington, DC: University Press of America.

Levinger, G., & Rands, M. (1985). Compatibility in marriage and other close relationships. In W. Ickes (Ed.), *Compatible and incompatible relationships* (pp. 308-332). New York: Springer-Verlag.

Lewis, R. (1973). A longitudinal test of the developmental framework for premarital dyadic formation. *Journal of Marriage and the Family, 35,* 16-25.

Mace, D. (1982). *Close companions: The marriage enrichment handbook.* New York: Continuum.

Mace, D. (1986). Three ways of helping married couples. *Journal of Marital and Family Therapy, 13,* 179-185.

Mace, D., & Mace, V. (1976). The selection, training and certification of facilitators for marriage enrichment programs. *The Family Coordinator, 25,* 117-125.

Mace, D., & Mace, V. (1986). The history and present status of the marriage and family enrichment movement. In W. Denton (Ed.), *Marriage and family enrichment* (pp. 7-18). New York: Haworth.

Markman, H. (1979). The application of a behavioral model of marriage in predicting relationship satisfaction of couples planning marriage. *Journal of Consulting and Clinical Psychology, 47,* 743-749.

Markman, H. (1981). Predicting marital distress: A 5-year follow-up. *Journal of Consulting and Clinical Psychology, 49,* 760-762.

Martin, T., & Bumpass, L. (1989). Recent trends in marital disruption. *Demography, 26,* 37-51.

Matter, M., McAllister, W., & Guerney, B. G. (1984). Relationship enhancement for the recovering couple: Working with the intangible. *Focus on Family and Clinical Dependency, 7,* 21-23.

McGoldrick, M. (1989). The joining of families through marriage: The new couple. In B. Carter & M. McGoldrick (Eds.), *The changing family life cycle* (pp. 209-234). Boston: Allyn & Bacon.

Meadows, M., & Taplin, J. (1970). Premarital counseling with college students: A promising triad. *Journal of Counseling Psychology, 17,* 516-518.

Miller, S. (Ed.). (1975). *Marriages and families: Enrichment through communications.* Beverly Hills, CA: Sage.

Miller, S., Nunnally, E. W., & Wackman, D. B. (1975). *Minnesota Couples Communication Program: Instructor's manual.* Minneapolis, MN: Interpersonal Communications Program.

Mudd, E., Freeman, C., & Rose, E. (1941). Premarital counseling in the Philadelphia marriage counsel. *Mental Hygiene, 25*(1), 98-119.

Murstein, B. (1976a). Qualities of desired spouses: A cross-cultural comparison between French and American students. *Journal of Comparative Studies, 7,* 455-469.

Murstein, B. (1976b). *Who will marry whom? Theories and research in marital choices.* New York: Springer.

Murstein, B. (1980). Mate selection in the 1970's. *Journal of Marriage and the Family, 42,* 777-792.

Murstein, B., & Christy, P. (1976). Physical attractiveness and marital adjustment in middle-aged couples. *Journal of Personality and Social Psychology, 34,* 537-542.

Nickols, S., Fournier, D., & Nickols, S. (1986). Evaluations of a preparation for marriage workshop. *Family Relations, 35,* 563-571.

Noller, P., & Fitzpatrick, M. (1990). Marital communication in the eighties. *Journal of Marriage and the Family, 52,* 832-843.

Oates, W., & Rowatt, W. (1975). *Before you marry them.* Nashville, TN: Broadman.

Olson, D., Fournier, D., & Druckman, J. (1982). *PREPARE-ENRICH counselors manual* (rev. ed.). (Available from PREPARE-ENRICH, P.O. Box 1363, Stillwater, OK 74076) (Original work published 1979)

Otto, H. A. (1969). *More joy in your marriage.* New York: Hawthorne.

Otto, H. A. (Ed.). (1976). *Marriage and family enrichment: New perspectives and programs.* Nashville, TN: Abingdon.

Parish, W. (1990, October). *A quasi-experimental evaluation of the premarital assessment program for premarital counseling.* Poster presentation, American Association for Marriage and Family Therapy Annual Meeting, Washington, DC.

Pasley, K. (1985). Stepfathers. In S. Hanson & F. Bozett (Eds.), *Dimensions of fatherhood.* Beverly Hills, CA: Sage.

Pasley, K., & Ihinger-Tallman, M. (1982). Stress in remarried families. *Family Perspective, 16*(4), 181-189.

Peck, J., & Manocherian, J. (1988). Divorce in the changing family life cycle. In B. Carter & M. McGoldrick (Eds.), *The changing family life cycle* (2nd ed., pp. 335-370). New York: Gardner.

Pill, C. (1981). A family life education group for working with stepparents. *Journal of Contemporary Social Work, 62*(3), 159-166.

Preston, J. D., & Guerney, B. G. (1982). *Relationship enhancement skill training.* (Available from the Department of Human Development and Family Studies, Catherine Beecher House, Pennsylvania State University, University Park, PA 16802)

Regula, R. B. (1975). Marriage Encounter: What makes it work? *The Family Coordinator, 24,* 153-159.

Reis, H., & Shaver, P. (1988). Intimacy as an interpersonal process. In S. Duck (Ed.), *Handbook of personal relationships* (pp. 367-389). London: Academic Press.

Rice, F. (1990). *Intimate relationships, marriages and families.* Mountain View, CA: Mayfield.

Rolfe, D. (1975). *Marriage preparation manual.* New York: Paulist Press.

Rolfe, D. (1976). Premarriage assessment of teenage couples. *Journal of Family Counseling, 4,* 32-39.

Rolfe, D. (1977). Techniques with premarriage groups. *British Journal of Guidance and Counseling, 5,* 89-97.

Rolfe, D. (1985). Preparing the previously married for second marriage. *The Journal of Pastoral Care, 34,* 110-122.

Rusbult, C. (1980). Commitment and satisfaction in romantic associations: A test of the investment model. *Journal of Experimental Social Psychology, 16,* 172-186.

Rusbult, C. (1983). A longitudinal test of the investment model: The development (and deterioration) of satisfaction and commitment in heterosexual involvements. *Journal of Personality and Social Psychology, 45,* 101-117.

Rutledge, A. (1968). An illustrative look at the history of premarital counseling. In J. Peterson (Ed.), *Marriage and family counseling.* New York: Association Press.

Sager, C. (1989). Treatment of the remarried family. In M. Textor (Ed.), *The divorce and divorce therapy handbook* (pp. 351-368). Northvale, NJ: Jason Aronson.

Salts, C. (1989). Group therapy for divorced adults. In M. Textor (Ed.), *The divorce and divorce therapy handbook* (pp. 285-300). Northvale, NJ: Jason Aronson.

Sawin, M. M. (1986). The family cluster approach to family enrichment. In W. Denton (Ed.), *Marriage and family enrichment* (pp. 47-57). New York: Haworth.

Schaap, C., Buunk, B., & Kerkstra, A. (1988). Marital conflict resolution. In P. Noller & M. Fitzpatrick (Eds.), *Perspective on marital interaction* (pp. 203-244). Clevedon, England: Multilingual Matters.

Schellenberg, J. (1960). Homogamy in personal values and the "field of eligibles." *Social Forces, 39,* 157-162.

Schumm, W., & Denton, W. (1979). Trends in pre-marital counseling. *Journal of Marital and Family Therapy, 5,* 23-32.

Shanteau, J., & Nagy, G. (1976). Decisions made about other people: A human judgment analysis of dating choice. In J. Caroll & J. Payne (Eds.), *Cognition and social judgment* (pp. 221-242). Hillsdale, NJ: Lawrence Erlbaum.

Sherwood, J. J., & Scherer, J. J. (1975). A model for couples: How two can grow together. In S. Miller (Ed.), *Marriages and families: Enrichment through communication.* Beverly Hills, CA: Sage.

Shonick, H. (1975). Premarital counseling: Three years experience of a unique service. *The Family Coordinator, 24,* 321-324.

Sillman, B., & Schumm, W. (1989). Topics of interest in premarital counseling: Clients' views. *Journal of Sex & Marital Therapy, 15,* 199-205.

Stahmann, R., & Hiebert, W. (1980). *Premarital counseling.* Lexington, MA: Lexington.

Stahmann, R., & Hiebert, W. (1984). Process and content in prewedding counseling. In R. Stahmann & W. Hiebert (Eds.), *Counseling in marital and sexual problems* (pp. 237-248). Lexington, MA: Lexington.

Stahmann, R., & Hiebert, W. (1987). *Premarital counseling: The professional's handbook* (2nd ed.). Lexington, MA: Lexington.

Surra, C. (1985). Courtship types: Variations in interdependence between partners and social networks. *Journal of Personality and Social Psychology, 56,* 357-375.

Surra, C. (1987). Reasons for changes in commitment: Variations by courtship style. *Journal of Social and Personal Relationships, 4,* 17-33.

Surra, C. (1990). Research and theory on mate selection and premarital relationships in the 1980's. *Journal of Marriage and the Family, 52,* 844-865.

Textor, M. (1989). The divorce transition. In M. Textor (Ed.), *The divorce and divorce therapy handbook* (pp. 3-43). Northvale, NJ: Jason Aronson.

Thomas, J., & Farnden, R. (1991). *Teaching about marriage preparation: A resource package for teachers.* Vancouver: British Columbia Council for the Family.

Trainer, J. (1979). Pre-marital counseling and examination. *Journal of Marital and Family Therapy, 5,* 61-78.

Turnbull, S., & Turnbull, J. (1983). To dream the impossible dream: An agenda for discussion with stepparents. *Family Relations, 32*(2), 227-230.

Ulrici, D., L'Abate, L., & Wagner, V. (1981). The E-R-A model: A heuristic framework for classification of skill training programs for couples and families. *Family Relations, 30,* 307-315.

Waldo, M. (1986). Group counseling for military personnel who batter their wives. *Journal for Specialists in Group Work, 2,* 132-138.

Whitaker, C., & Keith, D. (1984). Counseling the dissolving marriage. In R. Stahmann & W. Hiebert (Eds.), *Counseling in marital and sexual problems* (pp. 49-62). Lexington, MA: Lexington.

White, L. (1990). Determinants of divorce: A review of research in the eighties. *Journal of Marriage and the Family, 52*(4), 904-912.

Winch, R. (1954). The theory of complementary needs in mate selection: An analytic and descriptive study. *American Sociological Review, 19,* 241-249.

Winch, R. (1967). Another look at the theory of complementary needs in mate-selection. *Journal of Marriage and the Family, 29,* 756-762.

Wright, N. (1977). *Pre-marital counseling.* Chicago: Moody.

Zimpfer, D. (1988). Marriage enrichment programs: A review. *Journal for Specialists in Group Work, 13,* 44-53.

3

Sexuality Education

John W. Engel
Marie Saracino
M. Betsy Bergen

IN THE PAST, sexuality education was sometimes limited to stories about "birds and bees" and the "facts of life" that were focused on biological basics and unspecified dangers. In effect, sexuality was defined in terms of anatomy and reproduction. Today, however, it is increasingly recognized that human sexuality involves much more than anatomy, coitus, and reproduction. Within the context of family life, sexuality is usually associated with love, trust, and commitment, and recognition is given to the many components of sexuality, including knowledge, beliefs, attitudes, values, skills, decisions, behaviors, emotions, and relationships as well as anatomy and reproduction. Because sexuality is an important dimension and foundation of family life, sexuality education is also a critical component of family life education.

The purpose of this chapter is to review the major approaches to sexuality education over the life span as these are offered in schools, organizations and agencies, churches, and clinics. The chapter begins with a brief developmental perspective on sexual development and learning and then identifies the implications of this perspective for sexuality education. Sexuality education programs are discussed and the outcomes of evaluation studies are identified. The chapter concludes with a discussion of issues in sexuality education.

A DEVELOPMENTAL PERSPECTIVE

It is useful to begin this chapter with a succinct overview of human sexual development from conception to death as these major developments have implications for sexuality education. Readers who wish details on life span sexual development should consult references such as Hyde (1990) or Katchadourian (1989).

The foundations of sexuality develop early. The ability to respond physiologically to stimulation and to stimulate oneself begins to appear during prenatal development (Masters, Johnson, & Kolodny, 1982; Montague, 1971). During infancy, these physiological response patterns continue to develop (Hyde, 1990; Katchadourian, 1989), and, in addition, abilities related to the formation and maintenance of social relationships appear (Lefrancois, 1990). Infants become increasingly aware of the feelings and attitudes of caregivers, and they acquire feelings that later become associated with values and attitudes toward genitals, nudity, bodily functions, sensuality, and self. Thus their sexuality education (intentional or not) has already begun.

During childhood, there are increasing opportunities to explore and learn about oneself and others and about how one's social environment and culture views and values sexuality. Social norms and values are learned from adult reactions to questions and behaviors. Through interaction with peers/friends, children also learn to deal with feelings and develop communication and relationship-building skills that will be associated in adulthood with love/romantic/sexual relationships.

During puberty and adolescence, sexual development is more dramatic and the need for sexuality education becomes more obvious. The physical changes of puberty often have implications for the development of identity and self-concept and are accompanied by both positive and negative psychological reactions and adjustments. Some of the most negative reactions appear to be associated with the absence of appropriate preparatory education (Hyde, 1990). Preparatory educational efforts, however, are complicated by the varied timing of pubertal changes, both between sexes and between individuals within each sex.

During adolescence, there is increased sexual interest in dating and rehearsal for adult gender roles. Most adolescents begin to masturbate during this period, and involvement in a range of heterosexual experiences increases. Most males and females become sexually active during their adolescent years (Forrest & Singh, 1990; National Research Council, 1987). A small percentage may also have homosexual experiences (DeLamater & MacCorquodale, 1979).

For most young adults, dating involves a cycle of formation and termination of relationships. Through this process, young adults confirm their sexual identity, clarify their sexual likes and dislikes, and develop greater comfort, confidence, and capacities for intimacy and commitment. In many cases, dating develops into pre- or nonmarital cohabitation. The majority of young adults are sexually active (Hunt, 1974; Hyde, 1990; Zelnick & Kantner, 1980) and must face issues of responsibility (e.g., birth control) and safety (e.g., prevention of STDs).

Most Americans marry, and, of those who divorce, most remarry (Cherlin, 1981). Most married people (men slightly more than women) report being satisfied with their sexual relationships (Hyde, 1990). At the same time, as married life progresses, many couples experience changes in feelings, with some couples finding that sexual satisfaction increases and others that it decreases. Some may have extramarital affairs, and special efforts are sometimes needed to maintain or enrich sexual interest and vitality in marriage.

The physical changes of aging require both cognitive and emotional adjustments. Although women gradually lose their fertility, and sexual intercourse may become less comfortable for some, their physical capacity for orgasm remains the same (Hyde, 1990). Middle-aged men may experience psychological and social changes that can be very stressful (Brim, 1976; Levinson, 1978; Ruebsaat & Hull, 1975). With aging, there may be some decline in sexual interest and frequency of sexual behaviors (Blumstein & Schwartz, 1983; Hyde, 1990). There is no biological age limit to sexual activity, however (Brecher et al., 1984; Bretschneider & McCoy, 1988). In general, given the opportunity, both men and women continue to engage in sexual activity and to enjoy it as they age.

This developmental perspective has important implications for the content, process, and timing of sexuality education. Because sexuality has psychological, ethical, and sociocultural dimensions as well as biological ones, an individual's total sexuality education and learning over a lifetime would ideally be comprehensive, including all of these dimensions. Thus the content of comprehensive sexuality education should include knowledge, feelings, beliefs, values, attitudes, skills, behaviors, and relationships. Comprehensive sexuality education needs to recognize that the significance of human sexuality is expressed in the total adjustment of an individual in interpersonal relationships, family, and society.

What is learned about sexuality is often mediated or complicated by process, by how information is presented. Humans hear and perceive not only words and their meanings but also feelings and attitudes that are expressed nonverbally. Therefore comfort and attitudes are important variables to be considered in the training and selection of professional sexuality educators.

Timing is also a critical issue in sexuality education. Education that is offered too early, when the potential learner is not yet ready to learn, interested, or capable of understanding, is ineffective. According to developmental theory, humans learn, need to learn, and are capable of learning different things at different times. Ideally, sexuality education should be provided when learners are developmentally ready, and the content and process of sexuality education should be modified to fit the learner's needs and developmental maturity. Awareness of how children's sexual understanding matures and develops in stages (Bernstein, 1976; Bernstein & Cowan, 1975) and of typical questions asked by children at various ages/grades (Bruess & Greenberg, 1988; Hyde, 1990) may help educators provide appropriate information at appropriate times. Similarly, sexuality education may not be effective if provided too late. Appropriately timed preparatory education may facilitate adjustment to developmental transitions (e.g., menarche) and prevent problems (e.g., unwanted pregnancy, sexually transmitted disease, or sexual dysfunction). A comprehensive understanding of normal sexual development over the life span, including variation as well as group averages, should help educators estimate when preparatory education is most appropriate.

Increasing social/sexual problems related to adolescent pregnancy, AIDS, and sexual abuse have resulted in widespread concern and call for preventive education. In each case, education has been seen as a potential solution to reduce or prevent the problem.

SEXUALITY EDUCATION PROGRAMS

Formal sexuality education in North America is provided in various contexts, including schools, youth-/family-serving organizations and agencies, religious groups and churches, and medical/health organizations such as family planning clinics. In this section, the major approaches to sexuality education and evidence concerning their effectiveness will be presented. Attention will be given both to sexuality education in particular settings and to programs designed to address the issues of adolescent pregnancy, sexually transmitted diseases, and child sexual abuse. Chapter limitations preclude detailed descriptions of these programs, but key references are provided for readers who wish further information on these programs.

Sexuality Education in the Schools

Most states now require (others recommend) some sexuality and/or AIDS education in the public schools and provide curricula or curricular guidelines for use in local implementation. A 1990 review of state sexuality and AIDS education curricula found considerable variation in curricular comprehensiveness, currency, accuracy, and tone or attitude (de Mauro, 1990). A large proportion of the curricula were not comprehensive (less than half provided adequate/thorough information on family planning) and a large proportion were out of date, particularly with respect to AIDS education. Others have also found considerable state-to-state variation in program objectives, design, implementation, and evaluation and little evidence that comprehensive and effective programs have been implemented at the local level (Kenny, 1989; Kenny, Guardado, & Brown, 1989).

It appears that the majority of young people today receive some formal sexuality education before they leave school. A national survey of school districts in large cities found that three quarters of the districts provided some sexuality education in their junior and senior high schools and two thirds provided such education in their elementary schools (Sonenstein & Pittman, 1984). Another national survey found that, by age 18, 68% of 15- to 19-year-old women had received some formal education about pregnancy and contraceptive methods, 16% had received instruction on pregnancy (only), and only 16% received no formal education on either topic (Dawson, 1986). Similarly, Marsiglio and Mott (1986) found 60% of women and 52% of men to have had some formal sexuality education in school by age 19. Although it appears that most young people receive some formal sexuality education in schools, at least some (although a minority) receive little or no formal sexuality education.

Questions have been raised about the breadth and timing of sexuality education. According to Sonenstein and Pittman (1984), most school systems offer only short programs (10 hours or less), often integrated into health or physical education courses. Very few schools offer comprehensive sexuality education programs (more than 40 hours), and, when they do, not all students enroll. Kirby (1984) estimates that less than 10% of young people experience a comprehensive sexuality course provided by the schools.

Forrest and Silverman (1989) surveyed 4,241 junior and senior public school teachers who teach in the areas of biology, health education, home economics, physical education, and school nursing to assess what sexuality content is being taught. The vast majority (93%) reported that some sex or AIDS education was provided in their schools; 77% reported both sex and AIDS education; 8% reported sex education but not AIDS education; and another 8% reported AIDS education but not sex education. When sex education was offered, it was offered as a separate course in only 10% of the cases.

Nearly all the teachers surveyed by Forrest and Silverman (1989) believed that public school sex and AIDS education should cover a wide variety of sexual topics related to prevention of pregnancy and STDs/AIDS, such as sexual decision making, abstinence, and birth control methods. In practice, however, teachers were given little time for sexuality education (an average of 6.5 hours per year) and, as a result, the information provided was not comprehensive. Although 97% of the teachers believed that sex education should include information on where to go for contraceptives, this information was provided in less than half of the schools. Although most teachers believed that sex education should be provided by grade 7 or 8, before most adolescents become sexually active, in most schools sex education was not offered until grade 9 or 10.

School-based sexuality education programs and curricula have been described and evaluated in the literature (e.g., Parcel, Luttman, & Flaherty-Zonis, 1985). Pre- and posttest research on the effectiveness of school-based curricula usually report evidence of increased knowledge but little or less evidence of changed attitudes or behaviors. Thus it appears that, while school-based curricula may be effective in accomplishing the traditional educational goals of schools (i.e., to increase knowledge), other interventions may be necessary to accomplish social and health-related goals (i.e., behavior change and problem prevention).

Sexuality Education in Other Organizations and Agencies

Youth-serving agencies and organizations also provide sexuality education programs for young people. Several exemplary youth organization sexuality education programs have been reviewed and are reported in Scales and Kirby (1981) and Tabbutt (1987). Agencies and organizations such as the American Red Cross, American Home Economics Association, Boys Clubs of America, Girls Clubs of America, Girl Scouts of the USA, March of Dimes Birth Defects Foundation, National Congress of Parents and Teachers' Association, National Network of Runaway and Youth Services, and YWCA of the USA have all developed sexuality education programs for their local affiliates (Dietz, 1990). These programs vary in length (from 5 to 30 hours), and, although all focus on developing sexual knowledge and skills, they also vary considerably in comprehensiveness. Topics typically covered in these programs are the consequences of adolescent pregnancy, sexually transmitted diseases, anatomy, menstruation, family relationships, drugs and alcohol, myths and stereotypes, and dating. Skills such as communication, avoiding risky behaviors, decision making, clarifying values, and assertiveness are also included. These programs, however, appear to neglect topics such as homosexuality, abortion, adoption, and skill areas such as listening, employment, contraception, and assessment of health care systems. Little is known about how well affiliates implement these programs at the local level.

Churches and religious organizations also provide some sexuality education. Several exemplary church-based programs were reviewed by Scales and Kirby (1981), and church-based programs designed to enhance communication between adolescents and parents have been described by Green and Sollie (1989) and by Isberner and Wright (1988). For a discussion of the advantages and limitations of church-based sexuality education, see Green and Sollie (1989).

Family planning agencies and clinics such as Planned Parenthood traditionally offer sexuality education and counseling services. These services are typically designed to meet the needs/demands of clients, who are usually sexually active adolescents or adults seeking contraceptive information and services. Sexuality education in this context may be more focused on pregnancy prevention than on a comprehensive approach to sexuality education. For a review of several exemplary family planning agency-based programs, see Scales and Kirby (1981). During the 1980s, many family planning agencies abandoned traditional group classes and adopted individualized educational methods. For an evaluation and comparison of individualized versus group educational methods as used in family planning agencies, see Johnson (1985).

Adolescent Pregnancy Prevention Programs

In addition to the programs described above, other efforts and programs have been directed specifically toward prevention of adolescent pregnancy. Most attempt to increase knowledge; improve assertiveness, communication, or decision-making skills; influence attitudes and motivation; or increase access to contraceptive and other services. Some try to improve self-esteem, increase interest or success in school, or facilitate youth employment. And some attempt to combine and integrate school, community, and home-based approaches in a comprehensive way.

Barth, Middleton, and Wagman (1989) described a 15-day skill-building program being piloted in 25 California high schools. While there is some evidence that the program increases knowledge, more research is needed to determine whether or not it can prevent adolescent pregnancy.

Numerous programs have been designed and implemented to prevent adolescent pregnancy by encouraging abstinence from sexual activity until marriage, that is, to "just say no" (e.g., Trudell & Whatley, 1991). While most if not all adolescent pregnancy prevention programs encourage abstinence, some are limited to this approach by their institutional context or funding sources. This applies particularly to demonstration projects funded by the Adolescent Family Life Act (AFLA) passed by Congress in 1981 (Roosa & Christopher, 1990). The popular abstinence-based programs "Project Taking Charge" and "Success Express" have been found to increase knowledge but not to change self-esteem, attitudes, behavioral intentions, or family communication (Jorgensen, 1991; Roosa & Christopher, 1990). Although there is some evidence that other abstinence-based programs may have effects on attitudes as well as on knowledge (Adamek & Thoms, 1991; Olson, Wallace, & Miller, 1984), it appears that attitudinal changes may be temporary (Donahue, 1987). Unfortunately, program evaluations seldom report data on behavioral change (either sexual activity or pregnancy rate). When they do, findings typically show no change in behaviors (Donahue, 1987; Roosa & Christopher, 1990). Thus it appears that pregnancy prevention programs that are limited to encouragement of abstinence have questionable and limited effectiveness.

During the late 1980s, school-based health clinics proliferated throughout the United States, typically established in or near public junior and senior high schools. Although clinic programs and services varied widely from clinic to clinic, they tended to be comprehensive in their health orientation and included family planning information and counseling. There is growing evidence that school-based health clinic services may increase the use of contraceptives (Dryfoos, 1988; Kirby, 1985) and may reduce pregnancy rates (Kirby, 1985; Zabin, Hirsch, Smith, Streett, & Hardy, 1986). It is important to note, however, that not all clinics have been successful ("Taking on," 1987). For a general description and evaluation of over 100 school-based health clinics, including services, implementation, organization, and funding, see Dryfoos (1985, 1988). For a thorough description and evaluation of an exemplary school-based health clinic (the Baltimore pregnancy prevention program), see Zabin et al. (1986) and Zabin et al. (1988).

Programs designed to prevent adolescent pregnancy indirectly, by "enhancing life options" (National Research Council, 1987) through improving self-esteem, increasing interest/success in school, or facilitating youth employment, also appear to be attaining some success ("Taking on," 1987). The Teen Outreach Program (TOP), implemented in at least 17 cities across the United States, uses lectures, role-playing, group exercises, and volunteerism to encourage career planning, increase resistance to peer pressure, and boost self-esteem. The Summer Training and Education Program (STEP), implemented in at least 5 cities, offers "life skills" courses (including training in decision making) and academic tutoring as means of building self-esteem.

A comprehensive/integrated school- and community-based pregnancy prevention program in South Carolina has been found to be effective in reducing adolescent pregnancy rates (Vincent, Clearie, & Schluchter, 1987; Vincent & Dod, 1989). This program is focused on decision-making and communication skills, self-esteem, and values as well as on knowledge. The long-term goal of the program is prevention/reduction of adolescent pregnancy, with two key behavioral objectives: (a) the postponement of first coitus among youth who are not already sexually active and (b) the consistent use of effective contraception among youth who are already sexually active. In this educational intervention, teachers were first trained and then supported as they implemented sexuality education in all subjects in kindergarten through the 12th grade. Clergy and parents and later peer educators from the high school were also involved. Adolescent pregnancy rates in the school/community intervention area dropped by more than 50%, while pregnancy rates in demographically similar control group areas increased.

An integrated approach to preventing adolescent pregnancy was found to be effective in a university setting (Fisher, 1990). Lectures, videotapes, and written materials were developed to provide useful information about contraception, communication, and health services. Lectures were provided in dormitories, and videotapes (written and produced by students) were made available for classes, fairs, and other student use. Written materials were provided to all incoming students and as supplements to lectures and videotape showings. Following implementation of the program, the pregnancy rate in the student population dropped approximately 40% while similar changes did not occur in the control group, a general population of student-age females.

In summary, two key points can be made about adolescent pregnancy prevention programs. First, programs that are unidimensional and that limit intervention efforts, curricula, or modalities seem to have limited results, while multidimensional and multimodal (comprehensive or integrated) programs appear more effective in preventing unwanted adolescent pregnancy. Second, there continues to be a great need for evaluative research on the effectiveness of adolescent pregnancy prevention programs. All too often, programs are funded and implemented without being evaluated for effectiveness.

STD/AIDS Prevention Programs

Some of the school and organizational programs (e.g., Fisher, 1990) discussed earlier may have an STD/AIDS prevention component. Many school-based clinics offer a variety of health-related services directed toward prevention of both STDs/AIDS and pregnancy. These programs include intermediate goals such as delayed initiation of sexual activity, training in sexual communication and decision-making skills, encouragement of self-esteem and health, and access to resources (e.g., information, counseling, condoms).

In schools, a majority (54%) of high school students experience some HIV/AIDS education (Anderson et al., 1990), although the amount and kind seems to vary tremendously. According to Calamidas (1990), STD/AIDS education has been incorporated into the school curricula only to a minimal extent, and teacher effectiveness is hindered by lack of sufficient time, resources, preparation, and support.

In general, STD/AIDS prevention programs attempt to provide complete and accurate information regarding STD/AIDS transmission and prevention. Some programs also address personal values and responsibility issues, behavior change, communication or decision-making skills, or services/resources related to intervention and treatment. Educational efforts may focus on the reduction of behaviors that increase risk of infection or the encouragement of behaviors that minimize risk. For information about developing or evaluating STD/AIDS education/prevention programs, consult curricular guidelines published by the Centers for Disease Control (1988) and SIECUS (National Guidelines Taskforce, 1991).

A developmentally based approach to providing AIDS/HIV education to school-age children focuses on children's thought processes and the ways in which they understand and learn (Walsh & Bibace, 1990). The focus of the program is on reducing fears in younger children, on increasing knowledge and correcting myths in intermediate-aged children, and on strategies for AIDS prevention in older children.

Valentich and Gripton (1989) described a program designed to help parents understand the sexual development of their children, to anticipate sexual questions and needs for information, and to communicate effectively about sexuality and AIDS. A list of questions about AIDS typically asked by children in varying age groups was provided.

As with pregnancy prevention programs, there is a great need for research on the effectiveness of STD/AIDS prevention programs. An evaluation of one health behavior-focused school STD curriculum found that, although knowledge increased and attitudes changed in the direction of increased health, the changes diminished over a 6-week follow-up period (Yarber, 1988). It may be that effects last longer when STD/AIDS education is incorporated into comprehensive sexuality education programs. No data or any efforts to obtain data on behavioral change were reported.

It appears that today's youth are more knowledgeable about STDs/AIDS than were youth in previous years (Adame, Taylor-Nicholson, Wang, & Abbas, 1991), but many are still uninformed and lack basic knowledge regarding HIV transmission and protection (Negy & Webber, 1991; Stevenson & Stevenson, 1990). As well, many students still hold beliefs or attitudes that may put them at risk (Adame et al., 1991; Anderson et al., 1990). Despite greater knowledge, many students still engage in risky behaviors (MacDonald et al., 1990).

There is some evidence that knowledge about HIV/AIDS (whether obtained through formal education or otherwise) may reduce the incidence of risky sexual behaviors. Anderson et al. (1990) found that high school students who knew more about HIV transmission were less likely to report risky behaviors (having multiple sexual partners) and more likely to report consistent use of condoms. Similarly, in a study of Canadian college students, MacDonald et al. (1990) found insufficient HIV knowledge to be associated with not using condoms. Associations with other risky behaviors such as having multiple sexual partners or anal intercourse were less clear. Analysis of data on STD as well as HIV knowledge and overall prevalence of risky behavior in this student population led these researchers to conclude that "many students know the basic facts concerning STD/HIV yet most do not practice safer sex" (p. 3159).

It is increasingly clear to many sexuality/STD/AIDS researchers and educators that increased knowledge alone is not sufficient to prevent AIDS, but what is needed to supplement knowledge is still not clear. As in pregnancy prevention, decision-making and communication skills, values, self-esteem, and other variables such as motivation may be important. In their research on Canadian college students, MacDonald et al. (1990) found significant correlations between communication difficulties (in saying "no" and discussing use of condoms) and risky behaviors (having multiple partners and not using condoms). Thus communication skills may facilitate avoidance of risky sexual behaviors.

Recent research may help to clarify motivations for safe as opposed to unsafe sexual behaviors. For example, Klitsch (1990) reported that adolescent intentions to use condoms are associated with short-term social considerations (e.g., popularity with peers) but not with health concerns (i.e., prevention of STDs/AIDS or pregnancy). Similarly, Mac-Donald et al. (1990) found that fear of AIDS did not significantly influence condom use by Canadian college students. Others (Brandt, 1988; Haffner, 1988, 1989) have also concluded that fear is not an effective means of changing sexual behaviors. Thus health concerns or fears may not be effective motivators for safer sexual behaviors.

AIDS prevention efforts have been remarkably successful for gay men, resulting in the widespread adoption of safer sexual behaviors (DeMayo, 1991). (Three HIV/AIDS prevention programs specifically designed for gay men are described by DeMayo, 1991.) It appears that prevention programs may be more successful when designed specifically for a targeted clientele, when the clientele's subculture is taken into account. Indeed, it is increasingly clear that minorities and other subgroups differ in important ways that mediate AIDS infection and prevention. Accordingly, there is a growing literature that addresses the sexuality and HIV-/AIDS-related cultures, concerns, needs, motivations, problems, and issues of various minorities or subgroups, including blacks (Alexander, 1990-1991; Negy & Webber, 1991), Latinos (de la Vega, 1990; Lifshitz, 1990-1991; Maldonado, 1990-1991), Asians and Pacific Islanders (Lee & Fong, 1990), Native Americans (Rowell, 1990), women (Cole & Cooper, 1990-1991; Osborn, 1990-1991), lesbians (Cole & Cooper, 1990-1991), heterosexuals (Greenspan & Castro, 1990), and gay men (DeMayo, 1991).

Haffner (1988, 1989) has concluded that AIDS prevention programs should have five primary goals: (a) to eliminate misinformation and reduce panic, (b) to help youth delay premature sexual intercourse, (c) to encourage condom use among sexually active youth, (d) to warn about dangers of drug use, and (e) to encourage compassion for people with AIDS or infected with HIV. She also identified eight principles that should underlie effective AIDS education programs; they should (a) "be integrated into comprehensive health or sexuality education programs," (b) "be designed to reach all children, not just those in middle class communities," (c) "be offered in multiple sessions at each grade level and through numerous mediums," (d) "emphasize increasing teenagers' perceptions of their vulnerability to HIV infection rather than the provision of biomedical information," (e) "provide ample opportunity for behavioral skill development," (f) "be value based," (g) "be sexuality positive," and (h) "be empowering" (Haffner, 1989, pp. 200-202). Educators may find these goals and principles useful in designing or evaluating AIDS education programs.

Child Sexual Abuse Prevention Programs

During the 1980s, programs directed at prevention of child sexual abuse proliferated in North America. For an overview of programs in the United States and Canada, see Torjman (1989). These programs vary in location, content, methods, length and number of sessions, age of student, and teacher orientation and qualifications.

Most child sexual abuse prevention programs focus on the basic concepts of personal safety, including variations of the following messages: (a) Children have a right to control their own bodies; (b) there are different kinds of touch, good and bad, and not all need be tolerated; (c) children can trust their own feelings and recognize inappropriate touching; (d) children can (or can learn to) say "no" to touching that makes them feel uncomfortable or afraid and can run away; (e) children should tell an adult they trust about confusing or inappropriate touching; (f) the abuser may be someone the child knows, not a stranger; (g) "secrets" about touching need not be kept; and (h) children need to know that abuse is not their fault (Bales, 1988; Graham & Harris-Hart, 1988; Woods & Dean, 1986). Numerous curricula are available for teachers (e.g., West, 1984).

Methods used in child sexual abuse prevention programs include classroom instruction, reading materials (sometimes comic books), coloring books, media (films/tapes), theater, puppets, role-playing, and coached training sessions. It is generally recognized that methods (as well as content) should be appropriate for the student/audience, but there is little research on comparative method effectiveness (see Woods & Dean, 1986, for an exception).

Little is known about the overall effectiveness of sexual abuse prevention programs. Research (e.g., Woods & Dean, 1986) does indicate that programs can be effective in increasing knowledge. Knowledge retention, however, particularly in younger children, may be short-lived and require later reinforcement for long-term effectiveness (Bales, 1988; Graham & Harris-Hart, 1988). There is no convincing evidence, however, that knowledge per se changes behaviors or that increasing knowledge will prevent abuse. Beliefs and attitudes are also assumed to be important. Skill training, role-playing, and so on that includes practice in identifying inappropriate touch and saying "no" effectively may have greater potential for behavioral change and long-term prevention. There is some evidence of skill or behavioral learning resulting from some programs (e.g., refusal to go with a stranger on the playground, successful termination of an uncomfortable/prolonged handshake; Graham & Harris-Hart, 1988). For a review of research on program effectiveness, see Gentles and Cassidy (1988).

In addition to questions of effectiveness, concerns regarding the potential negative effects of abuse prevention programs continue to arise. Anecdotal evidence (Bales, 1988; Krivacska, 1991) suggests that some children may become overly fearful or that their relationships with significant adults/parents may be harmed in some way. Krivacska (1991) points out that some of the concepts (e.g., continuum of touch and empowerment) taught in many programs are appropriate for adults but not children and in fact may be harmful when misunderstood or understood incompletely. To date, research on the potential side effects (e.g., Wurtelle & Miller-Perrin, 1987) has found no evidence that the specific programs studied increased fear or relationship problems at home.

The focus of most child sexual abuse prevention programs is on children, based on the assumption that, with appropriate education or training, children can avoid abuse. It may be that programs would be more effective if they focused on adults (parents and teachers) as well as children. Gilgun and Gordon (1985) point out that current prevention programs overlook the offender and describe how a program might be designed to focus more on adult offenders rather than on or in addition to children.

Most child sexual abuse prevention programs serve two purposes: early intervention and prevention. Generally, programs that focus on teaching children how to recognize or identify abuse and what to do about it are more pertinent to early intervention than to prevention. Thus most child sexual abuse "prevention" programs are more intervention than prevention programs (Krivacska, 1991; Whatley & Trudell, 1989). In some schools, abuse education may be the only sexuality education that children receive (Krivacska, 1991; Whatley & Trudell, 1989). In the absence of positive sexuality education, the focus on the negative aspects of sexuality (i.e., on abuse) may be harmful, as children may learn only negative messages about sexuality. To avoid this, abuse intervention programs should be offered in the context of (or as a component of) comprehensive health-focused sexuality education.

Educators concerned about child sexual abuse prevention may find the following resources helpful. Graham and Harris-Hart (1989) review prevention programs in North America and provide information about relevant conferences and resources. Ferguson and Mendelson-Ages (1988) describe and review prevention programs in Canada. SIECUS (1990) publishes relevant bibliographies.

Summary

While formal sexuality education programs are offered in various settings, such as schools, youth organizations, churches, and clinics, they are seldom comprehensive and not all young people participate. Although programs have been designed specifically to prevent adolescent pregnancy, STDs/AIDS, or sexual abuse, their effectiveness is still questionable.

Research shows that formal sexuality education can increase knowledge (Barth et al., 1989; Dawson, 1986; Eisen, Zellman, & McAlister, 1990; Jorgensen, 1991; Kirby, 1985; Parcel et al., 1985; Woods & Dean, 1986; Yarber, 1988; Zabin et al., 1986). Knowledge may not be retained without reinforcement, however (Bales, 1988; Donahue, 1987; Graham & Harris-Hart, 1989; Yarber, 1988).

While some programs or approaches appear to change beliefs or attitudes (Adamek & Thoms, 1991; Olson et al., 1984; Yarber, 1988), many do not (Eisen et al., 1990; Jorgensen, 1991; Kirby, 1985; Parcel et al., 1985; Roosa & Christopher, 1990; Zabin et al., 1986).

Some programs have been found to increase communication between parent and child (Dawson, 1986; Green & Sollie, 1989; Kirby, 1985), while others have not (Furstenberg, Moore, & Peterson, 1985; Jorgensen, 1991).

There is some evidence that formal sexuality education may change behaviors. Education has been found to delay or reduce sexual activity in some cases (Eisen et al., 1990; Furstenberg et al., 1985; Zabin et al., 1986) but not in others (Dawson, 1986; Marsiglio & Mott, 1986). Some programs (particularly those that include health clinic services) have been found to increase use (i.e., consistency and effectiveness) of contraceptives (Dawson, 1986; Dryfoos, 1988; Kirby, 1985; Marsiglio & Mott, 1986; Zabin et al., 1986). Whether education can reduce behaviors that increase the risk of AIDS is unclear (Anderson et al., 1990).

Reductions in adolescent pregnancy rates have been reported for some programs (usually comprehensive integrated school, clinic, and community programs; Fisher, 1990; Kirby, 1985; Vincent & Dod, 1989; Vincent et al., 1987; Zabin et al., 1986), while not for others (Dawson, 1986; Marsiglio & Mott, 1986). There is still little evidence that education is effective in prevention of STDs/AIDS or child sexual abuse in the general population, however.

CHALLENGES AND FUTURE DIRECTIONS

To provide effective, comprehensive sexuality education in the future, educators will need to face several challenges related to goals, politics, methods, results, evaluation, and training.

Goals and Objectives

There is still no consensus, among professionals or laypeople, regarding appropriate goals for sexuality education, and objectives and content vary by educator, program, and context. In many cases, programs are narrowly focused on negative aspects of sexuality and their prevention. It is increasingly clear, however, that the focus on negative aspects of sexuality and their prevention is too limited, perhaps even harmful. "Sexual health" has been proposed as a more appropriate primary goal for sexuality education, because it leads to a more comprehensive focus on positive as well as negative aspects of sexuality. For discussions of sexual health as value, concept, or construct, see Maddock (1989) and Scales (1986). Given health as a primary goal, the objectives of comprehensive sexuality education should address information, attitudes, values, insights, relationships, interpersonal skills, and responsibility (Bruess & Greenberg, 1988; National Guidelines Taskforce, 1991).

Political Realities

It is increasingly clear that educators must face political challenges to gain support for and overcome opposition to comprehensive sexuality education (Scales, 1989; Yarber, 1987). Educators may have to convince employers, institutions, or communities that the goals, objectives, and content of comprehensive sexuality education are appropriate and important. The success of programs may depend upon the active involvement and support of parents and community networks (Rienzo, 1989).

Methods: Context, Timing, and Clientele

For sexuality education to be developmentally appropriate and comprehensive, educators will need to give more attention to multiple contexts, times, and underserved audiences or clienteles.

There is still no consensus regarding where sexuality education should take place. While some people still believe that sex education for young children by parents in the home is sufficient, most now recognize the need for formal education in schools as well (Gallup, 1985). This can be seen as progress, but it may not go far enough. Research findings suggest that educational programs that integrate school, health clinic, home, and community are more effective than those that are more limited in scope. To maximize success, educators may need to give more attention to programming in community agencies, organizations, churches, and clinics as well as schools.

The timing of sexuality education is another challenge for sexuality educators. While many, although a minority, of young people still receive little or no sex education, many of those who do receive education in school are receiving it after they have become sexually active (Marsiglio & Mott, 1986). For some, this may be too late. The timing of group sexual education is complicated by the fact that individuals develop and mature at different rates. Nevertheless, a comprehensive understanding of normal sexual development over the life span, including variation as well as group averages, should help educators predict when education is developmentally appropriate. For guidelines or examples of sex education curricula that outline content appropriate for different grade levels or ages, see Bruess and Greenberg (1988), Hyde (1990), McCaffree (1986), or National Guidelines Taskforce (1991).

Sexuality education must face the challenge of neglected audiences and clienteles. Not all potential learners are children or students. Adults are also a potential clientele for sexuality education. Indeed, sexual development theory suggests that sexual learning occurs and continues from conception to death, in whatever contexts people live. Not only do adults continue to learn about their own sexuality, but those that become parents are also expected to function as sexuality educators for their children. When ignorance or misinformation expresses itself in sexual dysfunction, education may occur in the form of counseling or therapy. Adults may "return to school" and take sexuality courses at colleges or universities. Such courses tend to be focused on the interests and needs of the typical student, however, who tends to be an adolescent or young adult. A correspondence course has been designed for adults, which facilitates private study at home (Engel, 1983). In general, however, there seems to be a dearth of preventive or health-focused educational programs designed for adults as they mature and age. Programs for parents might be offered in school or church settings. Programs for older adults might be offered through the auspices of adult or senior citizen organizations or centers, churches, clinics, or nursing homes. At any rate, more attention to the needs of the potential older adult clientele is called for.

Results: Effectiveness

Sexuality educators may have to deal with questions regarding the effectiveness of sexuality education. There is some tendency in the popular media to conclude that sexuality education doesn't work. For example, according to *Newsweek* (December 9, 1991, p. 52), the "prevalence (of STD/AIDS) represents an apparent failure of the quintessential liberal solution to social problems, education." On the one hand, educators may have to face the issue of whether the solution of major social problems is an appropriate goal/objective for sexuality education. On the other hand, to maximize effectiveness, educators need to know what is effective, when, and for whom.

Indeed, there is a growing body of literature reporting research on the effectiveness of programs that suggests that education *can* be effective but often isn't. Education appears to be more effective toward some objectives (to increase knowledge) than toward others (to change attitudes or behaviors). The research also shows that some types of programs (comprehensive integrated school, clinic, and community programs) are more effective than others ("just say no," abstinence-only programs). As in other educational endeavors, the degree of effectiveness will depend upon other variables such as program comprehensiveness, objectives, design, methods, implementation, student and educator characteristics, school/clinic/community integration, and institutional and other contextual support.

Results: Concerns Regarding Negative Effects

Sexuality education also faces challenges related to concerns about potential negative effects. Critics of formal sexuality education in the schools fear that sex education may encourage or promote early sexual activity and promiscuity. Research, however, has suggested that in most cases such fears are unfounded. Study after study has indicated that sexuality education does not elicit or increase sexual activity (Scales, 1987). Only two exceptions to this conclusion could be found in the research literature. Christopher and Roosa (1990) found some evidence that virgin males increased their precoital sexual behaviors during involvement in an abstinence-only pregnancy prevention program. Marsiglio and Mott (1986) found that adolescent women who had sexuality education were slightly more likely to initiate sexual activity at ages 15 and 16. In general, however, studies find that sexuality education either has no effect on timing or amount of sexual activity (Dawson, 1986; Kirby, 1980; Kirby, Waszak, & Ziegler, 1991) or actually delays/

reduces sexual activity (Eisen & Zellman, 1987; Eisen et al., 1990; Furstenburg et al., 1985; Zabin et al., 1986). Thus there is very little evidence that sexuality education encourages or promotes premarital sexual activity or promiscuity.

Concerns regarding potential negative effects of child sexual abuse prevention programs (e.g., Bales, 1988; Krivacska, 1991) were discussed in an earlier section. Some harm may result from programs/methods that narrowly focus on negatives without the larger context of comprehensive sexuality education. While research on one program found no evidence of negative effects (Wurtelle & Miller-Perrin, 1987), research is needed on other programs and methods to reinforce generalizability of findings. Educators must take more responsibility for evaluating methods and programs and ensuring that they are appropriate and do no harm.

Evaluation and Research

Sexuality education must face the challenge that there remains a great need for more and better evaluation research. Continuation of support and funding for individual programs may depend upon research evidence that a program has met its objectives. As well, research is needed to determine what methods are effective (and how effective), when, and for whom. Evaluation research to date suffers from various deficiencies that ideally would be corrected in future research. While space limitations proscribe a comprehensive discussion of research methods, the following suggestions may be helpful. Program objectives should be clearly specified, ideally in operational terms, and evaluation instruments should be designed to measure the objectives specified. For accurate results, researchers should be independent, objective, and in no way personally invested in the success of the program/method being evaluated. Comparison or control groups should be used in the research method. Measures of change should occur at multiple times, to catch effects that take more time to surface and to ensure that effects are lasting. For additional suggestions on evaluation strategies, see Card and Reagan (1989), National Research Council (1987), or Philliber (1989).

Qualifications and Training of Sexuality Educators

Professional sexuality educators must take responsibility for ensuring that sexuality education is provided by appropriately trained and qualified educators. This will become an increasingly difficult challenge as sexuality education becomes more comprehensive and pervasive in schools and communities. Professionals may have a greater overall impact by training or supervising other educators (e.g., child care workers, elementary/secondary school teachers, volunteers) as opposed to providing education directly themselves. At any rate, professional sexuality educators should assume responsibility for determining and publicizing the qualifications needed by (and required of) educators at various levels and in various contexts.

Hyde (1990) described three qualifications that are important for a sexuality educator: (a) comfort in sexual communication; (b) an ability to listen, understand questions, and assess needs; and of course (c) appropriate education and knowledge about human sexuality. The amount of training and knowledge that a teacher needs depends upon the needs and age or maturity of students. Elementary school teachers do not need as much training as high school teachers, who do not need as much as university professors, and so on. A university course in human sexuality should provide a good knowledge base for elementary and high school teachers. Teachers of college students and other adults should have additional education and training. Professional family life educators are required to have specific sexuality and related course work to qualify for certification by the National Council on Family Relations (NCFR). Professional sexuality educators must have extensive sexuality course work, group work, supervised internship, graduate degree, and years of experience to qualify for certification by the American Association of Sex Educators, Counselors and Therapists (AASECT). In addition, the professional sexuality educators of the future may need skills in politics, public relations, fund-raising, and administration.

SUMMARY AND CONCLUSION

Sexuality has psychological, ethical, and sociocultural as well as biological dimensions. Sexual development and learning begins at conception and continues until death. Ideally, sexuality education should be comprehensive and developmentally appropriate.

Although formal sexuality education programs are offered in various contexts, such as schools, youth organizations, churches, and clinics, they are seldom comprehensive and not all young people participate. Programs have been designed specifically to prevent adolescent pregnancy, STDs/AIDS, or sexual abuse, but their effectiveness remains questionable.

Given today's many sexual concerns and problems, including unwanted pregnancies and AIDS, there is an even greater need now than there was in the past for effective, comprehensive, developmentally appropriate sexuality education that integrates contributions from home, school, and community. To provide such education in the future, sexuality educators will need to face several challenges related to goals, politics, methods, results, evaluation, and training and qualifications.

RESOURCES

- American Association of Sex Educators, Counselors, and Therapists (AA-SECT), Eleven Dupont Circle, N.W., Suite 220, Washington, DC 20036; tel. (202) 462-1171: AASECT certifies sex educators, counselors, and therapists and publishes the *Journal of Sex Education and Therapy*.
- National Council on Family Relations (NCFR), 3989 Central Ave. N.E., Suite 550, Minneapolis, MN 55421: NCFR certifies family life educators and publishes various educational resources including the applied journal *Family Relations*.
- Sex Information and Education Council of the United States (SIECUS), 130 W. 42nd Street, Suite 2500, New York, NY 10036: SIECUS publishes various educational resources, including the *SIECUS Report*.

REFERENCES

Adame, D. D., Taylor-Nicholson, M. E., Wang, M., & Abbas, M. A. (1991). Southern college freshman students: A survey of knowledge, attitudes, and beliefs about AIDS. *Journal of Sex Education and Therapy, 17*(3), 196-206.

Adamek, R. J., & Thoms, A. I. (1991). Responsible sexual values program: The first year. *Family Perspective, 25*(1), 67-81.

Alexander, V. (1990-1991, December-January). Black women and HIV/AIDS. *SIECUS Report, 19*(2), 8-10.

Anderson, J. E., Kann, L., Holtzman, D., Arday, S., Truman, B., & Kolbe, L. (1990). HIV/AIDS knowledge and sexual behavior among high school students. *Family Planning Perspectives, 22*(6), 252-255.

Bales, J. (1988, June). Child abuse prevention efficacy called in doubt. *APA Monitor*, p. 27.

Barth, R. P., Middleton, K., & Wagman, E. (1989). A skill building approach to preventing teenage pregnancy. *Theory into Practice, 28*(3), 183-190.

Bernstein, A. C. (1976). How children learn about sex and birth. *Psychology Today, 9*(8), 31.

Bernstein, A. C., & Cowan, P. A. (1975). Children's concepts of how people get babies. *Child Development, 46*, 77-92.

Blumstein, P., & Schwartz, P. (1983). *American couples*. New York: William Morrow.

Brandt, A. (1988). AIDS in historical perspective: Four lessons from the history of sexually transmitted diseases. *American Journal of Public Health, 74*(8), 367-371.

Brecher, E. M., & the editors of Consumer Reports books. (1984). *Love, sex, and aging*. Mount Vernon, NY: Consumers Union.

Bretschneider, J. G., & McCoy, N. L. (1988). Sexual interest and behavior in healthy 80- to 102-year-olds. *Archives of Sexual Behavior, 17*, 109-130.

Brim, O. G. (1976). Theories of the male mid-life crisis. *Counseling Psychologist, 6*(1), 2-9.

Bruess, C. E., & Greenberg, J. S. (1988). *Sexuality education.* New York: Macmillan.

Calamidas, E. G. (1990). AIDS and STD education: What's really happening in our schools? *Journal of Sex Education and Therapy, 16*(1), 54-63.

Card, J. J., & Reagan, R. T. (1989). Strategies for evaluating adolescent pregnancy programs. *Family Planning Perspectives, 21*(1), 27-30.

Centers for Disease Control. (1988). Guidelines for effective school health education to prevent the spread of AIDS. *Journal of School Health, 58*(4), 142-148.

Cherlin, A. (1981). *Marriage, divorce, remarriage.* Cambridge, MA: Harvard University Press.

Christopher, F. S., & Roosa, M. W. (1990). An evaluation of an adolescent pregnancy prevention program: Is "just say no" enough? *Family Relations, 39*(1), 68-72.

Cole, R., & Cooper, S. (1990-1991, December-January). Lesbian exclusion from HIV/AIDS education. *SIECUS Report, 19*(2), 18-23.

Dawson, D. A. (1986). The effects of sex education on adolescent behavior. *Family Planning Perspectives, 18*(4), 162-170.

DeLamater, J., & MacCorquodale, P. (1979). *Premarital sexuality: Attitudes, relationships, behavior.* Madison: University of Wisconsin Press.

de la Vega, E. (1990). Considerations for reaching the Latino population with sexuality and HIV/AIDS information and education. *SIECUS Report, 18*(3), 1-8.

de Mauro, D. (1990). Sexuality education 1990: A review of state sexuality and AIDS education curricula. *SIECUS Report, 18*(2), 1-9.

DeMayo, M. (1991, October-November). The future of HIV/AIDS prevention programs: Learning from the experiences of gay men. *SIECUS Report, 20*(1), 1-7.

Dietz, P. (1990). Youth-serving agencies as effective providers of sexuality education. *SIECUS Report, 18*(2), 16-20.

Donahue, M. J. (1987). *Promoting abstinence: Is it viable?* Paper presented at an Office of Adolescent Pregnancy Programs technical workshop, Washington, DC.

Dryfoos, J. (1985). School-based health clinics: A new approach to preventing adolescent pregnancy? *Family Planning Perspectives, 17*(2), 70-75.

Dryfoos, J. (1988). School-based health clinics: Three years of experience. *Family Planning Perspectives, 20*(4), 193-200.

Eisen, M., & Zellman, G. L. (1987). Changes in incidence of sexual intercourse of unmarried teenagers following a community-based sex education program. *Journal of Sex Research, 23,* 527-533.

Eisen, M., Zellman, G. L., & McAlister, A. L. (1990). Evaluating the impact of a theory-based sexuality and contraceptive education program. *Family Planning Perspectives, 22*(6), 261-271.

Engel, J. W. (1983). Sex education of adults: An evaluation of a correspondence course approach. *Family Relations, 32*(1), 123-128.

Ferguson, H. B., & Mendelson-Ages, S. (1988). *Evaluating child sexual abuse prevention programs.* Ottawa, Ontario: National Clearinghouse on Family Violence, Health and Welfare, Canada.

Fisher, W. A. (1990, April-May). All together now: An integrated approach to preventing adolescent pregnancy and STD/HIV infection. *SIECUS Report, 18*(4), 1-11.

Forrest, J. D., & Silverman, J. (1989). What public school teachers teach about preventing pregnancy, AIDS and sexually transmitted diseases. *Family Planning Perspectives, 21*(2), 65-72.

Forrest, J. D., & Singh, S. (1990). The sexual and reproductive behavior of American women, 1982-1988. *Family Planning Perspectives, 22*(5), 206-214.

Furstenberg, F. F., Moore, K. A., & Peterson, J. L. (1985). Sex education and sexual experience among adolescents. *American Journal of Public Health, 75*(11), 1331-1332.

Gallup, A. M. (1985, September). The 17th annual Gallup poll of the public's attitudes toward the public schools. *Phi Delta Kappan, 67*(1), 35-47.

Gentles, I., & Cassidy, E. (1988). *Evaluating the evaluators: Child sexual abuse prevention. Do we know it works?* Ottawa, Ontario: National Clearinghouse on Family Violence, Health and Welfare, Canada.

Gilgun, J. F., & Gordon, S. (1985). Sex education and the prevention of child sexual abuse. *Journal of Sex Education and Therapy, 11*(1), 46-52.

Graham, L., & Harris-Hart, M. (1988). Meeting the challenge of child sexual abuse. *Journal of School Health, 58*(7), 292-294.

Graham, L., & Harris-Hart, M. (1989). *Child sexual abuse prevention programs.* Ottawa, Ontario: National Clearinghouse on Family Violence, Health and Welfare, Canada.

Green, S. K., & Sollie, D. L. (1989). Long-term effects of a church-based sex education program on adolescent communication. *Family Relations, 38*(2), 152-156.

Greenspan, A., & Castro, K. G. (1990, October-November). Heterosexual transmission of HIV infection. *SIECUS Report, 19*(1), 1-8.

Haffner, D. W. (1988, July-August). The AIDS epidemic: Implications for the sexuality education of our youth. *SIECUS Report, 16*(6), 1-5.

Haffner, D. W. (1989). AIDS and sexuality education. *Theory into Practice, 28*(3), 198-202.

Hunt, M. (1974). *Sexual behavior in the 1970s.* Chicago: Playboy Press.

Hyde, J. S. (1990). *Understanding human sexuality.* New York: McGraw-Hill.

Isberner, F. R., & Wright, W. R. (1988). Sex education in Illinois churches: The Octopus Program. *Journal of Sex Education and Therapy, 14*(2), 29-33.

Johnson, J. H. (1985). Individual vs. group education in family planning clinics. *Family Planning Perspectives, 17*(6), 255-259.

Jorgensen, S. R. (1991). Project taking charge: An evaluation of an adolescent pregnancy prevention program. *Family Relations, 40*(4), 373-380.

Katchadourian, H. A. (1989). *Fundamentals of human sexuality.* Orlando, FL: Harcourt, Brace Jovanovich.

Kenny, A. (1989). *Sex education and AIDS education in the schools: A survey of state policies, curricula and program activities.* Washington, DC: Alan Guttmacher Institute.

Kenny, A. M., Guardado, S., & Brown, L. (1989). Sex education and AIDS education in the schools: What states and large school districts are doing. *Family Planning Perspectives, 21*(2), 56-64.

Kirby, D. (1980). The effects of school sex education programs: A review of the literature. *Journal of School Health, 50*(10), 559-563.

Kirby, D. (1984). *Sexuality education: An evaluation of programs and their effects.* Santa Cruz, CA: Network.

Kirby, D. (1985). The effects of selected sexuality education programs: Toward a more realistic view. *Journal of Sex Education and Therapy, 11*(1), 28-37.

Kirby, D., Waszak, C., & Ziegler, J. (1991). Six school-based clinics: Their reproductive health services and impact on sexual behavior. *Family Planning Perspectives, 23*(1), 6-16.

Klitsch, M. (1990). Teenagers' condom use affected by peer factors, not by health concerns. *Family Planning Perspectives, 22*(2), 95.

Krivacska, J. J. (1991, August-September). Child sexual abuse prevention programs: The need for childhood sexuality education. *SIECUS Report, 19*(6), 1-7.

Lee, D. A., & Fong, K. (1990). HIV/AIDS and the Asian and Pacific Islander community. *SIECUS Report, 18*(3), 16-22.

Lefrancois, G. R. (1990). *The lifespan.* Belmont, CA: Wadsworth.

Levinson, D. J. (1978). *The seasons of a man's life.* New York: Ballantine.

Lifshitz, A. (1990-1991, December-January). Critical cultural barriers that bar meeting the needs of Latinas. *SIECUS Report, 19*(2), 16-17.

MacDonald, N. E., Wells, G. A., Fisher, W. A., Warren, W. K., King, M. A., Doherty, J. A., & Bowie, W. R. (1990). High-risk STD/HIV behavior among college students. *Journal of the American Medical Association, 263*(23), 3155-3159.

Maddock, J. W. (1989). Healthy family sexuality: Positive principles for educators & clinicians. *Family Relations, 38*(2), 130-136.

Maldonado, M. (1990-1991, December-January). Latinas and HIV/AIDS. *SIECUS Report, 19*(2), 11-15.

Marsiglio, W., & Mott, F. L. (1986). The impact of sex education on sexual activity, contraceptive use and premarital pregnancy among American teenagers. *Family Planning Perspectives, 18*(4), 151-162.

Masters, W. H., Johnson, V. E., & Kolodny, R. C. (1982). *Human sexuality.* Boston: Little, Brown.

McCaffree, K. (1986, November-December). Sex education curricula: Selection for elementary and secondary school students. *SIECUS Report,* pp. 4-6.

Montague, A. (1971). *Touching: The human significance of skin.* New York: Harper & Row.

National Guidelines Taskforce. (1991). *Guidelines for comprehensive sexuality education, kindergarten-12th grade.* New York: Sex Information and Education Council of the United States.

National Research Council. (1987). *Risking the future: Adolescent sexuality, pregnancy, and childbearing.* Washington, DC: National Academy Press.

Negy, C., & Webber, A. W. (1991). Knowledge and fear of AIDS: A comparison study between white, black, and Hispanic college students. *Journal of Sex Education and Therapy, 17*(1), 42-45.

Olson, T. D., Wallace, C. M., & Miller, B. C. (1984). Primary prevention of adolescent pregnancy: Promoting family involvement through a school curriculum. *Journal of Primary Prevention, 5,* 75-91.

Osborn, J. E. (1990-1991, December-January). Women and HIV/AIDS: The silent epidemic? *SIECUS Report, 19*(2), 1-4.

Parcel, G. S., Luttman, D., & Flaherty-Zonis, C. (1985). Development and evaluation of a sexuality education curriculum for young adolescents. *Journal of Sex Education and Therapy, 11*(1), 38-45.

Philliber, S. (1989). *Evaluating your adolescent pregnancy program: How to get started.* Washington, DC: Adolescent Pregnancy Prevention Clearinghouse and Children's Defense Fund.

Rienzo, B. A. (1989). The politics of sexuality education. *Journal of Sex Education and Therapy, 15*(3), 163-174.

Roosa, M. W., & Christopher, F. S. (1990). Evaluation of an abstinence-only adolescent pregnancy prevention program: A replication. *Family Relations, 39*(4), 363-367.

Rowell, R. M. (1990). Native Americans, stereotypes, and HIV/AIDS. *SIECUS Report, 18*(3), 9-15.

Ruebsaat, H. J., & Hull, R. (1975). *The male climacteric.* New York: Hawthorn.

Safer Sex. (1991, December 9). *Newsweek,* pp. 52-56.

Scales, P. (1986). The changing context of sexuality education: Paradigms and challenges for alternative futures. *Family Relations, 35*(2), 265-274.

Scales, P. (1987). How we can prevent teen pregnancy (and why it's not the real problem). *Journal of Sex Education and Therapy, 13*(1), 12-15.

Scales, P. (1989). Overcoming future barriers to sexuality education. *Theory into Practice, 28*(3), 172-176.

Scales, P., & Kirby, D. (1981). A review of exemplary sex education programs for teenagers offered by nonschool organizations. *Family Relations, 30*(2), 238-245.

SIECUS. (1990, August-September). Child sexual abuse education, prevention, and treatment: A SIECUS annotated bibliography of available print materials. *SIECUS Report,* pp. 15-21.

Sonenstein, F. L., & Pittman, K. J. (1984). The availability of sex education in large city school districts. *Family Planning Perspectives, 16*(1), 19-25.

Stevenson, M. R., & Stevenson, D. M. (1990). Beliefs about AIDS among entering college students. *Journal of Sex Education and Therapy, 16*(3), 201-204.

Tabbutt, J. (1987, November-December). Empowering teens: The national YWCA's PACT program. *SIECUS Report,* pp. 8-9.

Taking on teen pregnancy. (1987, March 23). *U.S. News & World Report,* pp. 67-68.

Torjman, S. (1989). *Child sexual abuse overview: A summary of 26 literature reviews and special projects.* Ottawa, Ontario: National Clearinghouse on Family Violence, Health and Welfare, Canada.

Trudell, B., & Whatley, M. (1991). Sex respect: A problematic public school sexuality curriculum. *Journal of Sex Education and Therapy, 17*(2), 125-140.

Valentich, M., & Gripton, J. (1989). Teaching children about AIDS. *Journal of Sex Education and Therapy, 15*(2), 92-102.

Vincent, M. L., Clearie, A. F., & Schluchter, M. D. (1987). Reducing adolescent pregnancy through school and community based education. *Journal of the American Medical Association, 257*(24), 3382-3386.

Vincent, M., & Dod, P. S. (1989). Community and school based interventions in teen pregnancy prevention. *Theory into Practice, 28*(3), 191-197.

Walsh, M. E., & Bibace, R. (1990). Developmentally-based AIDS/HIV education. *Journal of School Health, 60*(6), 256-261.

West, P. F. (1984). *Protective behaviors: Anti-victim training for children, adolescents, and adults.* Madison, WI: Protective Behaviors, Inc.

Whatley, M., & Trudell, B. (1989). Sexual abuse prevention and sexuality education: Interconnecting issues. *Theory into Practice, 28*(3), 177-182.

Woods, S. C., & Dean, K. S. (1986, September). Sexual abuse prevention: Evaluating educational strategies. *SIECUS Report, 15,* 8-9.

Wurtelle, S. K., & Miller-Perrin, C. L. (1987). An evaluation of side effects associated with participation in a child abuse prevention program. *Journal of School Health, 57*(6), 228-231.

Yarber, W. L. (1987, July-August). School AIDS education: Politics, issues and responses. *SIECUS Report, 15*(6), 1-5.

Yarber, W. L. (1988). Evaluation of the health behavior approach to school STD education. *Journal of Sex Education and Therapy, 14*(1), 33-38.

Zabin, L. S., Hirsch, M. B., Smith, E. A., Streett, R., & Hardy, J. B. (1986). Evaluation of a pregnancy prevention program for urban teenagers. *Family Planning Perspectives, 18*(3), 119-126.

Zabin, L. S., Hirsch, M. B., Streett, R., Emerson, M. R., Smith, M., Hardy, J. B., & King, T. M. (1988). The Baltimore pregnancy prevention program for urban teenagers: I. How did it work? *Family Planning Perspectives, 20*(4), 182-187.

Zelnick, M., & Kantner, J. F. (1980). Sexual activity, contraceptive use and pregnancy among metropolitan-area teenagers: 1971-1979. *Family Planning Perspectives, 12*(5), 230-237.

4

Parent Education

Theory, Research, and Practice

Gregory W. Brock

Mary Oertwein

Jeanette D. Coufal

IN ALL ERAS and across cultures, parents have been educated in the general sense to fulfill their parental roles (Harmin & Brim, 1980). Gradually, this informal socialization has been supplemented or even replaced by formal educational programs called "parent education." One of the earliest aspects of the movement of family life education has been that of education for parenthood (Croake & Glover, 1977).

This interest in parent education should not be surprising. Most people become parents; most take the role seriously and want to be successful at it; and most seek some kind of guidance in fulfilling this role. Particularly in times of rapid social change, parents may face new circumstances and challenges that require that they reexamine their basic parental functions and assume new and different roles. Harmin and Brim have identified several social factors that contribute to the contemporary need for parent education: "The process of family nuclearization, erosion of community, role differentiation and specialization, geographical distancing of family generations, and the increased entry into the labor force—have created a new reality in which parents no longer benefit from traditional structure in their parenting roles"

(Harmin & Brim, 1980, p. 14). The increasing incidence of divorce and remarriage, child abuse and neglect, spouse abuse, runaways, emotional disturbance, and high incidence of teenage pregnancy have also been identified as current indicators of the need for parent education (Hicks & Williams, 1981).

The purpose of this chapter is to discuss the nature of parent education. This discussion begins with a brief historical overview to acquaint readers with a heritage that extends to antiquity. The theoretical basis for parent education will then be presented, followed by a review of major approaches to parent education. The chapter concludes with a brief summary and discussion of issues in the field.

There has been little consensus on a definition of parenthood education (Hicks & Williams, 1981). The result has been considerable variation in the goals, methods, and subjects toward which it is directed. In this chapter, parenthood education is defined as an organized, programmatic effort to change or enhance the child-rearing knowledge and skills of a family system or a child care system. This definition is a departure from earlier ones (Croake & Glover, 1977; Earhart, 1980; Hicks & Williams, 1981; McAfee & Nedler, 1976; Schlossman, 1976, 1983) that focused solely on parents, excluded both the children and any nonparents who might be involved in child care, and did not address themes such as skills training and family systems that the authors of this chapter believe are important elements of contemporary parent education.

HISTORICAL PERSPECTIVE

A written heritage of general education for parenthood began with the ancient Greek writers (Schlossman, 1983). Plutarch was perhaps the best example, although many others have also written about family life and about how to raise children (Garland, 1990). In the United States, parent education had its inception during the 1700s when the church and the government worked together to ensure that children were raised within standards imposed by the Bible (Schlossman, 1983). The earliest self-help groups appeared around 1800 and "how-to" books began to appear in the 1850s. Around the turn of the twentieth century, large numbers of child-study and mother-study groups appeared throughout the nation, especially on the East Coast. This study movement evolved into what is now known as parent teacher associations (PTAs) in the public school system (Schlossman, 1983).

Following World War I, there was a surge in parent education supported by private foundations, and an era began in which both charismatic personalities and scientific research on children provided the content for parent education. Themes and responsibilities for parents and children changed in the ensuing decades. During the 1960s and early 1970s, for example, research focused on parent behaviors that produced particular outcomes in child behavior and development, while in the later 1970s and 1980s, this view gradually changed to include child behaviors that precipitated parent responses. As a result, parent-child interaction is currently viewed from a systemic perspective, indicating that both relationships and individuals develop in an environment in which they influence and are in turn influenced by members of their intimate relationship system. This systemic view of relationship development both complicates the evaluation of what is known about these relationships and provides increased opportunities for educational intervention.

Currently, parenthood education is both preventive and remedial, and, within the past 10 years, parents, the courts, churches, and community mental health centers have turned to parenthood education as a remedy for some of the most challenging problems facing families. Parent education programs, for example, are now "common fare" among the services provided by community health centers. The courts frequently sentence abusive parents to parent education classes, and some courts require divorcing parents to attend parent education classes to teach them how to minimize the stress and destructive influences of divorce on their children. The programs to be discussed in this chapter, however, are those preventive programs that rest on several assumptions implicit in an educational model: (a) Increased knowledge and skill are a catalyst for change; (b) people wish to grow in positive and healthy ways; (c) growth is enhanced by clearly stated goals and objectives; and (d) optimum growth occurs when consumers select goals appropriate to their own perceived needs.

Currently, there is an extensive literature in parent education (research studies, program descriptions, evaluation reports), much of it generated by researchers and scholars in family science, human development, psychology, social work, and education over the past 30 years. As a measure of the quantity of that work, the authors' subject search of literature indexed by the Education Resources Information Center (ERIC) yielded more than 3,000 citations. Obviously, a single chapter such as this cannot do full justice to that literature. Rather, the intent is to summarize some of the key literature on major themes in parenthood education, to survey the most important parent education programs, and to introduce the issues currently facing the field.

THE THEORETICAL BASE FOR PARENT EDUCATION

Because changing parent-child interaction has been the focus of most parent education efforts, research on the interaction of children and their caretakers has been the subject of considerable attention. Several excellent reviews of the literature have been provided by Walters and Stinnett (1971), Walters and Walters (1980), Peterson and Rollins (1987), Van der Zanden (1989), Belsky (1990), and Hamner and Turner (1990). Three themes about parent-child relationships emerge from these reviews: nurturance, structuring, and patterns of interaction. These three themes provide a framework both for summarizing what is known about parent-child interaction and for discussing selected parenthood education programs.

Nurturance

Nurturance refers to a collection of parenthood behaviors (warmth, support, the recognition of each child as an individual, developmentally appropriate expectations, responsiveness to child-initiated interaction, attachment) that constitute the positive, empathic, caring aspect of parenting. Nurturing parental behaviors have been found to influence positively both parent-child interaction and child development. Among these positive effects are increased sharing and comforting (Bradley, Caldwell, & Rock, 1988; Bryant & Crockenberg, 1980), fewer behavioral problems (Pettit & Bates, 1989), the expression of positive emotions (Malatesta, Grigoryev, Lamb, Albin, & Culver, 1986), increased intellectual ability (Clarke-Stewart, 1977; Morrow & Wilson, 1961; Norris, 1968; Peppin, 1963), and the development of social competence (Rollins & Thomas, 1975; Staub, 1979). Bronfenbrenner (1990) has also taken the position that parental nurturance develops social competence and that normal child development, in all its aspects, requires a family context.

The significance of parental nurturance was illustrated in a study by McClelland, Constantian, Regalado, and Stone (1978), who did a follow-up of an earlier study of 379 mothers of kindergarten children in which the mothers were rated on 150 child-rearing practices (Sears, Maccoby, & Levin, 1957). The children of the original study were interviewed and were given psychological tests. McClelland and his associates did not find any particular child-rearing techniques that determined later adult behavior or attitudes. They did find, however, that nurturant behavior by parents was important to adult maturity. The findings of this study have particular significance for parenthood education, as it indicates that nurturance per se is more important than any particular method or technique of child rearing.

Many of the studies of nurturance have developed from Bowlby's (1969) theory of bonding and attachment, which stated that sensitive and responsive care during infancy is essential for infant attachment and the development of a sense of security. In a review of research on this theory, Belsky (1990) has concluded that the research generally supports the theory. He also found, however, that responsive care after infancy can mitigate the effects of deficits in early interactions between the parent and the child.

Structure

Structure in parent-child interaction consists of making and enforcing rules and includes limit setting, control, behavioral expectations, and follow-through. It is through structuring that a parent outlines the boundaries that enable a child to define him- or herself in a complex world. Coopersmith (1967) found that structure was as important as warmth (nurturance) for the development of self-esteem. He defined appropriate structures as those that set reasonable limits on a child's behavior, that communicate those limits in a clear and democratic style, and that include an attentive concern that the child conform.

The concept of structure is not as global as that of nurturance, nor are its effects as consistently supported in the literature. The difference appears to lie in how structure is maintained and communicated. Three subdimensions of structure (induction, coercion, love withdrawal) have been identified by several researchers (Hoffman, 1970; Rollins & Thomas, 1975; Staub, 1979). *Induction* involves efforts to have the child understand the reasons that a particular behavior is expected. It emphasizes process and decision making and assumes that children can eventually develop the capacity to choose appropriate behaviors on their own. Toner (1986) found that parents who use inductive restructuring methods have children who are less likely to disobey than other children. *Coercion* refers to forced compliance. The literature has consistently shown the negative effects of coercion. Moore (1965) found that the use of physical punishment by mothers was positively correlated with dependency in boys and that severe restrictions were correlated with dependency in girls. According to Delaney (1965), imposed restrictiveness by parents correlated with aggressive behavior in young children. Other studies have shown correlations between the use of physical punishment and aggression (Becker, Peterson, Luria, Shoemaker, &

Hellman, 1962; Lefkowitz, Waldner, & Eron, 1963). *Love withdrawal* is the temporary withdrawal of parental affection or support to ensure conformity with behavioral expectations. Recent studies of the effects of shame indicate that the long-term effects of this method on child development are negative (Kaufman, 1985; Miller, 1990).

The Baumrind Model of Authoritative Parenting

The Baumrind model of authoritative parenting is perhaps the best method of structuring in parent-child interaction. In several studies of nursery school children, Baumrind (1966, 1971) found that different styles of parental structuring (which she called permissive, authoritarian, and authoritative) were associated with particular child behaviors. Permissive parents, for example, were supportive and nurturant but avoided exercising controls. They allowed their children to make many choices and exerted few demands for the child to assume responsibility for orderly behavior. When necessary, permissive parents controlled through reason or by manipulation. Baumrind's work indicated that the children of permissive parents were less likely to be self-reliant, inquisitive, and self-controlled than were other children in her study.

According to Baumrind, the authoritarian parents used a standard for conduct to control their children. They valued obedience, used punitive and forceful measures to ensure compliance, restricted autonomy, and actively worked to overcome each child's self-will. Baumrind found that the children of authoritarian parents tended to be withdrawn, discontented, and mistrustful.

The authoritative parents in Baumrind's study used inductive child guidance methods but they also expected compliance with their expectations. They valued both self-will and conformity and encouraged verbal give-and-take. Reason, power, and reinforcement were used by authoritative parents to structure behavior. In Baumrind's study, the children of authoritative parents were self-reliant, self-controlled, explorative, and contented.

To be effective, structuring must be unambiguous, and the parent must act the same way when a child misbehaves. Erratic punishment rarely inhibits the forbidden behavior (Deur & Parke, 1970; Parke & Deur, 1972). Positive behaviors that a parent wishes to diminish must be consistently ignored, punished, or at least denied positive reinforcement through the use of "time-out." Intermittent reinforcement will maintain a behavior that is already learned but is not helpful during the initial phase of behavior change.

Most current parenthood education programs adhere to the research on structuring (especially the authoritative model), although different programs emphasize different aspects of creating structures. As many parents attend parenthood education classes because of difficulties with control, the structuring methods that they learn and the values underlying these methods are of considerable importance. The structuring methods emphasized in each of the major parenthood education programs will be described later in this chapter.

Patterns of Interaction

Twenty years ago, a discussion of parent-child interaction might have ended after the preceding paragraph because interaction was viewed as a linear process; that is, if parents do this, then children will do that. More recent research, however, has indicated that what parents do and how children respond is only one part of the process. Parents affect child behavior *and* child behavior influences parental behavior. Thus interaction between parents and children is reciprocal or systemic in character. Korner (1971) found, for example, that newborns initiated four out of five interactions with caregivers, with mothers' responses influenced by the infants' state, level of arousal, sex, and neurophysiological functioning. Clarke-Stewart (1973, 1978a) examined the developing patterns of interaction between infants and parents and reported that a child's expressions of pleasure (smiling, cooing, excitement) increased the parent's positive emotional responses. She traced this pattern over time and found that positive expressions by a child at 11 months led to positive parental behaviors 3 months later. Furthermore, positive experiences between a parent and child increased the positive expressions between the parents of that child.

R. O. Bell and Harper (1977) did extensive research on parent-child interactions in families in which abuse was present. They found that some physiological characteristics of a child substantially influenced parent-child interactions (e.g., children born with a low birth weight were more likely to be abused than other children). They also identified two types of child behavior patterns that evoked different parental responses: upper limit controls and lower limit controls. When a child's behavior exceeded a parent's expectations of intensity or frequency, for example, parents exercised upper limit controls to reduce or redirect the child's behavior. Examples of upper limit controls are demands ("Clean up your room") or threats and consequences ("If you don't . . ., then . . .") and were a common parental response to child behaviors such as restlessness, whining, uncontrolled activity, or aggression. Lower limit controls were provided to encourage behaviors that conformed to parental expectations and were less likely to elicit power struggles. Examples of lower limit controls include "I'd like you to clean up your room" or

"Here are your chores." According to Bell and Harper, parent-child interactions should include a balance of upper and lower limit controls. Other research has also supported this idea of two levels of parental control behavior (Anderson, Lytton, & Romney, 1986; Brunk & Henggeler, 1984; Buss, 1981).

Parent behavior is also influenced by wider contexts. Many studies have shown, for example, that spouse support affects both quality and satisfaction with parenting (Belsky & Isabella, 1988; Bristol, Gallagher, & Schopler, 1988; Goldberg & Easterbrooks, 1984). As well, studies by the American Humane Association (1978) have shown that child abuse and neglect are not only the result of intrafamilial processes but also are related to the community context. Families with insufficient income, inadequate housing, alcohol dependence, and social isolation are more likely than others to abuse or neglect their children. These general environmental deficits appeared to be correlated more closely with neglect than with abuse, however. Neglect, especially, appears to be a result of societal context.

All of these factors influencing parent-child interaction have significant implications for parenthood education. Because parents often enroll in programs because of difficulties with their children, they are seeking solutions to dilemmas that they define as child control problems. The recognition that such problems do not necessarily result solely from the behavior of children is important both for parenthood educators and for the parents with whom they work. Thus parenthood education efforts that focus *only* on changing the parents may not be sufficient. It may be that the children also need help and thus should be included in the educational process. Additionally, improving a marriage or an extended family relationship or increasing general social support may also have a positive effect on parenting.

The research on parent-child interaction summarized in this section provides a scholarly basis for the content of parent education programs. Because effective parenting includes nurturing, structuring, and an awareness of evolving interaction processes, these themes should be addressed in parent education programs. These themes will be integrated into the following discussion of group parent education programs.

CONTEMPORARY PROGRAMS IN PARENTHOOD EDUCATION

According to Harmin and Brim (1980), there are three major modes of instruction in parent education: the individual mode, the group mode, and the mass mode. The individual mode is addressed to individual parents or caregivers and is usually associated with counseling and guidance rather than with family life education. Thus, although it is an important mode of parent education, the individual mode will not be further discussed in this chapter.

The group mode of parent education is directed toward an audience organized into specific learning groups for the purposes of parent education (Harmin & Brim, 1980). In practice, parent education and group methods are practically synonymous (Croake & Glover, 1977). Thus major emphasis in this section will be given to these group modes, with attention focused specifically on those programs that have been evaluated by a number of studies.

The third mode of parent education, the mass mode, is that form of education that addresses anonymous, mass audiences through media such as books and pamphlets, magazines and newspapers, radio and television, and so on. Although this mode has received little attention in parent education, several studies will be reviewed that appear to have important implications for parent education.

The Group Mode of Parent Education

Contemporary parenthood education programs for groups originate from several sources. Theoretically, most are based on Baumrind's (1966, 1971) authoritative parenting model, on the practices of effective communication, and on the principles of behavior modification. All of the programs discussed in this section directly address the themes of nurturance and structure in parent-child relationships. Family processes are explicitly included in some programs and are implied in others. Thomas Gordon's Parent Effectiveness Training (PET; 1975, 1976) and Dinkmeyer and McKay's Systematic Training for Effective Parenting (STEP; 1976, 1989; Dinkmeyer, McKay, & McKay, 1987) were the first widely distributed contemporary group programs and have served as models for newer programs, many of which emphasize experiential learning, the direct involvement of children in the learning process, and the use of audiovisual aids.

In addition to nurturance, structure, and processes of interaction, several other themes are present in most programs. One is the development of the capacity to listen and respond to the emotions of children. Usually called "active" or "responsive" or "empathic listening," it is typically taught by having parents identify the feelings expressed in children's words or actions and acknowledge those feelings verbally. The reciprocal communication skill usually taught is that of the I-message or parent statement; that is, parents are taught to communicate clearly their needs, feelings, or expectations to a child in a way that facilitates a positive or compliant response. Some programs include negotiation skills, while others assume that parenting problems are better resolved without negotiation.

All of the parenthood education programs discussed in this chapter include techniques for discipline and structure. All assume that hitting is not the appropriate way to accomplish this task. Rather, corporal punishment is replaced by structuring to prevent the problem, by the positive reinforcement of good behavior, or by some version of time-out (removal of the child from the stimulus situation). Time-out functions to calm the child (and the parent), provides time to reflect on behavior, and subtly punishes inappropriate behavior.

Parent Effectiveness Training (PET)

Parent Effectiveness Training (PET) was developed by Thomas Gordon in 1962 and was the first widely publicized group parent education program. The major concepts of this program are presented in Gordon's two books, *Parent Effectiveness Training* (1975) and *P.E.T. in Action* (1976). By 1980, PET had reached over 400,000 people in communities across the United States and abroad (Doherty & Ryder, 1980). Instructors in the program were required to participate in a 5½-day training program.

There are several elements of the PET programs (problem ownership, flexibility rather than consistency, and no-lose conflict resolution) that are often not included in other parenthood education programs. Problem ownership is a skill used to determine who needs to work out a solution to the problem. Gordon believes that, to resolve a problem, it is sometimes necessary to redefine or transfer problem ownership from one individual in the family to another. For example, homework is often perceived as a parent problem because it is the parent who is upset. In PET, it is necessary to restructure this problem so that it becomes the child's problem and thus he or she can do something about it.

Gordon believes that parents are more likely to be too consistent rather than too inconsistent. For example, it may not always be necessary to go to bed at 9:00. Openness to negotiation on such issues enables a child to trust that his or her personal needs and ideas are considered. Such openness in families also enables other family members to develop as situations in the family change.

According to Gordon, the use of no-lose conflict resolution eliminates power struggles between parents and children. If a means can be negotiated in which both the parent and the child get something that they want (a win-win situation), then there is less need to win at all costs (a win-lose situation).

There was considerable research on the effectiveness of PET programs in the 1970s, and these studies generally found changes toward acceptance of child behaviors and egalitarian attitudes (Hamner & Turner, 1990). Hetrick (1979) and Therrien (1979) found significant changes in empathic communication when PET trained parents where compared with control groups. In a study comparing PET, behavior modification, and Adlerian programs with no-treatment control groups 1 year after completion of the program, Schultz and Nystul (1980) found that PET and behavior modification parents were more likely to provide for independence in a warm family climate than were those in the other two groups. No other significant differences were found.

Rinn and Markle (1977), however, noted that many of the studies of PET had design problems and were limited in scope. Doherty and Ryder (1980) noted four criticisms of PET: (a) the equation of effective parenting with communication techniques, (b) judgments of parents, (c) simplistic formulas for handling problems, and (d) simplistic and linear concepts of family interaction.

PET appears to have been a program of the 1970s and 1980s. Today, versions of the original program, such as *How to Talk So Kids Will Listen and Listen So Kids Will Talk* (Faber & Mazlich, 1980), have become popular. Effectiveness Incorporated, the organization that provides support for PET, now focuses more on business management training and offers only two PET leader training workshops per year.

Systematic Training for Effective Parenting (STEP)

Systematic Training for Effective Parenting (STEP) has evolved from the work of Alfred Adler, whose ideas were developed in the United States by Rudolf Dreikurs. Dinkmeyer and McKay (1976, 1989; Dinkmeyer et al., 1987) have developed Dreikurs's ideas into the comprehensive STEP parent education programs. These programs are probably the best known and most widely used parent education programs at the current time, and many other programs described in this chapter are based on the STEP curriculum.

The goals of children's misbehavior form the cornerstone for STEP programs. Four possible goals have been identified: attention getting, power, revenge, and expression of inadequacy. Parents are encouraged to examine the goal of the child's misbehavior and to respond in a way that will facilitate more positive behaviors and interactions. Two

assumptions are central: (a) that emotions in children leading to misbe-
haviors are often based on faulty interpretations of experiences and
events and (b) that, as parents change their behaviors to enable children
to have more accurate interpretations, child behaviors will change.
Methods for changing child behaviors are addressed in STEP programs,
and natural and logical consequences are emphasized. The program
concludes with the introduction of family meetings that encourage the
family to hold democratic discussions of family problems, activities, and
goals.

More research has been done on STEP than on any other parenthood
education program. A summary of 51 studies is available from American Guidance Service (1991). Most studies have included a pre- and
posttest design with alternate treatment and control groups and the use
of objective measures, and results generally have been positive. Studies
have examined the use of STEP with many groups, including abusive
parents and parents of learning disabled and behavior disordered children. The most significant results have been positive changes in parent-
child interaction (7 of 8 studies), parental attitudes (10 of 13 studies),
child behaviors (9 of 10 studies), and parent perceptions of child behaviors (11 of 15 studies). Research has also indicated greater improvement
in family climate when both parents attended sessions (American Guidance Service, 1991).

Active Parenting

The Active Parenting program was developed by Michael Popkin
(1983, 1987, 1989). The uniqueness of this program lies in its presentation
rather than its content, as it puts the major concepts of the PET and STEP
programs into contemporary, video format. The core of the program
involves discussion of 40 video vignettes of parent-child interactions,
with concepts applied through weekly family enrichment activities.
According to Popkin (1989), the video approach helps to (a) develop
group cohesiveness, (b) teach through metaphor and story, (c) analyze
parent-child dynamics, (d) model effective parenting skills, (e) assist
with generalization of skills, (f) develop empathy skills, (g) increase
group attendance, (h) provide simulated practice, and (i) motivate parents to take action.

At least three studies have investigated the effectiveness of Active
Parenting. Popkin (1989) conducted field tests of the program using a
posttest-only design and found that the majority of parents rated themselves positively on use of the skills, reported their children's behavior
had improved, and recommended the program to friends. Boccella

(1988) used a pretest, posttest, control group design to assess the effects of the program on changes in parental attitudes, perceived behavior change of children, and perceived change in family environment. She found only that parents' confidence improved. Sprague (1990) used a one-group, pretest-posttest design and found significant positive changes in moral reasoning and parenting skills.

Parenting Skills Training

Parenting Skills Training was developed by Louise Guerney (1975, 1977) from a program for foster parents. In addition to teaching parents about child development, the noteworthy concepts of the Parenting Skills program include structuring the environment and seeing problems from the child's point of view.

Structuring the environment is a method of anticipating difficulties and planning to circumvent them. It includes planning for a variety of activities; arranging the home for child safety, comfort, and play; talking about new or different experiences beforehand; showing children exactly what is expected of them and letting them practice; and redirecting a child to another activity when unwanted behaviors occur. Parents learn to look at problems from the child's viewpoint to determine whose feelings should take priority and then to choose from various nurturing or structuring responses.

The Parenting Skills Training program has been evaluated with foster parents of children aged 5 to 12 (L. Guerney, 1977). Compared with no-treatment control groups, parents completing the program held more accepting attitudes toward their children and used more effective parenting responses. An adaptation of the program was tested on a drug abuse prevention program (D'Augelli & Weener, 1978) and resulted in parents increasing their use of effective responses to drug-dilemma situations.

Parent-Child Relationship Enhancement (PCRE)

Parent-Child Relationship Enhancement (PCRE; Coufal & Brock, 1983) was derived from Filial Therapy (B. Guerney, 1964) to train parents as play therapists for children with serious adjustment problems. PCRE differs from Filial Therapy in that PCRE is time limited, is more structured, and may appeal to parents who are more interested in prevention than in remediation.

The goal of PCRE is a change in parent-child relationships through a change in interaction patterns. The program focuses directly on behaviors and skills and centers on supervised play sessions. As the child is given the parent's full attention in play sessions, he or she is encouraged to be expressive and self-directed in play. Parents are taught to be empathic and warm while at the same time setting clear limits on unacceptable behavior. After supervised group play sessions, parents implement the new interaction patterns in the home. Evaluation studies have shown that PCRE parents scored higher than no-treatment and alternate-treatment parents on personal involvement with their child, on acceptance and nonverbal affection displayed toward the child, and on allowing the child self-direction (Coufal, 1982; Coufal & Brock, 1984).

Parent Adolescent Relationship Development (PARD) is similar to PCRE and is one of the Relationship Enhancement programs developed by Bernard Guerney, Jr. (1977) to improve family communication and problem solving. PARD is designed for families in which the children are old enough to express their needs directly and to assume responsibility for their part in family interaction. Ginsberg (1977) found that participants in PARD improved significantly on communication, quality of relationship, and self-concept. Guerney, Coufal, and Vogelsong (1981) evaluated PARD with a population of middle- and low-income mothers and adolescent daughters. When compared with a discussion method and with no-treatment groups, PARD participants were superior on indexes of communication skills, communication patterns, and relationship quality. Gains were maintained at a 6-month follow-up (Guerney, Vogelsong, & Coufal, 1983).

Self-Esteem: A Family Affair

"Self-Esteem: A Family Affair" was developed by Jean Clarke as a follow-up to her book of the same name (1978). It combines methods for developing self-esteem with an understanding of transactional analysis techniques. The program centers on communication, styles and outcomes of parenting, personal beliefs, and affirmations. According to Clarke, affirmations are the core because, at each stage of development, there are key messages a child needs to receive in order to develop properly. These messages are linked to the developmental tasks of a stage (being, doing, thinking, identity and power, structure, identity-sexuality-separation, and interdependence), are communicated through parental words and actions, and provide the prime ingredients of self-esteem (i.e., nurturing for being and structure for doing). If the appropriate messages are not received, then the stage is set for lowered self-esteem and skewed development.

To carry out this task, parents must sometimes apply transactional analysis to their own belief systems, and the program demonstrates how to do so. This theme is further developed in *Growing up Again: Parenting Ourselves, Parenting Our Children* (Clarke & Dawson, 1989). The focus is on replacing old, nonaffirming messages with affirming ones. The procedure is currently being field tested, and the instructions are available in book form.

Bredehoft (1986) tested the Self-Esteem program and found significant changes in family adaptability, cohesion, and conflict. In two follow-up studies (Bredehoft, 1990; Centers, Jump, Murray, & Sarra, 1990) with high-risk or abusive parents, significant changes in self-esteem and parenting behaviors were confirmed. The Bredehoft study showed limited change in cognitive understanding of parenting concepts. This research is important because self-esteem usually changes slowly, and low self-esteem is linked to high risk for abuse (Rosen, 1978).

Nurturing

The nurturing programs are by far the most comprehensive parent education programs generally available at the current time. They include a family of programs developed by Stephen Bavolek and colleagues (Bavolek & Bavolek, 1989; Bavolek & Comstock, 1985) targeted toward parents who are abusive or at risk for abuse of their children. Although the programs are often used in court-referred parent education programs, the content is appropriate for other populations. Separate nurturing programs are available for parents with children ages 0-5 years, 4-12 years, and adolescents and for special groups such as teen parents, parents with special learning needs (mental retardation or emotional disturbance), Spanish-speaking parents, and foster and adoptive parents. Most of the programs are for groups, but the program for young families comes in two formats: one for 45 home visits with individual families and another for 23 group sessions.

This program is based on research about the characteristics of abusive parents (Bavolek, 1990a). Four characteristics are targeted: (a) inappropriate parental expectations of the child, (b) lack of empathic awareness of child needs, (c) high use of physical punishment, and (d) reversal of parent-child roles (i.e., parents use the children to take care of them; Steele, 1975; Susman, Trickett, Iannotti, Hollenbeck, & Zahn-Waxler, 1985). Goals of the program focus on the cognitive, affective, and behavioral aspects of these characteristics. Because many abusive parents may have limited academic backgrounds, the program centers on learning through activity. These activities also serve to facilitate positive parent-child interaction. The philosophy of the program is nonjudgmental toward parents and assumes that parents want to be nonabusive and nurturing but may lack the necessary self-development and skills. Thus, along with parenting skills, the program teaches self-expression, self-nurturance, and self-care.

All segments of the program involve both parents and children. Group sessions develop the same concepts in separate but concurrent groups of parents and children, and then the two groups combine for a portion of the session for family activities. Each session has homework assignments that reinforce the concepts introduced in the sessions. The in-home sessions include activities for children, for parents, and for the whole family.

Detailed reports of validating research are available from Family Development Resources (Bavolek, 1990b), including an evaluation of the curriculum for parents of children ages 4 to 12. Measures of family environment showed increases in cohesion, expressiveness, and independence and a decrease in family conflict, while children showed a significant increase in assertiveness, enthusiasm, and tough-poise (the tendency to solve problems under stress rather than react emotionally). There was also an increase in age-appropriate behaviors, empathy, beliefs in alternative methods of punishment, and a shift toward pleasing and meeting the needs of mother and father (Bavolek, 1990b).

Behavior Modification Programs

Behavior modification programs differ significantly from other strategies. They are founded on the large body of research on the effectiveness of controlled management of behavior antecedents and consequences. O'Dell (1974) reviewed more than 70 studies of training programs for parents within the behavior modification model. He outlined the following advantages: (a) Unskilled parents can learn the techniques in a short period of time; (b) group instruction is effective; (c) the model does not label either parent or child; and (d) techniques are applicable to a wide variety of child behaviors. Cagan (1980), however, has also noted several disadvantages to behavior modification: (a) possible insensitivity to a child's needs, emotions, and stage of development; (b) emphasis on consistency, which may limit flexibility, spontaneity, and responsiveness; (c) the assumption that parental behavioral expectations are automatically legitimate; and (d) the potential loss of person-to-person interaction (i.e., a parent's response is based on a set of program reinforcers rather than on the parent's feelings or a reciprocal child-parent interaction).

Effective behavior modification requires the selection of reinforcers that are truly rewarding to a child. It is also important to establish a baseline on the behavior to be modified. This process alone often redefines a problem because, when parents count a behavior and notice what precedes and follows it, they may respond spontaneously with changes in their own behavior and/or perceptions. This change may resolve the difficulty without further intervention.

An important principle in behavior modification is deliberate modeling. When parents intentionally focus on modeling appropriate behaviors, they often interact with their children in new and very positive ways. These aspects of behavior modification are often ignored by opponents.

There are a multitude of effective behavior modification programs for parents. Beginning in the 1960s, Gerald Patterson applied behavior change methods based on social learning theory to parental concerns. He organized the Oregon Social Learning Project to develop empirically based, low-cost treatments for use with families of aggressive and pre-delinquent children. Evaluation of Patterson's time-limited, group training approach has shown it to be effective in changing aggressive behavior in children (Patterson, Chamberlain, & Reid, 1982). More recently, Patterson's work has evolved to the development and testing of theory on antisocial and delinquent behavior (Patterson, 1986; Patterson, DeBaryshe, & Ramsey, 1989). Patterson's group now believes that prevention of delinquent behavior is possible through systematic programs that include parent training, child social skills training, and academic remediation (Patterson et al., 1989).

Seventeen behavioral programs for emotionally disturbed children are presented in the *Handbook of Parent Training: Parents as Co-therapists for Children's Behavior Problems* (Schaeffer & Briesmeister, 1989). Examples of programs for major categories of childhood behavior disorders are given, including research results of the effectiveness of the programs. While the effectiveness of parent training as an adjunct to marriage and family therapy is well documented (Schaeffer & Briesmeister, 1989), it is often overlooked as a significant segment of parent education. Schaeffer and Briesmeister's book offers a variety of methods to provide parent education to this population. As both therapy costs and the number of families in need increase, specialized programming such as this may well be a growing area for family life educators.

The Mass Mode of Parent Education

Harmin and Brim's third mode of parent education was the mass mode, or that form of parent education that addresses anonymous, mass audiences through media such as books and pamphlets, magazines and newspapers, radio and television, and so on. Several studies have identified the importance and relevance of this particular mode of parent education. A national assessment of parent education needs (Gotts, Coan, & Kenoyer, 1977) reported that reading was the method most preferred by parents for learning about child rearing. Clarke-Stewart (1978b) and Durio and Hughes (cited in Holcomb & Stith, 1985) have also documented the widespread use of popular print materials by parents for obtaining child-rearing advice.

Despite this apparent preference of parents for obtaining information via the mass mode, there has been little attention to the use or evaluation of this mode of parent education. One notable exception has been that of age-paced newsletters, which are used by the U.S. Department of Agriculture Cooperative Extension Service as a strategy for providing information to expectant and new parents (Cudaback et al., 1985; Riley, Meinhardt, Nelson, Salisbury, & Winnett, 1991). These newsletters are mailed to expectant parents prior to the projected date of birth and then monthly thereafter during the baby's first year (and sometimes beyond). Information in each newsletter is targeted to the baby's age, so that relevant information reaches the parents at what is likely a "teachable moment" (Riley et al., 1991). Newsletters may also include information regarding individual and parental needs (e.g., family communication, managing stress).

In the Cudaback et al. study (1985), evaluations of parental responses to these newsletters indicated that parents found the information to be useful, that over half of the parents kept the newsletters for future reference, and that at least one additional person read the newsletter regularly. Nearly two thirds of the respondents in the Riley et al. evaluation (1991) reported the newsletters to be very useful, and their usefulness was rated higher than other sources of child-rearing advice (such as physicians, relatives, books). Parents also reported that reading the newsletters led them to change their child-rearing behaviors. There was some evidence that parents in "risk groups" (e.g., first time parents, parents with low incomes or those with low education) benefited more from the newsletters than did other parents (e.g., experienced parents, parents with higher incomes or higher education).

Several advantages of newsletters as a mode of parent education have been identified. Not only can newsletters target a particular audience at a particular time, but they also are low cost when compared with other educational interventions. Newsletters may serve hard-to-reach families (those who might be unable or unwilling to attend courses and meetings) and can be shared and discussed by parents within their own social network (Riley et al., 1991). At the same time, a newsletter is a relatively small, impersonal intervention and by itself may not be a sufficient prevention tool. Nevertheless, beneficial results have been documented, especially for inexperienced parents and other risk groups, indicating that newsletters have the potential to be effective prevention tools. Additional support for the use of printed materials as an educational strategy has been reported in an evaluation of a learn-at-home delivery system for family life information (Hennon & Peterson, 1981).

Books are also an important source of information for parents, and the number of "how-to" books on parenting is expanding rapidly, with many new titles added to those traditional resources that may now have been published in several editions. Because these printed sources are one interface between the scholarly community and parents and because they may serve either as stand-alone interventions or as resources for group methods, the contents of these publications deserve careful scrutiny by parent educators (DeFrain, 1977).

Several studies have examined the content of parenting information. DeFrain (1977), for example, examined advice concerning who should bear direct responsibility for rearing children in 52 parenting books and found that 16 of these books either implicitly or explicitly accepted the traditional roles of fathers and breadwinners and mothers as nurturant caretakers, that only 2 of these books openly questioned the value and the basis for assuming differences between mothers and fathers in parenting behaviors, and that the remainder did not address sex roles in parenting at all, apparently leaving issues of responsibility up to parents to decide. In an analysis of advice to parents in selected Christian child-rearing manuals, Boggs (1983) found that the emphasis was placed on middle childhood and that there was a preoccupation with the concepts of identity and meaning. She also found that these books omitted any reference to the social context in which family life takes place and that they ignored the potential for guilt induction when advice to parents was validated in "moral" terms.

Infant Care is an important parent education pamphlet, first published by the U.S. government in 1914. It was the first attempt by the government to provide a source of parent education and thus was a significant advance in social policy. It is one of the four or five best-selling publications in the United States, with over 60 million copies distributed (Malone & Orthner, 1988). Changes in the content of the publication have been analyzed by Wolfenstein (1953), M. Gordon (1968), and Malone and Orthner (1988).

As might be expected, the publication has gone through significant transformations over time, reflecting changing conceptions of effective child-rearing practices, but, perhaps of greater importance, the two most recent editions have been directed toward disadvantaged parents (e.g., lower socioeconomic parents and those who might have less education; Malone & Orthner, 1988). *Infant Care* thus makes important information available to parents who may not be able to take advantage of other more costly parent education resources or other modes.

One of the tasks of parent educators may be to focus on the usefulness and acceptability of printed materials to parents (Holcomb & Stith, 1985). Two studies have examined the readability of selected parent education materials (Abram & Dowling, 1979; Holcomb & Stith, 1985), as readability (ease of understanding or comprehension due to the style of writing) may be one factor in the selection and use of a book by parents. Abram and Dowling developed mean readability scores for 50 frequently read parent education books, and, although they noted several cautions in using these scores, the authors believed that the scores were potentially of value to educators in helping to match the reading skills of parents with the readability of the books.

PARENT EDUCATION FOR ADOLESCENTS

Although most parenthood education programs are targeted to adult populations, it is important to give brief attention in this chapter to those parent education programs designed specifically for adolescents. There are two forms of this education: parent education for those adolescents who are already parents and parent education for those adolescents who may become parents sometime in the future.

Clewell, Brooks-Gunn, and Benasich (1989) have provided a useful overview of programs for teenage parents. They identified three different types of programs: (a) home visitor programs that provide counseling and anticipatory guidance for the parent and well-baby care for both mother and baby (e.g., Field, 1981; Gutelius, Kirsch, MacDonald, Brooks, & McErlean, 1977); (b) center-based programs found in schools (e.g., Bennett & Bardon, 1977; Roosa, 1984) or in hospitals (e.g., Furstenberg, Brooks-Gunn, & Morgan, 1987; Osofsky & Osofsky, 1970) that provide a wide range of educational, medical, social, and parenting services; and (c) those programs that combine home- and center-based interventions (e.g., C. A. Bell, Casto, & Daniels, 1983). In their review, Clewell et al. (1989) noted that all of these programs were intended to alter parenting skills and that some also included goals concerning changes with respect to schooling and jobs. Evaluations of these different types of programs have indicated that home visits can be an effective approach in educating teen parents but that, when compared with the home visit approach, center-based programs may be more effective, especially for high-risk teens. In the conclusion to their review, the authors suggested that a true assessment of parenting education programs for adolescent parents must take into account several broader outcomes: child outcomes (social, cognitive, and health measures), maternal outcomes (educational progress, economic independence, subsequent pregnancy), and parenting outcomes (parenting skill, expectations, use of community services). This kind of evaluation approach is consistent with the systemic perspective discussed earlier in this chapter.

School-based parent education programs for future parents have been available in U.S. (and other) schools for some time (Kerckhoff, Habig, and *The Family Coordinator* Family Life Education Panel, 1976). In addition to numerous local and state parent education curriculum guides, there is a federally funded curriculum titled *Exploring Childhood*, developed in 1972 by the then U.S. Office of Education and the Office of Child Development. These various programs typically combine instruction in child development and child-rearing topics (e.g., physical development, discipline, parent-child communication) with field experiences involving the study or observation of children. The rationale for including these programs in the schools tends to emphasize the importance of preparing adolescents for their future child-rearing tasks.

Although many of these programs are well established in the schools, several important cautions have been raised about this form of parent education. Harmin and Brim (1980) suggested that, because adolescents have no children of their own and because they are still themselves being raised by their parents, they may compare their new knowledge with their own child-rearing experience, with potential unintended negative consequences for their own family interactions. As well, de Lissovoy (1978) challenged parent education in the schools, indicating that, although the objectives (i.e., better prepared parents) were sound, the target audience was open to question. He based his concern on knowledge about adolescent development, suggesting that the majority of adolescents are not maturationally ready to understand or resolve the developmental tasks of parenthood. He also questioned whether adolescents who were likely seeking freedom from parental control were prime prospects for learning about the tasks of parenthood. In de Lissovoy's view, the best parent education for adolescents would be preparental education, focusing on the *precursors* of successful parenting—issues of self, interpersonal relationships and skills, and values within a democratic society.

CONCLUSION

Parent education is a well-established form of family life education, with the greatest attention given to group parent education programs. At the current time, there is almost no evidence to support the effectiveness of one group parent education program over another. Based on current research evidence, all programs are effective (e.g., Medway, 1989; Rinn & Markle, 1977). Thus other variables (e.g., cost, session format, thematic emphasis) may be the most appropriate criteria for implementing a particular program. The task of the practitioner is to make a good match between the needs of the parents and their children and the particular program. Given that there probably are diverse needs within any parenthood education group, this task is not an easy one.

The trend over the past 25 years has been toward greater specificity. The earliest programs were presented as appropriate for all parents of all children. Over time, the content of these programs has been adapted for children of different ages and for parents with different backgrounds and different needs. Assuming that this trend continues, the generic parent education program (one that does not differentiate among parent subcultures, child guidance problems, or the social context in which the family lives) may not meet the needs of parents. In spite of this trend, there are many common family problem areas, in particular those related to divorce and remarriage, that are not directly addressed by well-known and readily available programs. Although some programs have been reported on, adequate research evidence concerning their effectiveness has not been carried out. This is clearly an area in need of attention.

A related issue has to do with the adaptation of the authoritative model of parent education to various cultural groups. Is this model as applicable for black, Hispanic, Native American, and other culturally diverse families as it may be for the cultural majority? Evolving research indicates that there are some significant differences in family structures, values, and needs among different subcultures. Thus, while nurturance, structure, and process may be important across cultural groups, the methods of implementing and teaching these concepts may need to be adapted to the significant mores of each group.

One of the major issues facing parent education is the integration of family systems theory into the content of programs. Despite research evidence, most program designers fail to recognize the role of the family system in determining child and parent behavior. By and large, most programs still assume linearity; that is, parents are still taught that their behavior controls their child or that, if they will only use time-out properly, their child management problems will go away. According to systems theory, pattern changes are not always that simple. The child may respond with rebellion, comply in one instance and then resort to old behavior a short time later, or come up with a new more disturbing behavior. Unless systemic phenomena such as this are addressed in parent education, it may create premature discouragement for parents or put undue pressure on family members. Thus it is essential that ways be developed to integrate family systems understanding into parent education programs.

There are some indications that family systems theory is already influencing the structure and content of parent education programs, as several programs do include children. The advantage of course is that this provides an opportunity to create more realistic situations for both parents and children to practice their new skills. Simply adding children (or other family members for that matter) does not, however, fully incorporate the family systems orientation. The analysis of sibling relationships, marital difficulties, or extended family issues must become an important part of the content of parent education so that parents might more fully understand the targeted child behavior patterns.

Another most important issue focuses on delivery methods. Although most parent education programs reported in this chapter are packaged programs (i.e., have a specifically designed curricula), local practitioners may find that they must in fact formulate their own programs rather than follow materials that have been prescribed by the program's authors. Some parents can't or won't commit to attending the required 8 to 10 sessions of most packaged programs; many parents are interested in particular issues rather than in general skills; and many parents have life-styles that make it difficult to attend typical group parent education sessions. These conditions present particular challenges for parent education. It may be time to move parent education groups to settings such as the workplace or the day-care center or even to replace the traditional discussion groups with mass mode alternatives that are as well designed as the car and beer commercials on television.

In all areas of family life education, there is a need for more and better research, and many questions remain unanswered concerning program effectiveness and impact. Does match between program and parental needs make a difference? What are the long-range impacts of parenthood education on family systems? Does inclusion of children make a difference, and, if so, what kind of difference? How best do parents learn and under what conditions? What prevents new knowledge and skill from being included in family interaction patterns? Answers to these and similar questions are required to strengthen the already important contribution of parent education to family life education.

REFERENCES

Abram, M. J., & Dowling, W. D. (1979). How readable are parenting books? *The Family Coordinator, 28*, 365-368.

American Guidance Service. (1991). *STEP research studies*. Circle Pines, MN: American Guidance Service.

American Humane Association. (1978). *National analysis of official child neglect and abuse reporting*. Denver, CO: American Humane Association.

Anderson, K. E., Lytton, H., & Romney, D. M. (1986). Mothers' interactions with normal and conduct-disordered boys: Who affects whom? *Developmental Psychology, 22*, 604-609.

Baumrind, D. (1966). Effects of authoritative parental control on child behavior. *Child Development, 37*, 887-907.

Baumrind, D. (1971). Current patterns of parental authority. *Developmental Psychology Monographs, 4*, 1-103.

Bavolek, S. (1990a). *A handbook for understanding child abuse and neglect*. Park City, UT: Family Development Resources.

Bavolek, S. (1990b). *Research and validation report of the nurturing programs*. Park City, UT: Family Development Resources.

Bavolek, S., & Bavolek, J. (1989). *Nurturing program for parents and children: Birth to five years*. Park City, UT: Family Development Resources.

Bavolek, S., & Comstock, C. (1985). *Nurturing parent handbook*. Park City, UT: Family Development Resources.

Becker, W. C., Peterson, D. R., Luria, Z., Shoemaker, D. J., & Hellman, L. A. (1962). Relations of factors derived from parent interview ratings to behavior problems of five year olds. *Child Development, 33*, 509-535.

Bell, C. A., Casto, G., & Daniels, D. S. (1983). Ameliorating the impact of teen-age pregnancy on parent and child. *Child Welfare, 62*, 167-173.

Bell, R. O., & Harper, L. V. (1977). *Child effects on adults*. New York: John Wiley.

Belsky, J. (1990). Parental and nonparental child care and children's socioemotional development: A decade in review. *Journal of Marriage and the Family, 52*, 885-903.

Belsky, J., & Isabella, R. (1988). Maternal, infant, and social contextual determinants of attachment security. In J. Belsky & T. Nezworski (Eds.), *Clinical implications of attachment*. Hillsdale, NJ: Lawrence Erlbaum.

Bennett, V. C., & Bardon, J. I. (1977). The effects of a school program on teenage mothers and their children. *American Journal of Orthopsychiatry, 47*, 671-678.

Boccella, E. (1988). *Effects of the "Active Parenting" program on attitudinal change of parents, parent perceived behavioral change of children, and parent perceived change of family environment*. Unpublished doctoral dissertation, Temple University.

Boggs, C. J. (1983). An analysis of selected Christian child rearing manuals. *Family Relations, 32*, 73-80.

Bowlby, J. (1969). *Attachment*. New York: Basic Books.

Bradley, R. H., Caldwell, B. M., & Rock, S. L. (1988). Home environment and school performance: A ten-year follow-up and examination of three models of environmental action. *Child Development, 59*, 852-867.

Bredehoft, D. J. (1986). An evaluation of self-esteem: A family affair. *Transactional Analysis Journal, 16*, 175-181.

Bredehoft, D. J. (1990). An evaluation study of self-esteem: A family affair program with high-risk abusive parents. *Transactional Analysis Journal, 20*, 111-117.

Bristol, M. M., Gallagher, J. J., & Schopler, E. (1988). Mothers and fathers of young developmentally disabled and nondisabled boys: Adaptation and spousal support. *Developmental Psychology, 24*, 441-451.

Bronfenbrenner, U. (1990). Discovering what families do? In D. Blankenhorn, S. Bayme, & J. Elshtain (Eds.), *Rebuilding the nest: A new commitment to the American family* (pp. 27-38). Milwaukee, WI: Family Service America.

Brunk, M. A., & Henggeler, S. W. (1984). Child influences on adult controls: An experimental investigation. *Developmental Psychology, 20*, 1074-1081.

Bryant, B. K., & Crockenberg, S. B. (1980). Correlates and dimensions of prosocial behavior: A study of female siblings and their mothers. *Child Development, 51*, 520-544.

Buss, D. M. (1981). Predicting parent-child interaction from children's activity level. *Developmental Psychology, 17*, 59-65.

Cagan, E. (1980). The positive parent: Raising children the scientific way. *Social Policy, 10*, 41-48.

Centers, K. L., Jump, J. L., Murray, S. E., & Sarra, D. W. (1990, September). *Preventing child abuse through systemic reform: A grass roots approach.* Paper presented at the 8th International Congress on Child Abuse & Neglect, Hamburg, Germany.

Clarke, J. I. (1978). *Self-esteem: A family affair.* New York: Harper & Row.

Clarke, J. I., & Dawson, C. (1989). *Growing up again: Parenting ourselves, parenting our children.* San Francisco: Hazeldon.

Clarke-Stewart, K. A. (1973). Interactions between mothers and their young children: Characteristics and consequences. *Monographs of the Society for Research in Child Development, 38* (Serial No. 153).

Clarke-Stewart, K. A. (1977). *Child care in the family: A review of research and some propositions for policy.* New York: Academic Press.

Clarke-Stewart, K. A. (1978a). And daddy makes three: The father's impact on mother and young child. *Child Development, 49*, 466-478.

Clarke-Stewart, K. A. (1978b). Popular primers for parents. *American Psychologist, 33*, 359-369.

Clewell, B. C., Brooks-Gunn, J., & Benasich, A. A. (1989). Evaluating child-related outcomes of teenage parenting programs. *Family Relations, 38*, 201-209.

Coopersmith, S. (1967). *Antecedents of self-esteem.* San Francisco: Freeman.

Coufal, J. (1982, October). *An experimental evaluation of two approaches to parent skills training: Parent-child participation versus parents only.* Paper presented at the National Council on Family Relations Annual Meeting, Washington, DC.

Coufal, J., & Brock, G. (1983). *Parent-Child Relationship Enhancement: A 10 week education program.* Menomonie: University of Wisconsin.

Coufal, J., & Brock, G. (1984). A model for including children in parent skills training. *Parenting Studies, 1*(2), 55-59.

Croake, J. W., & Glover, K. E. (1977). A history and evaluation of parent education. *The Family Coordinator, 26*, 151-157.

Cudaback, D., Darden, C., Nelson, P., O'Brien, S., Pinsky, D., & Wiggins, E. (1985). Becoming successful parents: Can age-paced newsletters help? *Family Relations, 34*, 271-275.

D'Augelli, J., & Weener, J. (1978). Training parents as mental health agents. *Community Mental Health Journal, 14*, 87-96.

DeFrain, J. D. (1977). Sexism in parenting manuals. *The Family Coordinator, 26*, 245-251.

Delaney, E. J. (1965). Parental antecedents of social aggression in young children. *Dissertation Abstracts, 26*, 1763.

de Lissovoy, V. (1978). Parent education: White elephant in the classroom? *Youth & Society, 9*, 315-338.

Deur, J. L., & Parke, R. O. (1970). Effects of inconsistent punishment on aggression in children. *Developmental Psychology, 2,* 403-411.

Dinkmeyer, D., & McKay, G. (1976). *Systematic training for effective parenting: Parent's handbook.* Circle Pines, MN: American Guidance Service.

Dinkmeyer, D., & McKay, G. (1989). *Parenting young children.* Circle Pines, MN: American Guidance Service.

Dinkmeyer, D., McKay, G., & McKay, J. (1987). *New beginnings: Skills for single parents and stepfamily parents.* Circle Pines, MN: American Guidance Service.

Doherty, W., & Ryder, R. (1980). Parent effectiveness training (PET): Criticism and caveats. *Journal of Marital & Family Therapy, 42,* 409-419.

Earhart, E. (1980). Parent education: A lifelong process. *Journal of Home Economics, 72,* 39-43.

Faber, A., & Mazlich, E. (1980). *How to talk so kids will listen and listen so kids will talk.* New York: Avon.

Field, T. M. (1981). Intervention for high-risk infants and their parents. *Educational Evaluation and Policy Analysis, 3*(6), 69-78.

Furstenberg, F. F., Jr., Brooks-Gunn, J., & Morgan, P. (1987). *Adolescent mothers in later life.* New York: Cambridge University Press.

Garland, R. (1990). *The Greek way of life from conception to old age.* Ithaca, NY: Cornell University Press.

Ginsberg, B. G. (1977). Parent-adolescent relationship development. In B. Guerney (Ed.), *Relationship enhancement* (pp. 227-267). San Francisco: Jossey-Bass.

Goldberg, W. A., & Easterbrooks, M. A. (1984). Role of marital quality in toddler development. *Developmental Psychology, 20,* 504-514.

Gordon, M. (1968). Infant care revisited. *Journal of Marriage and the Family, 30,* 578-583.

Gordon, T. (1975). *Parent effectiveness training.* Berkenfield, NJ: Penguin.

Gordon, T. (1976). *P.E.T. in action.* New York: Putnam.

Gotts, E. E., Coan, D. L., & Kenoyer, C. (1977). *Developing instructional television products for effective parenting: A national assessment of parent educational needs.* Paper presented at the annual meeting of the American Educational Research Association. (ERIC Document Reproduction Service, No. ED 136 788)

Guerney, B. G. (1964). Filial therapy: Description and rationale. *Journal of Consulting Psychology, 28,* 303-310.

Guerney, B. G. (1977). *Relationship enhancement.* San Francisco: Jossey-Bass.

Guerney, B., Coufal, J., & Vogelsong, E. (1981). Relationship Enhancement versus a traditional approach to therapeutic/preventive/enrichment parent-adolescent programs. *Journal of Consulting & Clinical Psychology, 49,* 927-939.

Guerney, B., Vogelsong, E., & Coufal, J. (1983). Relationship Enhancement versus traditional treatment: Follow-up & booster effects. In D. Olson & B. Miller (Eds.), *Family studies review yearbook.* Beverly Hills, CA: Sage.

Guerney, L. (1975). *Parenting: A skills training manual.* State College, PA: IDEALS.

Guerney, L. F. (1977). A description and evaluation of a skills training program for foster parents. *American Journal of Community Psychology, 5,* 361-371.

Gutelius, M. F., Kirsch, A. D., MacDonald, S., Brooks, M. R., & McErlean, T. (1977). Controlled study of child health supervision: Behavioral results. *Pediatrics, 60,* 294-304.

Hamner, T. J., & Turner, P. H. (1990). *Parenting in contemporary society* (2nd ed.). Englewood Cliffs, NJ: Prentice-Hall.

Harmin, D., & Brim, O. G., Jr. (1980). *Learning to be parents: Principles, programs, and methods.* Beverly Hills, CA: Sage.

Hennon, C. B., & Peterson, B. H. (1981). An evaluation of a family life education delivery system for young families. *Family Relations, 30,* 387-394.

Hetrick, E. (1979). Training parents of learning disabled children in facilitative communication skills. *Journal of Learning Disabilities, 12*, 275-277.

Hicks, M., & Williams, J. W. (1981). Current challenges in educating for parenthood. *Family Relations: Journal of Applied Family and Child Studies, 30*, 579-590.

Hoffman, M. L. (1970). Moral development. In P. H. Mussen (Ed.), *Carmichael's manual of child psychology* (3rd ed.). New York: John Wiley.

Holcomb, C. A., & Stith, M. (1985). Readability of selected parent education publications. *Family Relations, 34*, 151-159.

Kaufman, G. (1985). *Shame: The power of caring*. Rochester, VT: Schenkman.

Kerckhoff, R. K., Habig, M., & *The Family Coordinator* Family Life Education Panel. (1976). *The Family Coordinator, 25*, 127-130.

Korner, A. F. (1971). Individual differences at birth: Implications for early experience and later development. *American Journal of Orthopsychiatry, 41*, 608-619.

Lefkowitz, M. M., Waldner, L. O., & Eron, L. (1963). Punishment, identification, and aggression. *Merrill-Palmer Quarterly of Development & Behavior, 9*, 159-174.

Malatesta, C. Z., Grigoryev, P., Lamb, C., Albin, M., & Culver, C. (1986). Emotion socialization and expressive development in preterm and full-term infants. *Child Development, 57*, 316-330.

Malone, D. M., & Orthner, D. K. (1988). *Infant Care* as a parent education resource: Recent trends in care issues. *Family Relations, 37*, 367-372.

McAfee, O., & Nedler, S. (1976). *Education for parenthood: A primary prevention strategy for child abuse and neglect*. Denver, CO: Education Commission of the States.

McClelland, D. C., Constantian, C. A., Regalado, D., & Stone, C. (1978). Making it to maturity. *Psychology Today, 12*(6), 42-45.

Medway, F. (1989). Measuring the effectiveness of parent education. In M. J. Fine (Ed.), *The second handbook on parent education: Contemporary perspectives* (pp. 237-255). San Diego, CA: Academic Press.

Miller, A. (1990). *Banished knowledge: Facing childhood injuries*. New York: Doubleday.

Moore, J. (1965). Antecedents of dependency and autonomy in young children. *Dissertation Abstracts, 26*, 1966.

Morrow, W. R., & Wilson, R. C. (1961). Family relations of bright high achievers and underachieving boys. *Child Development, 32*, 501-510.

Norris, N. P. (1968). Parental understanding, parental satisfaction and desirable personality characteristics in preadolescent boys. *Dissertation Abstracts*, 4709-4710.

O'Dell, S. (1974). Training parents in behavior modification: A review. *Psychological Bulletin, 81*, 418-433.

Osofsky, H. J., & Osofsky, J. D. (1970). Adolescents as mothers: Results of a program for low-income pregnant teenagers with some emphasis upon infants' development. *American Journal of Orthopsychiatry, 40*, 825-834.

Parke, R. D., & Deur, J. L. (1972). Schedule of punishment and inhibition of aggression in children. *Developmental Psychology, 7*, 266-269.

Patterson, G. (1986). Performance models for antisocial boys. *American Psychologist, 41*, 432-444.

Patterson, G., Chamberlain, P., & Reid, J. (1982). A comparative evaluation of a parent-training program. *Behavior Therapy, 13*, 638-650.

Patterson, G., DeBaryshe, B., & Ramsey, E. (1989). A developmental perspective on antisocial behavior. *American Psychologist, 44*, 329-335.

Peppin, B. H. (1963). Parental understanding, parental acceptance and the self-concept of children as a function of academic over-and-under achievement. *Dissertation Abstracts, 23*, 4422-4423.

Peterson, G. W., & Rollins, B. C. (1987). Parent-child socialization. In M. B. Sussman & S. K. Steinmetz (Eds.), *Handbook of marriage and the family* (pp. 471-508). New York: Plenum.

Pettit, G., & Bates, J. E. (1989). Family interaction patterns and children's behavior problems from infancy to 4 years. *Developmental Psychology, 25,* 413-420.

Popkin, M. (1983). *Active parenting handbook.* Atlanta, GA: Active Parenting Publishers.

Popkin, M. (1987). *Active parenting: Teaching courage, cooperation, and responsibility.* New York: Harper Collins.

Popkin, M. (1989). Active Parenting: A video based program. In M. J. Fine (Ed.), *The second handbook on parent education: Contemporary perspectives* (pp. 77-98). San Diego, CA: Academic Press.

Riley, D., Meinhardt, G., Nelson, C., Salisbury, M. J., & Winnett, T. (1991). How effective are age-paced newsletters for new parents? A replication and extension of earlier studies. *Family Relations, 40,* 247-253.

Rinn, R. C., & Markle, A. (1977). Parent effectiveness training: A review. *Psychological Reports, 41,* 95-109.

Rollins, B. C., & Thomas, D. L. (1975). A theory of parental power and child compliance. In R. Cromwell & D. Olson (Eds.), *Power in families.* Beverly Hills, CA: Sage.

Roosa, M. W. (1984). Short-term effects of teenage parenting programs on knowledge and attitudes. *Adolescence, 19,* 659-666.

Rosen, B. (1978). Self-concept disturbance among mothers who abuse their children. *Psychological Reports, 43,* 323-326.

Schaeffer, C. E., & Briesmeister, J. M. (Eds.). (1989). *Handbook of parent training: Parents as co-therapists for children's behavior problems.* New York: John Wiley.

Schlossman, S. (1976). Before home start: Notes toward a history of parent education in America, 1897-1929. *Harvard Educational Review, 46,* 436-467.

Schlossman, S. (1983). The formative era in American parent education: Overview and interpretation. In R. Haskins & D. Adams (Eds.), *Parent education and public policy* (pp. 7-39). Norwood, NJ: Ablex.

Schultz, C., & Nystul, M. (1980). Mother-child interaction behaviors as an outcome of theoretical models of parent group education. *Journal of Individual Psychology, 36,* 315.

Sears, R., Maccoby, E., & Levin, H. (1957). *Patterns of child rearing.* New York: Harper & Row.

Sprague, J. R. (1990). *The impact of the Active Parenting program on the moral development and parenting skills of parents.* Unpublished master's thesis, North Carolina State University.

Staub, E. (1979). *Positive social behavior and morality* (Vol. 2). New York: Academic Press.

Steele, B. (1975). *Working with abusive parents from a psychiatric point of view.* Washington, DC: Government Printing Office.

Susman, E., Trickett, P., Iannotti, R., Hollenbeck, B., & Zahn-Waxler, C. (1985). Child rearing patterns in depressed, abusive, and normal mothers. *American Journal of Orthopsychiatry, 55,* 237-251.

Therrien, M. (1979). Evaluating empathy skill training for parents. *Social Work, 24,* 417-419.

Toner, T. (1986). Punitive and non-punitive discipline and subsequent rule following in young children. *Child Care Quarterly, 15*(1), 27-37.

Van der Zanden, J. W. (1989). *Human development* (4th ed.). New York: Knopf.

Walters, J., & Stinnett, N. (1971). Parent-child relationships: A decade review of research. *Journal of Marriage and the Family, 33,* 70-103.

Walters, J., & Walters, L. (1980). Parent-child relationships: A review, 1970-1979. *Journal of Marriage and the Family, 42,* 807-822.

Wolfenstein, M. (1953). Trends in infant care. *American Journal of Orthopsychiatry, 23*(1), 120-130.

5

Educating for Family Resource Management

Kathryn D. Rettig
Marilyn Martin Rossmann
M. Janice Hogan

CONTEMPORARY FAMILIES face a number of challenging issues, some of which arise from the social and economic environments in which they live. Parents find it difficult to develop good interpersonal relationships with children when economic resources are insufficient to provide for the basic needs of safety and comfort. It is challenging to be patient and tolerant in communicating with a family member when one is exhausted from working two jobs to make a living. Parents are currently realizing that the commonly shared goals of making a living, creating a comfortable home, maintaining healthy bodies and minds, finding some enjoyment in life, and encouraging growth and development are goals that are harder to achieve with the resources available in current economic environments. Many well-paying production jobs have been lost and jobs in the service economy are providing lower incomes.

The money incomes available for families affect not only their current level of living but also the investments that can be made in learning new skills or acquiring new competencies. If families can also take advantage of their community resources, time, abilities, talents, and material things, however, then they can often accomplish their impor-

AUTHORS' NOTE: Research time was supported by the Minnesota Agricultural Experiment Station (Project 52-054).

115

tant goals. The problem-solving and decision-making competencies that are needed to meet these challenges are becoming increasingly more important in complex and rapidly changing environments.

Because the purpose of family life education is to help individuals and families develop their capacities as family members and meet their needs for family living over the life span (Arcus, 1990), family life educators are involved in resource management education any time they are assisting others in identifying values conflicts, prioritizing goals, developing resource awareness and alternative-mindedness about resource uses, and strengthening decision-making competencies. The ultimate goal of family resource management education is to assist people in reducing the discrepancies between their wants and expectations and the resource realities of their lives.

Management has several purposes in family living, but, in general, it seeks to provide some degree of control over the events of everyday family living (Paolucci, Hall, & Axinn, 1977). It enables families to mobilize resources toward their values and central life purposes and to consciously address changing goals and concerns over their life span (Arcus, 1984). The use of conscious decision-making processes not only enhances the strength of family groups and produces capable people, it also brings about nondisruptive changes, reduces tension levels, and resolves conflicts (Deacon & Firebaugh, 1988; Paolucci et al., 1977). Through management processes, families seek balance and proportion in the attention given to the needs and interests of various family members; material and humanistic achievements; work, rest, and leisure; and meeting current and future needs (Liston, 1966).[1]

The focus of this chapter is on the internal dynamics of family decision-making processes, that is, the thinking involved in the *processes* of family resource management. This area is a vital component of family life education programs as identified in the Framework for Life-Span Family Life Education (Arcus, 1987; J. Thomas & Arcus, 1992) and is one of the topic areas of importance in preparing family life educators (Arcus, 1984).

COMPONENTS OF FAMILY RESOURCE MANAGEMENT

The assumptions, definitions, and explanations of family resource management need to be explicitly stated to provide the theoretical background to guide family educators in this area and for readers to have shared meaning of the content with the authors.

Assumptions About Resource Management Content

The major premise underlying family resource management education is that the use of conscious values and goals and deliberate decision-making processes will improve the effectiveness with which human resources are produced, exchanged, and used and will also increase the effectiveness with which nonhuman resources are allocated, consumed, exchanged, invested, or conserved.[2]

The following are five assumptions about the *content* of resource management. Resource management

(a) enables individuals and families to have some degree of control over their lives and some freedom to choose goals and to allocate resources;

(b) involves conscious problem-solving and decision-making processes that differ across families in styles and extensiveness of use;

(c) permeates all aspects of family living from everyday activities to infrequent, unusual, and perplexing problems;

(d) involves diverse applications based on the unique cultural milieu, decision situation, and family goals and resources; and

(e) requires a conscious understanding of the economic functions of families for society, as well as for individuals, as these functions are integrated with biological and social-psychological family functions.

There are also assumptions about learning processes and program delivery identified later in the chapter. The content, learning, and program assumptions influence how educators structure programs to focus on resource management issues.

Definitions and Explanations

Definitions of family resource management as a field of study have been surprisingly consistent over time. Family resource management was described in the 1930s as including the processes of "planning, guiding, and directing of human and material resources for the optimal development of individual members and the family within the home and in their relations with other individuals and groups" (Coon, 1938, p. 8). In 1967, family resource management involved the "accomplishment of work, made possible better use of money and abilities, released time and energy from work to allow time for recreational activities, improved the choice and use made of goods, influenced the establishment of reasonable standards, and integrated human values into living as changed conditions affect family life" (Nickell & Dorsey, 1967, p. 106).

Currently, the field continues to define its focus as the goal-directed behaviors of families, using decision making, valuing, planning, communicating, and organizing activities to guide resource use for improving quality of life (A. S. Rice & Tucker, 1986).

It is important for educators who are planning to include resource management content in family life education programs to realize what it means to view the family from an economic perspective. In addition, educators must also understand that management involves many interrelated and interdependent processes that occur sequentially, simultaneously, and at differing levels of abstraction or specificity. The central processes of management are problem solving, decision making, and decision implementation. Definitions of an economic unit and everyday processes (such as decision making) will vary somewhat in the different social sciences of anthropology, sociology, or economics. Therefore it seems important to establish some shared understanding of the family as an economic unit before proceeding to define central management concepts and processes.

An *economic unit* is any entity that can both maintain a set of goals and carry out the economic activities required for reaching these goals such as production, consumption, allocation, investment, and exchange of resources (Diesing, 1976). Diesing's definition of an economic unit means that *all goals* are economic and there is no such thing as a "noneconomic goal." All goals are economic because they require (at the very least) human resources for their accomplishment. Human and nonhuman resources are used or channeled even when one is working toward the goals of developing more empathy, strengthening a parent-child relationship, or providing emotional support for an unemployed spouse.

The above definition of an economic unit highlights some mistaken assumptions held by many family life educators: "In order to be economic, the resource to be managed must be money"; "money is the only economic resource"; and "consumption is the only economic activity of families." Family resource management is concerned about the development, use, and investment of human resources (Liston, 1975) and defines economic resources more broadly than money. Economic resources are those that are scarce, can be measured by neutral means outside the self, and can be allocated to various goals. An economic resource cannot be allocated unless it can be measured (Diesing, 1976). Economic resources include time, human energy, fossil fuel energy, and money.

Families are important economic units in society because of the necessary economic activities in which they engage. To reach goals, resources must be mobilized for various kinds of activities. Family life educators are typically most aware of the consumption activities of families, which involve purchasing and using resources for the satisfaction of needs and desires, but educators are less likely to think of families as production units, distributors of income and wealth, or investors.

Families are primarily responsible for the "production" of people and their human resources like health and the ability to speak the language of the culture. Families also produce goods and services, such as prepared meals and child care, which have a dollar value when purchased in the marketplace. These goods and services produced at home for family use are considered nonmoney income. Other examples of nonmoney income produced by families include clean clothes, refinished furniture, repaired cars, counseling services, and physical care during illness.

Families also produce and distribute monetary wealth to various members within and across generations. Monetary investments in the health and education of family members that have economic returns to the family and to society at a later time are called "human capital investments." Families set and achieve goals and produce, consume, allocate, exchange, and invest resources in the course of their everyday activities.[3]

Some of the textbooks used in family relationships courses at the college level do identify the family as an economic system (Cox, 1990; F. P. Rice, 1990; Strong & DeVault, 1992). The typical approach, however, involves one chapter devoted only to the management of money income and wealth. Little attention is given to other economic functions of families, such as producing human resources and nonmoney income or investing in acquiring new skills, or to the management of time, human energy, or fossil fuel energy. The economic resources needed to accomplish human relationship goals, such as time for teaching children or human energy for family activities, are assumed to be outside of the economic realm, not part of family resource management, or not important influences on family relationships.

The economic activities of families require both coordination and organization to make life satisfying. The decision makers (managers) perform this function and the managerial subsystem of any family involves the processes through which decisions are made about important policies, future directions, and how to mobilize resources for various goals and activities. The major elements of managerial subsystems of families include decision situations, decision makers, and decision processes (Rettig, 1988). Family resource management is also concerned with the content of problems and decisions, family members' roles in decision processes, and decision outcomes. Management includes the many processes through which families deal with problems that emerge from changes in the environment and changes within themselves.

Concepts

The central concepts of family resource management include problems, values, goals, standards, resources, decisions, and plans. Definitions and examples of the central concepts and subconcepts are described in Table 5.1. The central concepts of family resource management are sometimes confusing because management is not a static concept but consists of a combination of dynamic processes. Each of the central concepts of management is included in many different processes. For example, the concept of "problems" is included in the processes of problem recognition, problem definition, and problem solving. The concept of "values" is part of the processes of value identification, value prioritization, and value mediation and is also part of standard setting and standard maintenance. The combination of processes that are part of resource management is described below.

Processes

The central processes of family resource management are problem solving, decision making, choice, and decision implementation. Management is an adjustment process that begins and ends with change. The decision maker(s) either must respond to changes in the environment that require deliberation, or the desired changes are initiated by the decision maker(s) and later affect the environment. Although problem solving, decision making, and decision implementation are central processes occurring during the adaptation behaviors that characterize management, numerous other processes are also part of family resource management and include the following (see box):

Family Resource Management Processes[4]

Problem solving, decision making, choice, and decision implementation

Valuing, standard setting, and standard maintaining

Goal identifying, agreeing, and prioritizing

Resource producing, allocating, consuming, conserving, investing, and exchanging

Information accessing, processing, and sharing

Planning, organizing, facilitating, and implementing

Coordinating, controlling, checking, adjusting, evaluating, and innovating

Communicating, integrating, negotiating, mediating

Leading, motivating, supervising, learning, and socializing

TABLE 5.1. Central Concepts of Family Resource Management

Concept	Definitions	Examples
Problems	Problems are situations that call for analysis and action to produce a specific change (Tallman, 1988). Problems occur when there is a discrepancy between what is and what the person or group prefers (A. S. Rice & Tucker, 1986).	What should be done about improving the health of family members? What should be done about providing more support for an elderly parent?
Values	Conceptions of what is desirable, right, and good; what is worthy, important, or best; and what one feels a commitment toward (Paolucci, et al., 1977): Values are the reasons *why* people act.	
Personal	Character, or the manner in which individuals respond to everyday living (theoretical, economic, aesthetic) (Paolucci et al., 1977, pp. 65-66)	Competence, achievement, punctuality, goal directedness, self-discipline, decisiveness
Moral	A sense of right and wrong and responsibility to live in ways that protect the freedom and rights of others	Honesty, tolerance, and integrity
Social	Relationships with other people	Cooperation, support, justice, benevolence, equity, respect
Goals	The ends toward which people are willing to work; arise from values but are more definite than values because they can be accomplished in short, intermediate, or long-term time ranges (A. S. Rice & Tucker, 1986): Goals are *what* people *do* to work toward values.	Family goal: Increase physical activities during family leisure time to promote improved strength and endurance

continued

TABLE 5.1. *(continued)*

Concept	Definitions	Examples
Standards	Measures of value or worth, which represent how long, how much, or how often the behaviors must change to accomplish the goals that actualize values	Individual's standard: Walk 50 minutes at a brisk pace every-day at 5:00 p.m.
Resources	The *means* available for reaching goals, maintaining standards, and solving problems (Hogan & Buehler, 1984). Concepts of resources and goals are *defined interdependently*. For goal accomplishment, resources must be available (possession utility) at the time they are needed (time utility), at the place they are needed (place utility), and in a useful form (form utility).	
Nonhuman	Available means of supply or support one can use for reaching goals and solving problems	Economic resources such as time and money; environmental resources such as climate, water; technological resources such as computers
Human	Personal attributes an individual possesses to fulfill his or her changing roles (Liston, 1975)	Affective qualities such as enthusiasm; cognitive qualities such as judgment and initiative; psychomotor qualities such as communication abilities; temporal qualities such as pace and time orientation (A. S. Rice & Tucker, 1986, p. 110)
Decisions	A decision is a conscious and nonroutine process of comparing alternative objects or courses of action, selecting one of the alternatives, and making a commitment to that alternative until a subsequent evaluation is made (Tallman, 1988).	

Technical[a]	Effective accomplishment of one goal. The processes involve mobilizing resources, coordination with others, checking progress, and adjusting plans.	Planning and having a major family reunion involving a four-generation family
Economic[a]	Allocating scarce and measurable economic resources among multiple competing goals that must be prioritized. The processes begin with an understanding of the problem and known goals and proceed by seeking and processing information about alternatives and consequences.	Deciding how time can be allocated to meet personal needs, work demands, needs of family members, and requests of friends
Social[a]	Two or more people must make one decision that resolves value, goal, standard, and role conflicts to integrate the group. Process begins with discomfort, proceeds to define the problem in terms of personal needs and clarification of values, and ends with agreed-upon goals.	Agreeing on value priorities and deciding on goals for retraining both husband and wife for a changing work environment
Plans	Scheme, program, or method developed prior to and for the purpose of goal attainment (A. S. Rice & Tucker, 1986)	Development of a timetable for a savings plan for the education of children beyond high school

a. This section based on Diesing (1976) and Rettig (1986).

The following definitions of central processes of family resource management are presented in an order from most comprehensive to most specific.

> *Management* includes the many processes through which families strive for goal achievement and for reduction of the degree of tension and disequilibrium as well as the processes through which they plan for transcending their current dimensions (Liston, 1964).[5]
>
> *Problem solving* is the process of removing, ending, or overcoming some barrier, obstacle, or impediment to attaining a goal (Tallman, 1988). The problem-solving process may involve various kinds of decision-making processes.
>
> *Decision making* is the process of comparing alternatives in terms of the actor's subjective estimates of the probable costs and benefits associated with each alternative and selecting the alternative that provides the best assurance of attaining the expected satisfaction (Tallman, 1988).
>
> *Choice* is the act of choosing or selecting among alternatives.
>
> *Decision implementation* is the process of putting decisions into action by planning and carrying out plans for change.

Family resource management is concerned with facing situations and opportunities that may change the status quo, threaten achievement of desired standards and levels of living, or offer challenges for personal growth. Liston (1966) indicated that resource management problems are perplexing situations that involve doubt, uncertainty, or difficulty and call for a choice of action leading to an adjustment. The concerns surrounding each problem vary due to the content of the problem, degrees of urgency, risk of undesirable consequences, amount and number of resources required, and human resource availabilities and limitations of the family members involved.

Family resource management views the family as a problem-solving group where management is a *means* of engaging some of the most prized qualities of life. Family managers are concerned not only with the problem situations that call for rational uses of resources but also with the social processes involved in dealing judiciously with these problems (Liston, 1966, p. 7). The wide diversity in *types* of managerial problems faced by families is outlined in Table 5.2. The orientation dimension refers to the goal of responding to the concern as preventive, remedial, or growth. Comprehensiveness means the level of complexity of the issue, and, finally, the content orientations of problems are identified. Problems can exist with any of the resources being managed: time, money, human resources, property, and community resources (Liston, 1966, pp. 11-17).[6]

TABLE 5.2. The Dimensions of Practical Problems Requiring Management of Family Resources

Orientations or Targets	Comprehensiveness Levels	Content Orientation
Preventive and maintenance problems: aim to avoid situations in the future or reduce the seriousness of problems	Technical problems: involve how to do something and can often be solved by acquiring information	Organization/control problems: concern decisions about the performance tasks or activities in the family such as what needs to be done, when, where, how, how well, and by whom
Remedial or corrective problems: seek a remedy to a situation that is less than acceptable according to personal/family standards	Elemental problems: involve a special segment of family living such as food or money management, housing, or recreational management	Allocation problems: concern decisions about the most productive ways of distributing resources among alternative goals; this involves deciding on the best "mix" of kinds and amounts of resources for achieving various goals selected as important
Growth and development problems: aim to make an acceptable situation better by taking advantage of resources	Integrative problems: involve meshing several elements of family life into a balanced and satisfying whole such as the coordination of family activities	Policy problems: concern the decisions in which two or more people must agree on which values are fundamental, which goals deserve prime attention, and which resources are available for use
		Interaction problems: concern the process decisions or group dynamics issues of communication, role responsibilities, supervision, motivation, and evaluation

SOURCE: Adapted from Liston (1966).

The managerial responses to problem situations are described specifically as perception of wanted or needed changes, problem facing, discussion of problem meaning/definition, developing agreement to solve the problem, identifying personal and group needs, negotiating and mediating the issues, agreeing on value and goal priorities and policies, creating or imagining desirable alternative outcomes, planning mobilization of resources for high-priority goals, implementing policies and plans, controlling and adjusting plans, and evaluating for future changes (Rettig, 1986, p. 52). These responses will involve several kinds of decision-making processes (social, economic, and technical), all of which are likely to include the steps of defining or conceptualizing the problem, seeking information about alternative courses of action, considering the consequences of alternatives, and selecting or creating a solution to be implemented (Deacon & Firebaugh, 1988; Paolucci et al., 1977; Rettig, 1986).

The inclusion of decisions as a central *concept* and problem solving, decision making, and decision implementation as central *processes* of family resource management departs from the assumptions of the Framework for Life-Span Family Life Education (Arcus, 1987). The framework assumed that the processes of communicating, problem solving, and decision making were "incorporated into all of the topic areas as an integral part of educational programs and, therefore, were not listed as separate concepts" (p. 7). The authors of this chapter agree that these concepts are an integral part of family life education programs. Problem solving and decision making are seen as *managerial* processes, however, regardless of the content of the problem or decision. For problems to be solved or decisions to be made, the result is that values are clarified, goals are identified, resources are located and directed, action is taken, and results are evaluated. As it permeates all areas, family resource management as described in this chapter could integrate all other content areas of family life education.

DEVELOPMENT OF FAMILY RESOURCE
MANAGEMENT EDUCATION

The development of family resource management education is difficult for many reasons. The subject is process as well as content centered. There is a need for application to make the cognitive decision-making and affective valuing processes become real for learners. Cognitive and affective processes inform each other in actual decision-making situations and there is a need to examine the interdependence of these processes. The managerial problems faced by families can be large and significant or small and inconsequential. Managerial processes are generally embedded in all aspects of everyday life and need to be raised to a level of consciousness that examines the underlying assumptions. There are also so many different kinds of resources for families to manage and the management of human and nonhuman resources involves very different values and processes.

The major concepts and processes of family resource management are not likely to be isolated in a single curriculum unit but will be an integral part of educational topics such as marriage preparation and enrichment, conflict resolution, marital dissolution, remarriage, and preparation for retirement. Therefore educational planners cannot easily isolate the subject content or locate a set of decision rules for the selection and organization of family resource management curriculum. The development of family life education programs with a resource management perspective involves several assumptions about learning resource management processes and requires several guiding conceptual frameworks for organizing the content. The assumptions about learning managerial processes are presented first.

Assumptions About Learning Management Processes

Effective learning of resource management *processes* requires the following:

1. *Learners examine problems in context* so that value priorities and conflicts can be articulated, goals and standards identified, alternative uses of resources and courses of action be examined, consequences of alternatives imagined, and plans made for implementing decisions. This human ecological approach to learning resource management processes has been advocated for some time by authorities in the subject matter (Bubolz & Sontag, 1993; Deacon & Firebaugh, 1988; Gross et al., 1980; Hogan, 1978; Melson, 1980; Paolucci et al., 1977; Rettig & Everett, 1982).

2. *Learners increase levels of consciousness* concerning valuing and decision-making processes, particularly with more consciousness about value priorities and conflicts, individual and shared goals, alternative uses of resources, and diversity in life-style possibilities (Liston, 1966; Paolucci, 1966). This rational, cognitive-affective approach to solving practical family problems encourages students to struggle with persistent problems confronted by humans across generations, as they are experienced by particular people at one time and place, and to name processes they have already used in the past.

3. *Learners use cognitive competencies of analysis, synthesis, and evaluation* in critical thinking processes that require challenging existing assumptions; considering multiple, interacting variables; weighing pro and con arguments of fact and value; mediating values; synthesizing divergent viewpoints and alternatives; and evaluating effectiveness and needs for future changes (Costa, 1985; Green, 1988; Iozzi & Cheu, 1979; Paolucci et al., 1977).

4. *Learners implement decisions and plans* to evaluate the effectiveness of the mental processes preceding actions toward the intended goals. Management processes begin with mental processes but are not completed until decisions are implemented and evaluated (Deacon & Firebaugh, 1988; Gross et al., 1980).

5. *Learners function mentally within the normal range* so that information is accessed and processed with some degree of objectivity and rationality, consequences of actions can be anticipated and understood, and actions can be delayed when necessary. Mental illness is often signaled by changes in information processing or impulse control and cognitive impairment also reduces decision-making and planning competence (American Psychiatric Association, 1987).

Conceptual Frameworks

The assumptions about learning managerial processes suggest the importance for management education of the human ecological systems perspective in solving practical problems that require critical thinking processes. The conceptual frameworks of ecological systems (Bronfenbrenner, 1979; Darling, 1987; Paolucci et al., 1977), practical problems (M. Brown & Paolucci, 1979) and critical thinking (Brookfield, 1987; Ennis, 1985, 1989) are at differing levels of conceptual abstraction from the most global and comprehensive ideas (ecological systems) to the most concrete and specific personal competencies (critical thinking). All three perspectives are important in the development of family resource management education for understanding management *processes*. In addition, the Framework for Life-Span Family Life Education (Arcus, 1987) can also serve as a *content* guide for developing programs and for the inclusion of resource management perspectives across the other family life education topic areas.

Human Ecological Systems Framework

The study of human ecology examines the interdependence of human communities (organisms) and their various environments, including the *natural, human-behavioral*, and *human-constructed environments* (Bubolz & Sontag, 1993). Families are viewed as energy transformation systems that transform resources from the environment (energy inputs) into useful goods and services for their own needs and into outputs to the environment of human capital, goods, information, and waste (Hogan & Paolucci, 1979). "The flow of energy to and through the family system activates the decision-making and decision-implementation processes. Internally, the energy is transformed to support the production, consumption, and socialization functions of the family. The outputs to the environment are used by other systems, activating reciprocal exchanges and bonds of interdependence" (M. P. Andrews, Bubolz, & Paolucci, 1980, p. 35).

The emphasis on the interdependence of organisms and environments means that family decisions, as well as individual growth and development and family relationships, are seen to be influenced by and to influence various environments. Family decisions are influenced by and also influence the water quality, food supply, energy availability, and waste disposal in the *natural environment*; belief systems, policies of major institutions, and support patterns of informal networks such as relatives in the *social environment*; and communication and transportation systems in the *human-constructed environment*.

An ecological perspective is taken in family resource management education because management involves the human processes of adapting to personal, group, and environmental changes. Both external and internal changes produce decision situations for managers. An ecological perspective in educational programs emphasizes that environments provide both opportunities and constraints for decision makers; resources for solving problems are simultaneously environmental, personal, and interpersonal; the physical resources base of families is critically important and influences economic and social-psychological resource availabilities; fundamental resources such as air, water, land, food, temperature, space, and energy are important factors in the decision situation because they influence perceptions of the problem and envisioned solutions (Rettig, 1988).

Family resource management curriculum with an ecological perspective is concerned about quality of life issues and asks questions to examine family decisions within the context of environmental opportunities and constraints. The most general questions concern: "What is the good life?" and "What is the environmental impact?" Questions at a more specific level would also be about the interaction of families and environments; for example, "How do we allocate time for children's needs, our own needs, and our employer's expectations?" "What plans need to be made to meet current necessities and future needs in a changing world?" "What life-style changes could be made to reduce energy consumption?" "How do the resources of new reproductive technologies affect our decisions about parenting?" "How do cumulative decisions about sexuality influence the belief systems of society and then influence our family values?" Questions about human resource development include such concerns as the following: "How can we educate our children in an environment where the quality of education appears to be declining and the costs are increasing?"

One obvious limitation to the ecological framework is that there may be no end to the family-environment interactions, similar to there being no end to the ripple effect when a pebble is dropped in an ocean. Program developers will need to select a few impacts of environments on family decisions and a few consequences of family decisions on environments, making certain, however, that attention is given to the *natural* environment as well as to the human-behavioral and human-constructed environments. Family life educators in past years have typically emphasized the importance of family systems theory in developing educational programs but have tended to describe the social ecology of the family without mention of the reciprocal interactions with the natural environment or the importance of natural resources for the social ecology (Berry, 1992; Strong & DeVault, 1992). Family professionals have tended to view the social issues of resource use and environmental protection as low-priority topics for inclusion in family life education programs (Smith & Ingoldsby, 1992).

Practical Problem-Solving Framework

Practical problems are value questions about what action should be taken in a particular context. They are "persistent problems confronted perennially from generation to generation that have their roots in the issues of being human and living in a human society" (M. Brown & Paolucci, 1979, p. 47). *Problems,* as the term is used here, are serious concerns or opportunities that require thoughtful attention. The conceptualization of practical problems helps the program planner to select content that has a high probability of recurring over time and applies to most families and individuals. It does not eliminate addressing issues that are more specific to place and people but guides the choice of examples when there is not enough time to include everything. Following a practical problem focus, curriculum in family resource management flows from a question such as the overarching one posed in the Minnesota guide for secondary school family life educators: "What should be done about enabling individuals and families to identify values, formulate goals, set standards, and make informed choices regarding the management of human and nonhuman resources?" (Torgerson, 1990, p. 5).[7]

The practical problem-solving focus with a resource management perspective can be applied to any *purpose* or *content area* of family life education, as Maskay and Juhasz (1983) demonstrated with the decision-making process model for adolescent sexual decisions for the purpose of prevention and education. Roosa, Gensheimer, Short, Ayers, and Shell (1989) also reported the effective teaching of problem-focused coping strategies (decision-making process) as preventive intervention for elementary-aged children in problem-drinking families. Tebes, Grady, and Snow (1989) taught parents to facilitate their adolescent child's decision-making ability as part of an intervention program. Gilbert (1990) also explained that practical problem solving can be used as a method to organize lecture presentations to large classes.

There are several limitations of the practical problem-solving conceptual framework. The practical problem perspective implies something negative (a *problem*) when what is intended may better be labeled a *concern* or *issue*. The purest application of the guide seems to eliminate all but *major* problems. The practical problem focus is useful in prioritizing the challenging issues needing attention, but family resource management education also addresses the concerns of daily life. Learners may not perceive that the concerns of daily life are also enduring problems across generations, despite changes in standards and technologies.

Critical Thinking Framework

Resource management educators need to develop curriculum in ways that promote competencies in critical thinking and encourage the development of "reasoning" individuals. Critical thinking is defined as "reasonable, reflective thinking that is focused on deciding what to believe or do" (Ennis, 1985, p. 46). Use of critical thinking means that assumptions are identified and challenged; practices, structures, and actions are understood in relationship to the context; the capacity to imagine and explore alternatives is encouraged; and participants in programs exhibit reflective skepticism (Brookfield, 1987). The use of critical thinking assists learners in becoming more effective in divergent thinking, weighing evidence, constructing pro and con arguments for propositions, detecting mistakes in reasoning (Green, 1988), and separating facts and values (Linck, 1982). Learners will need to move beyond acquiring managerial knowledge and comprehending managerial processes to being able to analyze problem situations, synthesize new alternatives and plans, and evaluate.

Family resource management education involves teaching processes that people have previously experienced as part of daily life in family settings. They may believe there is nothing new for them to learn. The educator is challenged to assist learners in becoming critically conscious of their valuing and decision-making processes because managerial processes cannot be improved without heightened levels of awareness. Learners need to be able to explicitly name values, consciously recognize differing value priorities or various decision processes, consider short-term and long-term consequences of alternative solutions to problems, and reflect on resource use in alternative life-styles.

The use of critical thinking encourages individuals to doubt what they are told and what they are read and to form their own conclusions. Further, educators will need to begin with themselves to "reflect on their own thought processes, their experiences of learning, misunderstanding, confusion and insight" (Paul, Binker, Martin, & Adamson, 1989). Developing critical thinking competencies requires a curriculum that emphasizes the "tools" of critical thinking such as checking assumptions, reasoning, and contradicting. Questioning in a critical mode would involve questions like these: "What does it mean to use time wisely?" "Can you think of cultures in which 'wise use of time' would not be a relevant question for anyone?" "Can you support the argument that all cultures and religions share the same values and then support the opposite point of view?"

Curriculum Implications

The development of family resource management education curriculum is complex, as is curriculum development in general. The ecological systems perspective in solving practical problems that require critical thinking processes involves three conceptual frameworks that provide useful guidelines. The fact remains, however, that criteria to direct selection of new material, and elimination of old material to make room for the new, is lacking. Also missing are directions on how to accomplish the integration of this area into other family life education courses (Brady, 1990). In the absence of agreed-upon criteria, the educator must be skillful in conducting needs assessments among students, defining the ideal state of learning, and preparing a program that fills the discrepancy between the existing situation and the ideal.

Educational evaluation is the systematic assessment of value, worth, or merit so that judgments can be made about continuing, terminating, or changing programs (Plihal, 1983). "Good" resource management within families can be evaluated from the perspective of the insider (the individual or family group) or the outsider (external evaluators). From the point of view of the insider, outcomes depend upon the effectiveness with which available resources have been used to attain valued goals. Caution needs to be exercised by outsiders, because it is nearly impossible to view others' values or human energy resources and thus errors are likely in making value judgments.[8]

The absence of evaluation of family life education programs has been noted by various authors (Small, 1990; Weiss, 1988) and the absence of evaluation specifically in family resource management education programs is notable. There are no existing models for the critique of family resource management curricula other than using the central concepts, processes, and content as guidelines. It may be possible to use criteria designed for general evaluation of family life education (Jacobs, 1988).[9] For example, Griggs (1981) generated lists to be used by educators when selecting materials and Ray (1986) created a model for critiquing curricula. Ray stated that "the ultimate goal of curriculum and of instruction is to make meaningful learning experiences available for learners. Simultaneously, the goal of evaluation or critique is to judge the potential of a given set of resource materials to provide the types of encounter originally intended by the curriculum builders" (1986, p. 112).

Participatory evaluation (Whitmore, 1991) may provide a possible approach to evaluating in the area of family resource management. This method has been used in parent education programs. It is based on the premise that participation by the students and the educator in the evaluation of programs fosters a sense of ownership. This empowerment would also be true of the design of programs. The assumption is that the *process* provides learning. The focus shifts from outcomes to an interactive, dynamic activity where program participants themselves define the questions, gather data, and determine meaning. For further information regarding planning, implementation, and evaluation of educational programs, see Chapter 5 in Volume 1 of the *Handbook of Family Life Education*.

DELIVERY OF FAMILY RESOURCE MANAGEMENT EDUCATION PROGRAMS

The concern in family life education is to deliver programs in all content areas that meet the needs of people across the life span. The assumptions about program delivery are listed first and are followed by a discussion of strategies for integrating resource management content into two topic areas of family life education.

Assumptions About Program Delivery

It is assumed that resource management programs can be effectively designed and delivered

(a) for children, adolescents, and adults;

(b) in formal and nonformal settings;

(c) to enhance any of the goals of family life education, including education, enrichment, prevention, intervention, remediation, or therapy;

(d) directly with the focus on family resource management content and processes or indirectly as resource management perspectives in other topic areas of family life education; and

(e) to enhance any topic area of family life education, including families and society, education about parenthood, family interaction, human development and sexuality, interpersonal relationships, and ethics.

Programs that are delivered directly with the focus of resource management content and processes are typically offered in the formal settings of high schools, colleges, and universities or nonformal Cooperative Extension Programs at state and county levels. Direct delivery of resource management programs in both formal and nonformal settings is typically provided, or at least guided, by professionals with specialized educational preparation in resource management. It is likely that educators with specialized training have given special thought to the issues of program development and delivery. Therefore the remainder of this section on program delivery will focus on programs that are delivered indirectly as resource management perspectives in other topic areas of family life education. Because the processes of communication, problem solving, and decision making are assumed to be included in all topic areas of family life education, and because management *processes* have been discussed at length in the earlier pages of the chapter, the following discussion will emphasize the integration of resource management *content* into other areas of family life education.

Integration of Resource Management Content

One of the assumptions of the Framework for Life-Span Family Life Education (Arcus, 1987) is that the content of family resource management can and/or should be separated from the topics of families and society, family interaction, human development and sexuality, interpersonal interaction, education about parenthood, and ethics. The separation does have the advantage of giving more visibility to family resource management but also may fail to convey to learners the *continuity* of

managerial processes in all dimensions of family life. The same controversy about whether it is best to deliver family resource management
education to maintain its separate identity, or as integrated into other
areas of family life education (or both ways), continues to be voiced
within the field of study, where there are realistic concerns about losses
of identity (Deacon, 1992; Garman, 1992; Hanna, 1992). Educators who
are interested in integrating resource management content into other
topic areas of family life education will find that the possibilities are
numerous. Strong and DeVault (1992), Burr, Day, and Bahr (1989), and
Foster, Hogan, Herring, and Gieseking-Williams (1994) for junior high
school students are examples of textbooks with a demonstrated commitment to the integration objective.

The improved integration of family resource management content in
delivering future family life education programs could be accomplished
in several ways. First, it will be important to explicitly *label* the resource
management content already present so that learners identify it as such.
Marriage enrichment programs typically encourage couples to communicate about their good personal qualities (human resources) and to
develop shared goals and future plans for accomplishing goals. These
are managerial processes, although most leaders of marriage enrichment do not label them as such. A second strategy is to highlight or
emphasize the existing content in ways that accurately represent the
literature in resource management. The developmental tasks of money
and time management are seldom reported in family life-cycle stages in
family relationship textbooks (Strong & DeVault, 1992) so that educators
must go to the management texts to find them (Deacon & Firebaugh,
1988). Third, the resource management content that is missing can be
added to content areas where it is judged to be particularly important.
The following paragraphs suggest a few of the many possibilities to
consider within two topic areas of family life education.

Families and Society

The discussions on family and society in family life education could
be enhanced by labeling the resources families provide for other institutions, emphasizing the proactive role of cumulative family decisions in
producing social change, and adding the ecological perspective to family systems theory. The ecological systems conceptual framework is
valuable in viewing families *in* an ecosystem of other societal institutions and *as* an ecosystem for individual development (Paolucci et al.,
1977). It is important to *label* the family institution as providing *resources*
for society, the *resource exchanges* that occur among families and societal

institutions, and the way families *manage* these interactions as family economics and resource management content. Family interactions with the economy and family adjustments to fluctuations in the business cycle[10] are of special interest in family resource management. The recently published sources that would be helpful to educators interested in family-economy interactions include Blumberg (1991), Chilman, Cox, and Nunnally (1988), Magrabi et al. (1991), and Voydanoff and Majka (1988). The adjustments of families to economic hardship can be brought to life for learners through the use of current articles and classical literature. McBreen and Johnson (1982) described how they used *The Grapes of Wrath* (Steinbeck, 1939) to assist students in understanding how families manage change and to demonstrate the basic concepts of values, goals, resources, and decision making.

Most discussions about families and the economy describe the various impacts of the economy on families (E → O) but fail to *emphasize* that the cumulative decisions of all families affect the economy and other societal institutions (O → E). The predominant viewpoint is thus promoted that families are passive reactors to environmental changes, and the proactive role of families as initiators of change is overlooked by learners. An example of how families initiate institutional changes can be seen in the growing number of decisions to divorce and the resulting changes in divorce laws that have occurred.

An understanding of the cumulative effects of family decisions on society is further diminished in discussions that indicate families have changed from producing to consuming units (F. P. Rice, 1990; Zinn & Eitzen, 1990). The *emphasis* on consumption rather than production creates a misconception that the economic function of production is no longer an important contribution of families to society. Strong and DeVault (1992) attempted to explain that families produce fewer raw materials and fewer goods, but there has been a shift to producing more services of shopping and transportation as evidenced by increased time allocations to these activities (Sanik, 1981). Cox (1990) reported an additional truth that these unpaid services are largely unrecognized by the larger society. The economic functions of production could also be highlighted rather than diminished by discussing the production of services by families and the economic costs to families of socializing the younger generation.

Discussions of family and society in future programs will need to *add* more resource management content by including the ecological perspective in family systems theory (Burr et al., 1989), the reciprocal interactions of families with the natural environment, and the importance of natural resources in influencing human interactions. The addition of this content is important for influencing the biological survival versus extinction of humans who must remain in balance with the resources of nature. The resources of the planet must be able to support the population. It is important for learners to understand that good food, pure water, and clean air produce the kind of health that is necessary for the human energy required for empathic listening or balancing work and family roles.

The role of the household in the production of waste is another important way in which families influence the natural environment. Learners need to be challenged to examine their energy-intensive lifestyles and the consequences of their consumption decisions. The consequences of decisions to produce fewer meals at home could include the production of significant amounts of waste when the meals are purchased from fast-food restaurants (Rettig & Everett, 1982).

Education About Parenthood

Some of the most famous efforts in education about parenthood in past decades have used a resource management approach that was not *labeled* as such (Dreikurs & Soltz, 1964; Gordon, 1975).[11] Parents were encouraged to use active listening when the child owned the problem and to confront or manage the environment when the parent owned the problem. Parent-child conflicts that could not be resolved with these methods required the "no-lose" method of resolving conflicts in which parents were taught to use principles of participatory management by involving children in decision-making processes to resolve the issues (Gordon, 1975). Family resource management language would call this a "social decision situation" in which two or more people must make one decision together to resolve a conflict in goals, values, standards, or roles. The social decision process involves mediating values to change desires, discovering value similarities, inventing creative alternatives, and collaborating to find a solution that meets the needs of all parties. A rational social decision is one in which creativity has provided a solution to meet the needs of all parties and the result is integration of the group (Diesing, 1976; Rettig, 1986).

The Adlerian approach to parent education (Dreikurs & Soltz, 1964) also advocated participatory management in a family democracy that is governed by family councils to make decisions (social, economic, and technical) about important family issues. The Adlerian philosophy articulated that self-esteem is the most important human resource parents can facilitate for their children and that cooperation is a high-priority value for parents to teach in the socialization process. The means for reaching these socialization goals were described and demonstrated in parent education groups. The advantages of democratic family councils are that children learn problem-solving and decision-making processes in the family setting.

Both of the above approaches to education about parenthood are practical problem-solving approaches that include an implicit assumption about managerial behavior that needs to be articulated: "It is often possible and also effective to attempt to have some control over the *environment* in an interaction situation, but not control of the other person(s)." In other words, it is important to know when *not* to manage and where *not* to be "controlling." Close relationships encounter difficulties when there are feelings of manipulation or control. Management applied in this way is not appropriate or helpful in nurturing good family relationships. The delivery of educational programs for parenthood will need to *emphasize* the importance of managing the environment while remaining free to experience the interpersonal interactions in a spontaneous and authentic way. Economic values (efficiency, control) need to be put aside and social values and decision processes need to be applied in the family life education topic areas of education for parenthood, interpersonal relationships, and family interaction.[12]

Resource management content that needs to be *added* to parent education concerns the direct and indirect costs of raising children that are only occasionally represented in family textbooks (F. P. Rice, 1990; Wells, 1991). The pervasive lack of knowledge in this area was established in a longitudinal study of divorce (Rettig & Yellowthunder, 1992) in which all three phases of data collection clearly demonstrated that judges, attorneys, mediators, and divorcing parties did not fully realize the direct costs of children and did not know where to locate the information or how to modify it for a particular divorce case.[13] The anger levels of child support obligors can easily rise higher when they do not have this factual information because raising children in single-parent families is even more expensive than in two-parent households (Rettig, Christensen, & Dahl, 1991). The Minnesota Extension Service has recently initiated educational programming in response to the identified need as well as a publication that will be distributed in the midwestern region of the United States (Dixon, Bauer, & Rettig, 1992).

ISSUES IN FAMILY RESOURCE MANAGEMENT EDUCATION

The topics identified below are challenges for educators that are not unique to one topic area in family life education but are highlighted as they apply to resource management.

Preparing Educators

Family resource management is a unique and challenging area of family life education because of the pervasive problems of too many needs and wants and too few resources. To address these significant problems, educators need a broad education to incorporate psychology, sociology, economics, anthropology, law, and philosophy and perspectives from the applied fields of family therapy and social work (Arcus, 1984). The topic areas that have been identified as guidelines for training family life educators all include family resource management content and processes (Arcus, 1984). For example, the area *internal dynamics of families* includes content about conflict management, decision making, and goal setting. Conflicts about money are especially challenging issues in family interaction (Strong & DeVault, 1992), particularly for remarried families (Lown et al., 1989). *Human sexuality* includes values and decision making. *Ethics* is very much concerned with valuing and value choices.

Educating for family resource management requires competence in both interactive and reflective practices when translating knowledge into action (Wilson & Vaines, 1985). Interactive practice requires that educators interact with learners to form common meanings and to view situations from the perspective of the person involved. The role of the "expert" is not fixed because participation with the "seeker of knowledge" forges a new consensus of understanding. "Throughout this process each party is open to the influence of the other and knowledge itself is arbitrated and not just accepted" (Wilson & Vaines, 1985, p. 352).

Reflective practice involves critique to reveal constraining forces and false social beliefs of contemporary situations that may not be apparent to those closely involved. Reflective practice strives to bring about long-term change in the individual as well as in the social order (Wilson & Vaines, 1985). Interactive and reflective practice competencies are important to family resource management educators who must continually participate with students in analyzing problem situations and synthesizing new alternative solutions.

Motivating Students

Another challenge for educators is motivating students to learn more about the application of management in everyday family life. Although the content of resource management is useful for all ages of learners, it seems to be of greater interest to older students who have already faced more of life's difficulties, experienced resource scarcities, and have had to make important personal decisions involving value and role conflicts. When a group is heterogenous and contains older learners who have struggled to manage a household and to balance family and work, they can usually give good examples of the management principles that are interesting and realistic to those who are younger. Educators must understand the developmental level of learners to match the learning content to students' interests. Managerial thinking also appeals more to people with analytic cognitive style preferences than to those with pragmatist preferences, thus educators need to present the content in alternative ways to interest students with diverse cognitive style preferences (Rettig & Schulz, 1991).

Generating Unbiased Curriculum

Education is best facilitated in an atmosphere of mutual respect that is free from ageism, sexism, racism, and other forms of prejudice and intolerance. There are some important steps to take to create humane learning climates. Participants in family resource management education need to learn to think critically and to speak up when they believe something is unfair. The curriculum needs to be antibiased and still be value based in the sense that assumptions are made that values differences are expected but oppressive ideas and behaviors are not (Derman-Sparks, 1989).

Values

The principles and processes of management are fairly universal, but the practice or application is not because the practice of management by individuals and families is closely tied to cultural values and the social environment where it takes place. Educators must be sensitive to cultural values, for example, differences in the importance of punctuality and carefully using every minute (Gross & Crandall, 1963). There are differing philosophical perspectives about time across various cultures (Owen, 1991) and a critical need for qualitative research describing variations in time perspectives and family resource management styles across cultures and life-styles.

The process of educating for family resource management requires that educators be sensitive to the valuing processes that are present in decision makers as they struggle to maintain balances between the conflicting values of stability and change, freedom and responsibility, independence and interdependence, uniqueness and conformity, cooperation and competition, control and flexibility, and regularity and variety (Rettig, 1988). These values conflicts are often present within the thinking of one person as well as across persons in a family whose members are involved in making joint decisions. The role of the educator is to assist students to clarify these values conflicts rather than to take a particular values stance. The importance of values as part of both content and processes of family life education and a value reasoning approach to teaching values were outlined by Arcus (1980).

One of the most difficult ideas for most resource management learners to grasp is the transcendent quality of values across decision situations in the life of any one person. Values differ from attitudes and beliefs in their consistency or transcendent quality in all of the decisions of a particular person. While they may be prioritized differently, they reappear as important criteria in all major decisions (Rokeach, 1979). One way to demonstrate transcendent values is to examine the life decisions of one person through the use of biography or autobiography. The value priorities that emerge over time in the difficult decisions that were made make the transcendent quality of values more visible. Through guided questioning, older adults can write their personal history to develop consciousness of consistent values across time and key decisions and role changes while examining basic life themes (de Vries, Birren, & Deutchman, 1990). Genograms (Bahr, 1990) can also allow students to diagram the key decisions, resource options, and intergenerational value shifts. For more information on values and family life education, please refer to Chapter 4 in Volume 1 of this handbook.

Cultures

Culture is the total way of life of any group of people who share similar characteristics such as language, diet, dress, customs, and ethics. The assumptions and resulting actions of family resource management are present in a particular culture's philosophy of life. Some cultures attribute greater power to fate, chance, and a Supreme Being in controlling human lives. This approach often results in a more reactive style of responding to change. Other cultures, such as are generally found in North America, tend to believe in more control over personal lives and the environment (Kluckhohn & Strodbeck, 1961; Northrup, 1960), which often results in a more proactive style of approaching life changes. Different approaches to change determine different resource management styles (Baker & Nelson, 1987; Haynes, Nixon, & West, 1990; Johnson, 1989).

Most of the management textbooks, curricula, and other available educational materials, particularly the financial management textbooks, have not been written with a multicultural context. It is as if the authors thought the materials were universally adaptable. The decision-making situations of African American, Asian American, Native American,

Hispanic American, and interracial families need to be explicitly included in family resource management materials and courses. New immigrants, who may be experiencing cultural shock in adapting to normative family resource management behavior, need to have their unique beliefs and goals included in these family life education programs. For further information regarding ethnicity and family life education, see Chapter 7 in Volume 1 of this handbook.

Levels of Living

Resource adequacy has an influence on family managerial behaviors. For example, family resource management is more easily implemented by people with resource adequacy. Biases in the management content toward philosophies of control and power and toward people who have resources need to be recognized by educators so that they can adjust and sensitize the processes of teaching and learning. People who are poor must devote their financial resources to meet basic needs. They have minimal freedom to allocate money, time, or human energy for other than immediate uses and have little to give toward planning for future needs. Families and individuals with lower levels of living have less freedom to decide, little control over resource access, and fewer opportunities for human resource development, and their use of material resources is significantly diminished. Families can be "poor," not only in material resources but also in human resources of imagination, initiative, self-discipline, and the ability to seek alternatives. Strong and DeVault (1992) discuss the issues surrounding poverty and the effects on family relationships. Deacon and Firebaugh (1988) include a chapter on management in low-income families.

Gender

The issues of gender are associated with "women's work" and "men's work" in the family (Strong & DeVault, 1992). Stereotypically, North American females manage resources in the areas of coordinating family members' schedules, planning and implementing the household work, and making decisions about child care. Management of resources for car care, household repairs, and yard work have been stereotyped as the male's role. Regardless of their employment status, women usually have the major responsibility for household work (Maret & Findlay, 1984; Spitze, 1986, 1991; Thompson & Walker, 1991) and management, including implementing the plans (Deacon & Firebaugh, 1988).

There is controversy about whether males and females should be socialized into different family resource management behavior. This value-laden question is answered differently by males and females, by various religious and political groups, and among cultural groups. Many family resource management authors ignore gender roles, but textbooks in family relationships do include the economic and managerial dimensions of gender role behaviors and socialization (Cox, 1990; F. P. Rice, 1990; Strong & DeVault, 1992). Hutter (1988) presents a cross-cultural perspective on gender roles that includes economic work roles, but the educator would need to be skillful in labeling the managerial content of family decision making that is implied but not described. At the very least, educators need to use gender-neutral language when discussing resource management perspectives concerning gender roles. Further discussion of gender and family life education may be found in Chapter 6 in Volume 1 of this handbook.

Merging Theory and Practice

Educating for family resource management had its historical origin in home economics and was unique because of the learning environments provided for students. Early home economists realized that the mental processes of management needed to be implemented in action for the most effective learning to occur. They had already discovered the "new realization that learning needed to be subjective, experiential, and that learners needed empowering involvement in the body of knowledge and its application" (Allen & Crosbie-Burnett, 1992). The evidence for this realization was that they considered both classroom and laboratory experiences to be a necessity for learners of all ages. Gunther (1912) wrote about the importance of establishing practical training that was representative of home living conditions that went "beyond present-day laboratory methods, whereby conditions may be met as they really exist" (p. 362).

There were at least three approaches to these laboratories in early history. The first was to create a living environment in the form of model cottages, houses, or apartments where students moved into the dwelling with the teacher for a period of time. These programs were primarily for single women so there was definitely a gender and marital status bias present. The second was to use the homes or dormitory living situations of learners as laboratories where educators visited (Gunther, 1912; Lawrence, 1922; Rivers, 1939) or, alternatively, planned with students the learning experiences to be initiated in their own dwellings (Drew & Tinsley, 1957; Luckhardt, 1978; Naylor, 1922). Cooperative

Extension agents who visited farm homes occasionally had contact with the male farmer but primarily worked with women. The third option was to take advantage of community agencies as laboratory environments for students (Taubin, 1973), where males were more likely to be included in the learning experiences.

Despite the excellent ideas concerning the value of integrating technical, economic, and social learning experiences in living environments, the *activities* and standards of housekeeping were often mistakenly emphasized over the cognitive-affective *mental* processes of values clarification, goals formation, planning, and decision making. The living laboratory then grew out of favor with administrators who had difficulties in justifying the high per-student costs of "in-residence" education.

The living laboratory is now rarely practiced although it is still desirable to make the learning situation as close to real life as possible. Educators who presently use the activities approach or the laboratory option for delivery of resource management programs still face the same risks that the physical activities of implementing decisions can be emphasized over the thinking and planning of decision-making processes prior to taking action. The result is that learners do not remember that management is decision making as well as decision implementation.

The gap between theoretical and practical approaches to developing family resource management is a pervasive issue. Some educators emphasize the processes of thinking about decision making, goal setting, and other concepts with cognitive approaches such as short stories or case studies to illustrate and apply the concepts. In contrast, to teach managerial skills, others use events in the student's life such as planning a family celebration, setting up a financial plan, caring for an aging parent, or preparing a meal. Both abstract and concrete approaches make important contributions and also have limitations, depending upon the learning style and maturity of the student or clientele group. Educators need to bring the "thinking" and "doing" approaches together, especially because in most families there is a mix of management and labor, frequently by the same person or persons.

Many family resource management educators are primarily assigned to teach and are located in agencies or institutions that do not have the interest or capability to hire separate researchers to build on the base of knowledge about family resource management. Family resource management researchers, on the other hand, have limited ongoing experience in working directly with families and may teach only a few specialized courses. This specialized model of knowledge production has too often resulted in journal articles that give little or no attention to application by practitioners and are read primarily by researchers. A paradigm called "action research" also has been developed that could help family resource management educators to conduct research for the purpose of improving practice (Corey, 1949). It is carried out by the educators themselves because they want to know whether or not their methods or their courses are achieving the intended purposes, as was recently demonstrated by Bahr (1990).

FUTURE EMPHASES IN FAMILY RESOURCE MANAGEMENT EDUCATION[14]

The managerial problems of future families are likely to center on the global issues of resource availabilities: "Over consumption by the wealthiest fifth of humanity is an environmental problem unmatched in severity by anything but perhaps population growth. The surging exploitation of resources threatens to exhaust or unalterably disfigure forests, soils, water, air, and climate" (Durning, 1991, p. 11). Durning (1991) suggested that in a fragile biosphere the ultimate fate of humanity may depend on whether a deeper sense of self-restraint can be cultivated, founded on a widespread ethic of limiting consumption, population, and finding nonmaterial enrichment (p. 13). The compulsion to consume is so pervasive in many countries that educating people to think in alternative ways will be a monumental task that history suggests is impossible. Durning (1991) reported that the Puritans, Quakers, Amish, and Shakers, who advocated a voluntary-simplicity life-style, were never successful in gaining more than a slim minority of followers; nor were countries such as China that used more brutal persuasion techniques. The goal of creating a sustainable culture of permanence is a challenge that will face the next several generations of humans. L. R. Brown, Flavin, and Postel (1992) compared humans to the passengers on the *Titanic*, who denied their problems for many hours:

> As the twentieth century draws near a close, the tale of the *Titanic* comes uncomfortably close to describing the perceptual gap we now face: Our inability to comprehend the scale of the ongoing degradation of the planet and how it will affect our future. Few understand the magnitude of the potential tragedy; fewer still have a good idea what to do about it. (p. 10)

Resource scarcities in the future will most likely make reduced consumption an absolute necessity (Brown et al., 1992). Unfortunately, the usual effects of lower consumption are increasing economic inequalities and unemployment rates. "One of the greatest challenges for sustainable societies is finding ways to ensure basic employment opportunities for all without having to stoke the fires of economic growth" (Durning, 1991, p. 15). These societal adjustments will have effects on the money income of families as well as on the roles of family members. The adjustments of accepting and living by sufficiency rather than excess will cause painful changes in value priorities as families struggle to change both their standards of living (ideals of what is important) as well as their levels of living, which is what they actually have and enjoy.

The scope of family resource management education must be broadened to ensure the mutual survival and well-being of all members of the human family. There are few examples in the literature of family resource management education programs that include a global resource perspective. The challenges for future educators are in learning how to create "teachable moments" that will result in major behavioral changes. How do we educate for sustainability? How do we develop curriculum that assists students in understanding the cumulative effects of family decisions on the natural environment? How do we help students to realize that "environmental quality is more than a question of quality of life; it is often a matter of life and death" (Brown et al., 1992, p. 12).

There will be *ethical* issues for future educators to consider as well. Do we have an obligation to help build a sense of social responsibility in such a way that increased education and economic well-being are not only for personal advancement but also contribute to the social good? Can people be assisted to understand that their "individual good" will be enhanced through increasing the "social good"? How and where can a social ethic of responsibility for society and for the environment be built? (M. M. Bubolz, personal communication, June 21, 1991).

The above issues are extremely challenging problems for education in the future and particularly for the area of family resource management, which is likely to grow in importance as an educational need for all age groups. The educators who are best prepared to meet these challenges will have some understanding of global economics and geography, foreign political systems, and foreign languages. Competencies in various decision-making processes, conflict resolution, and negotiation processes will be absolutely vital assets in meeting the educational needs of future students.

NOTES

1. For more complete reviews of the family resource management research literature, refer to Abdel-Ghany and Nickols (1984), Berger (1984), Israelsen (1990), and Nichols, Mumaw, Paynter, Plonk, and Price (1970).

2. Individuals can increase satisfactions from family living if they will "give thought to its goals and purposes, and practical consideration of the ways of achieving them." "Conscious deliberation and choice contribute to increased satisfaction, diminished negative consequences, and greater availability of resources" (Andrews, 1937, p. 1).

3. For a review of research and theory concerning families as economic units, please refer to Helmick (1986), Magrabi, Chung, Cha, and Yang (1991), A. S. Rice (1981), and Voydanoff and Majka (1988).

4. This is based on Buehler and Hogan (1986), Deacon and Firebaugh (1988), Gross, Crandall, and Knoll (1980), Liston (1964), Melson (1980), Paolucci et al. (1977), Rettig (1988), A. S. Rice and Tucker (1986), and Schlater (1967).

5. Family resource management includes family economics, financial management, and consumer economics. Resource management, however, includes a greater variety of resources and emphasizes the internal dynamics of family problem-solving, decision-making, and choice processes more than the interactions of families with the larger economy. A content focus on the interaction of families with the economy would be called "family economics." Consumer economics seeks to educate students about consumer protection measures, government regulatory activity, and the complexities of society and the marketplace (Herrmann, 1982).

6. For more information on managing money resources, refer to Godwin (1990), Hogan and Bauer (1988), Lown, McFadden, and Crossman (1989), and Rettig and Mortenson (1986). Information on time resources can be found in Nickols (1986) and Sanik (1981) and energy resources in Urich and Hogan (1985). For a new theory of planning, see Avery and Stafford (1991).

7. For other examples of curriculum based on a practical problem focus, refer to Hultgren and Wilkosz (1986), Hultgren (1986), Kister (1986), and Schwartz, Wilkosz, DeBoe, Grote, and Torgerson (1986).

8. For more information on issues of measuring managerial effectiveness in families, refer to Sharpe and Winter (1991).

9. For reviews of evaluation of consumer and homemaking programs at the high school level, refer to Rossmann (1983) and the problems of evaluation processes as discussed by Plihal (1983) and R. Thomas (1983). Evaluation of a remarried family educational program delivered by the Alabama Cooperative Extension Service was described by Fitzpatrick, Smith, and Williamson (1992) and included coping with economic issues.

10. The managerial strategies used by families include increasing income; decreasing expenditures; extending resources by producing goods and services, changing standards, recycling, or reducing consumption; substituting resources; pooling resources; improving shopping strategies; sharpening planning strategies; and making human capital investments (Rettig, 1982). The family adjustments represented in the stress literature are reported by Schnittger and Bird (1990) as cognitive restructuring, delegating, limiting avocational activities, subordinating career, compartmentalizing, avoiding responsibility, and using social support (p. 201). Coping with economic distress is also described by Strong and DeVault (1992, p. 412) and Dollahite (1992).

11. For more information concerning comparisons of differing theoretical perspectives on parenting issues, refer to Roberts (1990).

12. For more information about how management is different when applied to human relationships as compared with work environments, please refer to Burr et al. (1989) and Rettig (1987).

13. For more information, refer to *Family Economics Review*, which is published quarterly by the Family Economics Research Group, U.S. Department of Agriculture, Agricultural Research Service. The journal is available for sale from the Superintendent of Documents, U.S. Government Printing Service, Washington, DC 20402. See also Espenshade (1984).

14. For another viewpoint concerning the future of family resource management, please see Key and Firebaugh (1989), Deacon (1992), Garman (1992), and Hanna (1992).

REFERENCES

Abdel-Ghany, M., & Nickols, S. (1984). Consumer, consumption, and family economics/ household management research, 1972-1982: Survey of the past and outlook for the future. *Home Economics Research Journal, 12*(3), 265-276.

Allen, K. R., & Crosbie-Burnett, M. (1992). Innovative ways and controversial issues in teaching about families: A special collection on family pedagogy. *Family Relations, 41*(1), 9-11.

American Psychiatric Association. (1987). *Diagnostic criteria from DSM-III-R: Desk reference.* Washington, DC: Author.

Andrews, B. (1937). *Economics of the household: Its administration and finance* (rev. ed.). New York: Macmillan.

Andrews, M. P., Bubolz, M. M., & Paolucci, B. (1980). An ecological approach to the study of the family. *Marriage and Family Review, 3*(1-2), 29-49.

Arcus, M. E. (1980). Value reasoning: An approach to values education. *Family Relations, 29*(2), 163-171.

Arcus, M. E. (1984). Preparing family life educators: Guidelines for training programs. *Canadian Home Economics Journal, 34*(2), 78-80.

Arcus, M. E. (1987). A Framework for Life-Span Family Life Education. *Family Relations, 36*(1), 5-10.

Arcus, M. E. (1990). *The nature of family life education: Family life curriculum guidelines.* Minneapolis, MN: National Council on Family Relations.

Avery, R. J., & Stafford, K. (1991). Toward a scheduling congruity theory of family resource management. *Lifestyles: Family and Economic Issues, 12*(4), 325-344.

Bahr, K. S. (1990). Student responses to genogram and family chronology. *Family Relations, 39*(3), 243-249.

Baker, G., & Nelson, L. J. (1987). Resource allocation in the Third World: Conceptual approaches, strategies, and challenges. *Journal of Consumer Studies and Home Economics, 11*(2), 131-139.

Berger, P. S. (1984). Home management research: State of the art 1909-1984. *Home Economics Research Journal, 12*(3), 252-264.

Berry, J. O. (1992). Preparing college students to work with children and families with special needs. *Family Relations, 41*(1), 44-48.

Blumberg, R. L. (Ed.). (1991). *Gender, family, and economy.* Newbury Park, CA: Sage.

Brady, M. (1990). *What's worth teaching?* Albany: State University of New York Press.

Bronfenbrenner, U. (1979). *The ecology of human development.* Cambridge, MA: Harvard University Press.

Brookfield, S. D. (1987). *Developing critical thinkers: Challenging adults to explore alternative ways of thinking and acting.* San Francisco: Jossey-Bass.

Brown, L. R., Flavin, C., & Postel, S. (1992). A planet in jeopardy. *The Futurist, 26*(3), 10-14.

Brown, M., & Paolucci, B. (1979). *Home economics: A definition.* Washington, DC: American Home Economics Association.

Bubolz, M. M., & Sontag, M. S. (1993). Human ecology theory. In P. G. Boss, W. J. Doherty, R. LaRossa, S. K. Steinmetz, & W. R. Schumm (Eds.), *Sourcebook of family theories and methods: A contextual approach* (pp. 419-448). New York: Plenum.

Buehler, C., & Hogan, M. J. (1986). Planning styles in single-parent families. *Home Economics Research Journal, 14*(4), 351-362.

Burr, W. R., Day, R. D., & Bahr, K. S. (1989). *Family science.* Provo, UT: Alexander's.

Chilman, C. S., Cox, F. M., & Nunnally, E. W. (Eds.). (1988). *Families in trouble: Vol. 1. Employment and economic problems.* Newbury Park, CA: Sage.

Coon, B. (1938, October 10). *Some factors involved in the teaching of home management in colleges: A report of a series of conferences with a group of college teachers* (Miscellaneous Bulletin 2119). Washington, DC: U.S. Department of Health, Education and Welfare, Office of Education.

Corey, S. M. (1949). Curriculum development through action research. *Educational Leadership, 7,* 147-152.

Costa, A. L. (1985). *Developing minds: A resource book for teaching thinking.* Alexandria, VA: Association for Supervision and Curriculum Development.

Cox, F. D. (1990). *Human intimacy: Marriage, the family and its meaning* (5th ed.) St. Paul: West.

Darling, C. A. (1987). Family life education. In M. B. Sussman & S. K. Steinmetz (Eds.), *Handbook of marriage and the family* (pp. 815-833). New York: Plenum.

Deacon, R. E. (1992). The future of family resource management. In *Managing for a better future* (Proceedings, pp. 184-191). Columbus, OH: Southeastern Regional Association of Family Economics/Home Management.

Deacon, R. E., & Firebaugh, F. M. (1988). *Family resource management: Principles and applications.* Boston: Allyn & Bacon.

Derman-Sparks, L. (1989). *Anti-bias curriculum: Tools for empowering young children.* Washington, DC: National Association for the Education of Young Children.

de Vries, B., Birren, J. E., & Deutchman, D. E. (1990). Adult development through guided autobiography: The family context. *Family Relations, 39*(1), 3-7.

Diesing, P. (1976). *Reason in society: Five types of decisions and their social conditions.* Westport, CT: Greenwood.

Dixon, C., Bauer, J. W., & Rettig, K. D. (1992). *The cost of raising your children in rural and urban areas.* St. Paul: Minnesota Extension Service.

Dollahite, D. (1992). Family resource management and family stress theories: Toward a conceptual integration. *Lifestyles: Family and Economic Issues, 12*(4), 361-377.

Dreikurs, R., & Soltz, Y. (1964). *Children: The challenge.* New York: Hawthorne.

Drew, L. M., & Tinsley, W. V. (1957). Home management at home for the married student. *Journal of Home Economics, 49*(5), 367-368.

Durning, A. (1991). Limiting consumption: Toward a sustainable culture. *The Futurist, 25,* 11-15.

Ennis, R. H. (1985). A logical basis for measuring critical thinking skills. *Educational Leadership, 43*(2), 44-48.

Ennis, R. H. (1989). Critical thinking and subject specificity: Clarification and needed research. *Educational Researcher, 18*(3), 4-10.

Espenshade, T. J. (1984). *Investing in children: New estimates of parental expenditures.* Washington, DC: Urban Institute Press.

Fitzpatrick, J. A., Smith, T. A., & Williamson, S. A. (1992). Educating extension agents: An evaluation of method and development of a remarried educational program. *Family Relations, 41*(1), 70-73.

Foster, J., Hogan, M. J., Herring, B., & Gieseking-Williams, A. (1994). *Creative living: Basic concepts in home economics* (5th ed.). Philadelphia: Glencoe.

Garman, E. T. (1992). The future of family resource management. In *Managing for a better future* (Proceedings, pp. 192-193). Columbus, OH: Southeastern Regional Association of Family Economics/Home Management.

Gilbert, K. R. (1990). Innovative approaches to teaching large family science lecture courses. *Family Science Review, 3*(2-3), 77-85.

Godwin, D. D. (1990). Family financial management. *Family Relations, 39,* 221-228.

Gordon, T. (1975). *Parent effectiveness training.* New York: Peter H. Myden.

Green, K. (1988). Teaching critical thinking in home economics: Frontiers to be conquered. *Illinois Teacher, 31,* 182-183.

Griggs, M. B. (1981). Criteria for evaluation of family life education materials. *Family Relations, 30,* 549-555.

Gross, I. H., & Crandall, E. W. (1963). *Management for modern families* (2nd ed.). New York: Appleton-Century-Crofts.

Gross, I. H., Crandall, E. W., & Knoll, M. M. (1980). *Management for modern families.* Englewood Cliffs, NJ: Prentice-Hall.

Gunther, E. H. (1912). Practice fields in household and institutional management. *The Journal of Home Economics, 4*(4), 362-368.

Hanna, S. (1992). The future of family resource management. *Managing for a better future* (Proceedings, pp. 182-183). Columbus, OH: Southeastern Regional Association of Family Economics/Home Management.

Haynes, P., Nixon, J. C., & West, J. F. (1990). Time perception, and consumer behavior: Some cross cultural comparisons. *Journal of Consumer Studies and Home Economics, 14*(1), 15-27.

Helmick, S. A. (1986). Family as an economic unit: Research in times of transition. In R. E. Deacon & W. A. Huffman, *Human resources research 1887-1987: Proceedings* (pp. 149-157). Ames: Iowa State University, College of Home Economics.

Herrmann, R. O. (1982). The historical development of the content of consumer education: An examination of selected high school texts, 1938-1978. *The Journal of Consumer Affairs, 16,* 195-223.

Hogan, M. J. (1978). Values and the family ecosystem. *Counseling and Values, 2,* 121-126.

Hogan, M. J., & Bauer, J. W. (1988). Problems in family financial management. In C. Chilman, F. M. Cox, & E. W. Nunnally (Eds.), *Families in trouble: Vol. 1. Employment and economic problems* (pp. 155-172). Newbury Park, CA: Sage.

Hogan, M. J., & Buehler, C. A. (1984). *The concept of resources: Definitional issues.* Paper presented at NCR 116, revised from the Theory Construction and Research Methodology Workshop, National Council on Family Relations, Minneapolis, MN.

Hogan, M. J., & Paolucci, B. (1979). Energy conservation, family values, household practices, and contextual variables. *Home Economics Research Journal, 7*(4), 210-218.

Hultgren, F. (1986). Value reasoning design: The Pennsylvania State University curriculum project. In J. Laster & R. Dohner (Eds.), *Vocational home economics curriculum: State of the field* (American Home Economics Association Teacher Education Yearbook 6). Peoria, IL: Glencoe.

Hultgren, F., & Wilkosz, J. (1986). Human goals and critical realities: A practical problem framework for developing home economics curriculum. *Journal of Vocational Home Economics Education, 4*(2), 135-154.

Hutter, M. (1988). *The changing family: Comparative perspectives* (2nd ed.). New York: Macmillan.

Iozzi, L. A., & Cheu, J. (1979). Preparing for tomorrow's world: An alternative curriculum model for the secondary schools. In F. J. Kierstead, J. Bowman, & C. Dede (Eds.), *Educational futures: Sourcebook I*. (pp. 107-119). Washington, DC: World Futures Society.

Israelsen, C. (1990). Family resource management research 1930-1990. *Financial Counseling and Planning, 1,* 3-39.

Jacobs, F. (1988). The five-tiered approach to evaluation: Context and implementation. In H. Weiss & F. Jacobs (Eds.), *Evaluating family programs* (pp. 37-68). Hawthorne, NY: Aldine.

Johnson, P. J. (1989). Changes in financial practices of Southeast Asian refugees. *Home Economics Research Journal, 17*(2), 241-252.

Key, R. J., & Firebaugh, F. M. (1989, Spring). Family resource management: Preparing for the 21st century. *Journal of Home Economics, 81,* 1-17.

Kister, J. (1986). Practical action curriculum (PAC) design: Ohio curriculum project. In J. Laster & R. Dohner (Eds.), *Vocational home economics curriculum: State of the field* (American Home Economics Association Teacher Education Yearbook 6). Peoria, IL: Glencoe.

Kluckhohn, C., & Strodbeck, F. (1961). *Variations in value orientations*. Evanston, IL: Row-Peterson.

Lawrence, M. M. (1922). Home management work in the extension field. *Journal of Home Economics, 14*(10), 563.

Linck, S. (1982). What happened to values in consumer education and research? *The Journal of Consumer Affairs, 16,* 389-393.

Liston, M. I. (1964, June). Management in the family as a social process. In *Conceptual frameworks: Processes of home management* (Proceedings of a Home Management Conference, East Lansing, MI). Washington, DC: American Home Economics Association.

Liston, M. I. (1966). *Management in the family group, syllabus and sourcebook for home management 375*. Unpublished manuscript, Iowa State University, College of Home Economics, Ames, IA.

Liston, M. I. (1975). Research on human resource development. In North Central Regional Center for Rural Development, *Human resources and community miscellaneous report* (pp. 27-57). Ames: Iowa State University.

Lown, J., McFadden, J., & Crossman, S. (1989). Family life education for remarriage: Focus on financial management. *Family Relations, 38*(1), 46-52.

Luckhardt, M. C. (1978). Home management practicum at home. *Illinois Teacher of Home Economics, 21*(3), 149-150.

Magrabi, F. M., Chung, V. S., Cha, S. S., & Yang, S. (1991). *The economics of household consumption*. New York: Praeger.

Maret, E., & Findlay, B. (1984). The distribution of household labor among dual-earner marriages. *Journal of Marriage and the Family, 46,* 357-364.

Maskay, M. H., & Juhasz, A. M. (1983). The decision-making process model: Design and use for adolescent sexual decisions. *Family Relations, 32,* 111-116.

McBreen, E. L., & Johnson, C. A. (1982). Creative literature as a key to family management. *Illinois Teacher, 26,* 135-138.

Melson, G. F. (1980). *Family and environment: An ecosystem approach*. Minneapolis, MN: Burgess.

Naylor, R. B. (1922). Home problems for household management classes. *The Journal of Home Economics, 14*(8), 416-418.

Nichols, A., Mumaw, C. R., Paynter, M., Plonk, M. A., & Price, D. Z. (1970). Family management. In C. Broderick (Ed.), *A decade of family research and action 1960-1969* (pp. 91-97). Minneapolis, MN: National Council on Family Relations.

Nickell, P., & Dorsey, J. M. (1967). *Management in family living* (4th ed.). New York: John Wiley.

Nickols, S. Y. (1986). Human resources and household time allocation: A long-term view. In R. E. Deacon & W. E. Huffman (Eds.), *Human resources research 1887-1987: Proceedings* (pp. 173-182). Ames: Iowa State University, College of Home Economics.

Northrup, F. S. C. (1960). *The meeting of East and West*. New York: Macmillan.

Owen, A. (1991). Time and time again: Implications of time perception theory. *Lifestyles: Family and Economic Issues, 12*(4), 345-359.

Paolucci, B. (1966). Contributions of a framework of home management to the teaching of family relationships. *Journal of Marriage and the Family, 28*(3), 338-342.

Paolucci, B., Hall, O., & Axinn, N. (1977). *Family decision making: An ecosystem approach*. New York: John Wiley.

Paul, R., Binker, A. J. A., Martin, D., & Adamson, K. (1989). *Critical thinking handbook: A guide for redesigning instruction*. Rohnert Park, CA: Center for Critical Thinking and Moral Critique.

Plihal, J. (1983). What questions direct evaluation of consumer and homemaking programs and how do such questions relate to criteria in making evaluative judgments? *Journal of Vocational Home Economics Education, 1*(4), 48-57.

Ray, E. (1986). A model for critiquing curricula. In J. F. Laster & R. E. Dohner (Eds.), *Vocational home economics curriculum: State of the field*. Peoria, IL: Macmillan.

Rettig, K. D. (1982). Strategies for fighting inflation. *Illinois Research, 24*, 7-9.

Rettig, K. D. (1986). *Social decision making*. St. Paul: Minnesota Extension Service, University of Minnesota.

Rettig, K. D. (1987). Household production: Beyond the economic perspective. *Journal of Consumer Studies and Home Economics, 11*, 141-156.

Rettig, K. D. (1988, November). *A framework for integrating family relations and family resource management*. Paper presented at the Theory Construction and Research Methodology Workshop, National Council on Family Relations, Philadelphia.

Rettig, K. D., Christensen, D. H., & Dahl, C. M. (1991). Impact of child support guidelines on the economic well-being of children. *Family Relations, 40*(2), 167-175.

Rettig, K. D., & Everett, G. (1982). Management: Crucial subject matter for home economists in the '80's. *Canadian Home Economics Journal, 32*(1), 17-20.

Rettig, K. D., & Mortenson, M. (1986). Household production of financial management competence. In R. E. Deacon & W. E. Huffman (Eds.), *Human resources research 1887-1987: Proceedings*. Ames: Iowa State University, College of Home Economics.

Rettig, K. D., & Schulz, C. V. (1991). Cognitive style preferences and financial management decision styles. *Financial Counseling and Planning, 2*, 25-44.

Rettig, K. D., & Yellowthunder, L. (1992). *Economic consequences of divorce in Minnesota: Phase III telephone report*. St. Paul, MN: Department of Family Social Science.

Rice, A. S. (1981). An economic framework for viewing the family. In F. I. Nye & F. Berardo (Eds.), *Emerging conceptual frameworks in family analyses* (pp. 223-268). New York: Praeger.

Rice, A. S., & Tucker, S. M. (1986). *Family life management* (6th ed.). New York: Macmillan.

Rice, F. P. (1990). *Intimate relationships, marriages, and families*. Mountainview, CA: Mayfield.

Rivers, E. A. (1939). Preparation for home management consultation with low-income rural families. *Journal of Home Economics, 31*(3), 155-159.

Roberts, T. W. (1990). A systems perspective of parenting: The family's responsibility in misbehaving. *Family Science Review, 2*(1), 139-151.

Rokeach, M. (1979). *The nature of human values.* New York: Free Press.

Roosa, M. W., Gensheimer, L. K., Short, J. L., Ayers, T. S., & Shell, R. (1989). A preventative intervention for children in alcoholic families: Results of a pilot study. *Family Relations, 38,* 295-300.

Rossmann, M. M. (1983). Criteria used to evaluate consumer and homemaking programs. *Journal of Vocational Home Economics Education, 1*(4), 57-67.

Sanik, M. M. (1981). Division of household work: A decade comparison 1967-1977. *Home Economics Research Journal, 10,* 175-180.

Schlater, J. D. (1967). The management process and its core concepts. *Journal of Home Economics, 59*(2), 93-98.

Schnittger, M. H., & Bird, G. W. (1990). Coping among dual-career men and women across the family life cycle. *Family Relations, 39*(2), 199-205.

Schwartz, D. J., Wilkosz, J., DeBoe, J., Grote, A., & Torgerson, R. (1986). Problem posing curriculum model: Minnesota curriculum project. In J. Laster & R. Dohner (Eds.), *Vocational home economics curriculum: State of the field* (American Home Economics Association Yearbook 6). Peoria, IL: Glencoe.

Sharpe, D. L., & Winter, M. (1991). Toward working hypotheses of effective management: Conditions, thought processes, and behaviors. *Lifestyles: Family and Economic Issues, 12*(4), 303-323.

Small, S. A. (1990). Some issues regarding the evaluation of family life education programs. *Family Relations, 39,* 132-135.

Smith, S., & Ingoldsby, B. (1992). Multicultural family studies: Educating students for diversity. *Family Relations, 41*(1), 25-30.

Spitze, G. (1986). The division of task responsibility in U.S. households: Longitudinal adjustments to change. *Social Forces, 64,* 689-701.

Spitze, G. (1991). Women's employment and family relations: A review. In A. Booth (Ed.), *Contemporary families: Looking forward, looking back.* Minneapolis, MN: National Council on Family Relations.

Steinbeck, J. (1939). *The grapes of wrath.* New York: Viking.

Strong, B., & DeVault, C. (1992). *The marriage and family experience* (5th ed.). St. Paul, MN: West.

Tallman, I. (1988). Problem solving in families: A revisionist view. In D. M. Klein & J. Aldous (Eds.), *Social stress and family development.* New York: Guilford.

Taubin, S. (1973, June). Community resources to implement new concepts of home management. In *Actualizing concepts of home management: Proceedings, Family Economics, Home Management Subject Matter Section* (pp. 44-47). Washington, DC: American Home Economics Association.

Tebes, J. K., Grady, K., & Snow, D. L. (1989). Parent training in decision-making facilitation: Skill acquisition and relationship to gender. *Family Relations, 38,* 243-247.

Thomas, J., & Arcus, M. (1992). Family life education: An analysis of the concept. *Family Relations, 41*(1), 3-8.

Thomas, R. (1983). What are the alternative criteria for judging consumer homemaking programs? *Journal of Vocational Home Economics Education, 1,* 68-75.

Thompson, L., & Walker, A. (1991). Gender in families: Women and men in marriage, work, and parenthood. In A. Booth (Ed.), *Contemporary families: Looking forward, looking back.* Minneapolis, MN: National Council on Family Relations.

Torgerson, R. (1990). *Resource management curriculum examples for Minnesota secondary home economics*. St. Paul: Minnesota Department of Education.

Urich, J. R., & Hogan, M. J. (1985). Measuring changes in family energy management: Consumption or efficiency. *Journal of Consumer Studies and Home Economics, 9*, 161-172.

Voydanoff, P., & Majka, L. C. (1988). *Families and economic distress: Coping strategies and social policy*. Newbury Park, CA: Sage.

Weiss, H. (1988). Family support and education programs: Working through ecological theories of human development. In H. Weiss & F. Jacobs (Eds.), *Evaluating family programs* (pp. 3-36). Hawthorne, NY: Aldine.

Wells, J. G. (1991). *Choices in marriage and family* (2nd ed.). San Diego, CA: Collegiate.

Whitmore, E. (1991). Evaluation and empowerment: It's the process that counts. *Networking Bulletin: Empowerment and Family Support, 2*(2), 1-7.

Wilson, S. W., & Vaines, E. (1985). A theoretical framework for the examination of practice in home economics. *Home Economics Research Journal, 13*, 347-355.

Zinn, M. B., & Eitzen, D. S. (1990). *Diversity in families* (2nd ed.). New York: Harper & Row.

6

Teaching About Family Communication and Problem Solving

Issues and Future Directions

Dianne K. Kieren
Maryanne Doherty-Poirier

MANY AUTHORS HAVE ARGUED that communication is the basis for all human interaction, particularly for the intimate social group called the family (Johnson & Johnson, 1982; Rausch, Greif, & Nugent, 1979). The success of any family group is dependent upon its ability to exchange information and transmit meanings to one another. Through the use of communication, family members are enabled to develop rapport, understanding, and trust; to coordinate actions; to problem solve and resolve conflicts; and to transmit affection, joy, or distress. Because family life is dynamic rather than static, problem solving is also an essential process, helping family units to generate solutions and meet their adaptive functions. The case for communication and problem solving as basic or generic family life skills has been made by a number of family professionals (see, for example, Durlak, 1983; Fitzpatrick & Badzinski, 1985; Reid, 1985).

The importance of communication and problem solving as critical resources for family life can be traced as far back as the writings of Plato and Aristotle (see McKeon, 1941; Pangle, 1980), who directed parents to rear and educate children in an interactive manner as a means of building a utopia. The importance of these processes has also been well recognized in family life education since the beginnings of this movement (see Chapter 2 in Volume 1). For example, early efforts in parent education encouraged mothers to interact with their children through songs, games, and stories (see I. Gordon, 1977; Kessen, 1965), and organizations such as the Child Study Association of American and the National Council of Parent Education (see Hamner & Turner, 1985) were noteworthy in their emphasis on communication and problem solving (see Chapter 4 in this volume). More recently, attention has been given to these processes in the marriage enrichment movement (Calvo, 1975; Mace, 1975). In marriage enrichment, emphasis is placed on couple dialogue, whether in private or as part of an enrichment group, thereby elevating skills in communication to the center of this approach to family life education (see Chapter 2 in this volume).

Although communication and problem solving are often discussed as separate processes that affect family functioning, they are in fact inextricably linked. Without the internal resources of communication structure (who speaks to whom and when) and information processes structure (how information is shared), effective problem solving cannot be accomplished. Because of this relationship, the issues discussed in this chapter are assumed to be common to both processes. For the purposes of this chapter, *family communication* is defined as the process of receiving, sending, interpreting, and inferring the meaning of messages sent by family members. *Family problem solving*, on the other hand, is the process of finding a resolution to novel or unsettled matters.

The basic premise underlying this chapter is not only that communication and problem solving are generic family processes but that programs in family life education can empower families to develop and enhance these processes. This chapter focuses on family communication and problem solving in a variety of family life education contexts, whether these are directed to individual family members, to couples, or to parent-child, sibling, or entire-family units. The rationale and theoretical underpinnings of communication and problem solving are discussed and programs that use these processes are described and critiqued. Attention is given to both methodology and evaluation, and the chapter concludes with a discussion of issues and challenges that must be addressed by educators if they are to make this component of family life education more effective.

RATIONALE

There are several reasons to focus upon communication and problem solving in family life education programs. Five have been cited frequently enough to give them greater attention.

Changed Family and Societal Expectations

Society no longer holds the nineteenth-century view of a family that is inattentive to people's emotional needs. In the twentieth century, people expect the family to be an emotional refuge in an increasingly bureaucratic world. This shift in expectations, in which emotional and psychological factors have preeminence, places different demands on the interpersonal processes of communication and problem solving among family members. To function effectively, all family members are expected not only to share information but also to share thoughts and feelings with those closest to them.

Increased Complexity of Family Functions

Not only do these sociopsychological expectations for the family shape the interpersonal exchanges within the family, they also change the nature and content of that interaction. Family exchanges are different as a result of concurrent changes in the roles of other institutions such as the school, church, or social agencies. These groups carry out many functions that were previously assigned to the family unit (e.g., socialization of children, care of the aged). For example, the type and amount of communication and problem solving between adults and their aged parents differ when other caregivers are significantly involved. One would expect that communication exchanges would have less continuity, particularly when the parent lives in an institutional setting. Not all of the impacts of the involvement of other caregivers are negative. Problem solving may actually improve when other caregivers are available to generate alternatives or buffer emotional responses in the process. Similarly, parents who have young children in a day-care setting may find that the child's vocabulary, understanding of communication and problem-solving rules, as well as experience in handling conflict may expand, given this opportunity.

Recognized Impact on Effective Family Living

Both preventionists and therapists have affirmed the crucial importance of communication and problem solving and their related skills on effective family functioning. For example, the recent work on family strengths and resiliency incorporated the key role of communication and problem solving (McCubbin & McCubbin, 1988), and virtually all the studies of indicators of health in families have included clear references to communication. The emphasis on flexibility, decision making, crisis management, and time together include presumptions of the ability to engage in effective problem solving (see, for example, J. Lewis, Beavers, Gossett, & Phillips, 1976; Olson et al., 1983; Stinnett, 1985).

Additionally, studies of family resiliency and child outcomes have highlighted problem-solving ability as a protective skill that aids children in dealing with adversity in their lives. Durlak (1983) suggested that the potential value of effective problem-solving abilities included increased flexibility and adaptability in social situations, the ability to deal with stress, and the ability to create appropriate means to attain personal goals and satisfy needs.

Varied Family Performance

The considerable literature on family and marital dysfunction (see, for example, Jacob, 1975; Schaap, Buunk, & Kerkstra, 1988) has provided support for the claim that, although all families communicate and solve problems, not all of them do these well or even satisfactorily. In the area of marital communication, clear differences have been cited in self-reported communication between happy and unhappy couples (Christiansen, 1988). Thus family groups do appear to need knowledge and skill development concerning these processes.

Identified Lifelong Learning Potential

Human beings have potential to learn or refine interpersonal skills over the entire life cycle. Beginning at birth, a child begins to communicate and engage in problem solving to have needs met. A person's unique developmental as well as experiential life space create the demand for new or adapted communication and problem-solving skills.

THEORETICAL UNDERPINNINGS

Historically, there has been an uneasy relationship between family theory and family life education practice. There is, however, a strong potential link between research, theory, and education about family communication and problem solving. What have researchers and theorists contributed to understanding family communication and problem solving? How can these understandings guide the development and evaluation of educational programs?

Theories About Family Communication

General theories of individual and ad hoc group communication and problem solving had considerable influence on early family life education programming probably because it was assumed that there were similarities in individual and group communication. Even when individual and group differences were recognized, it was assumed that the family as a small group functioned in the same way as other small groups. Until family theoreticians and researchers challenged and tested these assumptions, the field was dependent upon general understandings of these complicated processes.

Use of the communication approach in understanding intimate relationships emerged in the 1950s and 1960s. *Pragmatics of Human Communication* (Watzlawick, Beavin, & Jackson, 1967) has become the single, most influential theoretical resource in this area. This work, and others based on it, changed the emphasis in communication study from a focus on the individual to that of the system. This systems theory emphasized the whole rather than its individual parts, emphasized current behavior rather than historical influences, minimized internal motivational factors, and recognized that the system was its own cause in the process of change. The pattern of interchanges (their consistencies and their changes) was given a primary role in understanding family communication.

Developmental theory also provided important theoretical contributions to the understanding of family communication (Duvall, 1957). Concepts such as role, role expectations, and perception helped clarify the communication process in the family group. The notion of norms and rules, communication patterns, and how these changed as developmental tasks evolved over the family life cycle were also important contributions.

Considerable theoretical work has been completed about family communication in the past 10 years. Rausch et al. (1979) have provided a concise review of theory related to communication in couples and families. The theoretical work by R. Lewis and Spanier (1979) on marital quality complements this work.

The Minnesota Couples Communication Program (Miller, Nunnally, & Wackman, 1972) illustrates the use of theory in developing educational programs in family communication. Family developmental theory guided the identification and development of skills that would equip couples to accomplish developmental tasks, to accommodate to change, and to stimulate change when necessary to keep the relationship continually growing. Systems and communication theory supported the proposition that systems that function most effectively are able to maintain some level of stability while allowing for a means of effecting change when necessary. Based on these theoretical tenets, the educational program focused on two sets of skills: those that allowed partners to understand their rules and interaction patterns (awareness skills) and those that enabled them to change their rules and interaction patterns (communication and problem-solving skills).

Theories About Problem Solving

Theoretical work in the area of family problem solving is also relatively new and was influenced strongly by systems principles. This theoretical work blends five different areas of scientific study: (a) the micro study of problem solving in small groups, (b) the macro study of the family and social problems, (c) the study of family crises and adaptation, (d) the study of organizational decision making, and (e) normal family development (Klein & Hill, 1979). Although these areas of study offered concepts useful to the development of family problem-solving theory, there was an early recognition of the unique nature of the family as a problem-solving group characterized, for example, by its historical perspective, patterns of dependency, and developmental nature (see, for example, Tallman, 1970; Weick, 1971).

A wide range of partial theories has been developed (see Aldous, Condon, Hill, Straus, & Tallman, 1971, and Klein & Hill, 1979, for detailed reviews) with only a few attempts to provide integration. The direct use of *family* problem-solving theory in family life education practice is particularly weak. No particular problem-solving program has been developed using these theories.

On the other hand, theory has provided the basis for programs in social problem-solving programming in a variety of interpersonal situations. Durlak's (1983) review has identified three different approaches to these programs (cognitive, developmental, task-specific), each based upon different theoretical views of problem solving. Because of their potential relevance to family life education, brief overviews of each approach are provided here.

Cognitive theorists perceive problem solving as a series of cognitive processes that can be generalized to many different situations. Particular attention is given to the component parts of problem solving and to their use as objectives for educational intervention. Programs are usually limited to a specified number of problem-solving skills. Educators who use this theoretical perspective assume that cognitive problem-solving processes are essential as mediators of human adjustment and that improving these processes through education results in better behavioral adjustment. Spivack, Platt, and Shure (1986) developed a program for preschoolers and young children in school settings that identified alternative thinking, consequential thinking, and means-end thinking as the critical cognitive skills that determine problem-solving success. Most school-based programs, such as in *Lions Quest Programs: Skills for Adolescents* (Quest International, 1985), do not specify but are congruent with this theoretical perspective.

The developmental approach shares the assumption with the cognitive approach that core skills have relevance for adjustment, but these theorists place cognitive skills in a place secondary to the primary skills of social perception, social sensitivity, and role taking. Such skills are primary because they enable one to assess a situation accurately and thus determine not only what is expected but also what is appropriate in the situation. Programs based on this approach assume that assisting individuals to develop abilities such as role taking and perception will enhance their interpersonal functioning, including their problem solving. One example of a developmental program is that developed by Elardo and Caldwell (1979) to teach fourth and fifth graders perspective-taking and problem-solving skills.

The third theoretical approach in social problem-solving programs is the task-specific approach. Here, the assumption is that different tasks or problems require different skills. Target skills for educational programs are identified through a task analysis of the situation or a review of the research that contrasts skilled and unskilled individuals. In these programs, it is common to see discrete skills such as assertiveness receive greater attention than specific problem-solving skills. Most of these programs do not support a common set of problem-solving skills that lead to adjustment but instead focus on situation-specific skills. For an example of this approach, see D'Zurilla and Goldfried (1971).

PROGRAM EMPHASES

There are many ways in which to categorize current educational program emphases in family communication and problem solving. This chapter will focus on the following: (a) programs with a specific focus on the entire processes, (b) programs that focus on one step associated with the process or on one skill in the process (e.g., goal setting, alternative generation, evaluating alternatives or sending, receiving, interpreting messages), and (c) programs that are situation specific in that they teach and apply the process to a particular situation or problem (e.g., child rearing, marital relations, marital or family enrichment, parent-adolescent conflict, assertiveness training).

Programs Focusing on the Whole Process

Programs that are organized solely around the entire communication or problem-solving process are more likely to be found in school than in community family life education programs. Often these programs are cognitively based and participants are encouraged to learn about the entire process because of its relevance to many different types of situations. The relative scarcity of such programs outside of school settings may demonstrate the need for greater specificity in developing adult education in these processes. It may also reflect an assumption that adult learners are already aware of these processes.

The study of decision-making or problem-solving and communication processes are often key components of a number of subject areas in elementary and secondary school curricula: social studies, health, and mathematics as well as family life education. In family life education, whether the unit is one dealing with relationships, sexuality, or career planning, it is common to introduce or review the communication and/or problem-solving processes as potential tools for resolving issues. One example of such a program is the intervention designed by Hains and Hains (1987) in which delinquent youth were taught a five-step model for social problem solving through application to social dilemmas. Durlak (1983) has listed a number of school-based programs designed to develop children's cognitive problem-solving skills. Examples of nonschool programs that focus on the entire problem-solving process are those dealing with marital decision making (Knopf & Reid, 1986) and problem solving in families with adolescent diabetics (Kieren, Hurlbut, Looney, Mahaffey, & Bowman, 1988).

Programs Focusing on One or More Aspects of the Process

Many programs are limited to a few aspects of the process or to several skills associated with the process. One interesting skill-focused program teaches a four-step model of problem-solving communication skills, including negotiation of solutions to specific disputes, remediation of negative communication patterns, cognitive restructuring of inappropriate attitudes, and practice in applying negotiation communication (Bright & Robin, 1981). Although these programs were originally designed for therapeutic intervention, this model could easily be applied to educational contexts. Blechman (1974) has designed a family problem-solving training intervention that is designed to promote a rational, democratic family atmosphere while handling immediate family problems. Emphasis is placed on the establishment of contracts for resolution of problematic situations. A board game, The Family Contract Game (Blechman, 1974), is used repeatedly during the training process to write new contracts and renegotiate old ones.

Similarly, the communication process is often broken into parts to focus upon such skills as empathic listening, self-disclosure, managing affective communication, and communication flexibility. While the labels for these skills may vary, programs generally focus upon one or two of these skills. Most well-developed family communication programs such as the Minnesota Couples Communication Program (Miller et al., 1972), the Relationship Enhancement program (Guerney, 1977), and Parent Effectiveness Training (T. Gordon, 1970) are examples of this type of emphasis.

There are several limitations of these programs. Issues such as gender and cultural differences in problem solving and communication have not been adequately addressed. As well, the development of a shared reality regarding family problems and of a balance in both aspects of problem-solving effectiveness (solution quality and solution acceptance) are noteworthy by their absence. The importance of ritual in the communication process has also been ignored. At their best, ritual behaviors seem to convey underlying commitments that allow conflict and disagreements to be expressed directly. Because much of communication has a here-and-now, interactive focus, adding rituals that express loyalty and commitment can enhance communication and problem-solving possibilities (see Imber-Black, Roberts, & Whiting, 1988, and Steinglass, Bennett, Wolin, & Reiss, 1987, for the power and influence of rituals in the lives of families).

Communication programs have also had an individual focus as reflected in methods. Burr (1990) has suggested the need to broaden communication concepts to capture the relationship aspects of family communication. He proposed the concept of "we statements" as an additional communication concept or skill that would reflect the togetherness aspects of a family system.

Programs Applying the Process to a Particular Issue

Many problem-solving and communication programs are organized around the resolution of a particular issue or problem. Hoopes, Fisher, and Barlow (1984) have provided several examples of problem- or situation-based programs.

Marriage and family enrichment programs are examples of this emphasis as well. Wackman (1983) has suggested that the basic approach for communication training for marriage and family has been the small group program designed for a particular subunit of the family—couples, parents, or the family as a whole. Marriage communication programs offered mainly as marriage enrichment programs are designed to build strengths in already satisfactorily functioning relationships. Many such programs have been designed (see Olson, 1975;

Wackman, 1983). The three largest and best known programs are Marriage Encounter (Boscoe, 1972), Minnesota Couples Communication Program (Miller et al., 1972), and Conjugal Relationship Enhancement Program (Guerney, 1977).

Family enrichment programs have typically been less skill oriented than marriage enrichment programs. Instead, educational experiences are designed to allow families to view their own family from different realities and to create shared educational experiences around different aspects of family life. The Family Cluster Model (Sawin, 1979), Understanding Us (Carnes, 1981), and the Family Relationship Enhancement Program (Vogelsong & Guerney, 1980) are examples of enrichment programs with prominent problem-solving and communication components.

Based on participation levels, family life education programs that have had the greatest impact of all family-oriented communication training programs have been parent education programs. T. Gordon's Parent Effectiveness Training (1970) and Dinkmeyer and McKay's (1976) Systematic Training for Effective Parenting are the most widely distributed programs. Guerney and his associates (Grando & Ginsberg, 1976) have also developed the Parent-Adolescent Relationship Development Program. These programs place a heavy emphasis on the development of listening skills to help parents resolve the issues of power struggles between parents and children.

Although the above categorization is useful in illustrating the different emphases in communication and problem-solving programs, it should be noted that many programs cross the artificial boundaries of these categories.

METHODS AND METHODOLOGICAL ISSUES

Many different methods can be used to teach communication and family problem-solving skills or the problem-solving process. Methods that are purely didactic are most appropriate when the intent is to help participants gain understanding of or insight into these processes. Most communication and problem-solving programs, however, also use experiential methods. Such methods enable participants to choose and practice skills most relevant for their family situation first in the activities of the program and then later in the family's own life space.

No single method can be expected to provide appropriate experiences to learn all components of communication and problem solving. Table 6.1 provides examples of innovative methods in educational practice.

TABLE 6.1. Innovative Methods in Family Communication and
Problem Solving

Method	Objective
Family Practice Model (Reid, 1985)	To help family members identify and understand their problems and to facilitate problem-solving actions
Family Sculpting (Papp, Silverstein, & Carter, 1973)	To use nonverbal means to express thoughts and feelings, particularly those that might generate strong emotional aspects or potentially hostile reactions
Enactments (Reid, 1985)	To allow family members to reproduce or replay common interactions for review or critique
Family diary (Kieren & Poon, 1986)	To allow family members to record and review ongoing daily interaction and share different perceptions of that interaction
Games/simulations (Johnson & Johnson, 1982)	To allow family members to practice or review behavior in a less threatening context
In-home practice	To reinforce learning and allow practice in a real-life context
Laboratory method (L'Abate, 1990)	To use standard operating procedures in a cost-effective way in evaluation and preventive methods, using a lattice and ladder of different personnel with varying levels of expertise
Teleconferencing	To allow families to remain at home and have the opportunity to talk with other families and experts for both support and information
Interactive video	To allow families nonthreatening opportunities to learn in their own life space and time frame

It is important to recognize that methods are not meaningful outside of the assumptions and objectives of a particular family life education program. Educators must therefore take into account the specific purpose or goal of the activity, the target family characteristics, the time available to complete the task and its debriefing, and the skills or competencies demanded of the educator as facilitator of the activity. Principles important in the selection of methods for problem-solving and communication programs include focusing on family needs and salient issues, building on family resources and strengths, processing family actions by helping family members to observe their actions as outsiders might, and building in both practice and follow-up in the natural family setting.

In any task-oriented or experiential approach, the development of session tasks are particularly important. Educators usually move from simple to more complex tasks and begin with tasks that are less threatening or demanding. For example, the use of written or videotaped vignettes as an initial session task can be helpful for the discussion of common family or problem-solving situations because these vignettes are engaging and nonthreatening and do not usually require a high level of risk taking. At a later time in the program, practice or the role-play of actual family situations may be employed.

Several special challenges face educators who wish to teach about communication and problem solving. Primary among these is the myth of naturalism (Vincent, 1973), which suggests that individuals learn key interpersonal competencies and skills naturally through life experiences rather than as a result of direct teaching in formal or informal settings. This myth is a strong feature of popular beliefs concerning personal and interpersonal requirements for effective family living and may prevent individuals and/or family groups from taking time to develop the processes required to maintain the group and to allow it to grow and respond to change.

As well, perceptions of the processes of communication and problem solving within a particular family may not be shared by all family members. When these perceptions are shared or when family group members work to develop these into a commonly understood view, then a *family* perception or view may exist. In many cases, however, family groups comprise a collection of discrepant views of these processes, and educators must be alert to discover the nature of family *realities*.

Additionally, the views that family members have of the processes of communication and problem solving may not coincide with the views of educators concerning these same processes. For example, many educators promote problem solving as a positive activity in families, but the word *problem* may be viewed negatively by participants, particularly when associated with their own family unit. Family members often do not wish to admit to problems, fearing that they may be labeled as dysfunctional. Educators are thus challenged to reframe problem solving as a positive, daily activity that can create opportunities for new avenues of adaptation, success, and satisfaction.

Family members are not always aware of the unique nature of the family group when it is compared with other groups. The historical perspective of the family, the wide variation in ability, age, and power, and the affectional bonds all create a communication and problem-solving environment that is unmatched in other human interaction. The family is both resourceful and cumbersome as it operates to carry out its functions. As a problem-solving unit, it has vast potential for unique solutions but may often use only a limited range of alternatives. Thus educators may be challenged by the tendency of families to use habitual communication or problem-solving responses rather than to engage in new efforts to find solutions to family problems.

Finally, the emphasis on communication skills in the popular literature has been so strong that many people have come to believe that the more a couple or family talked with one another about their relationship, the stronger and better the relationship. It was as if the tool of communication became the goal rather than serving as a means to the end of more effective family functioning. When participants hold such beliefs, educators must assist these individuals in moving beyond talking.

EVALUATION

For the most part, cognitively based problem-solving programs for children have generally reported discouraging results (Durlak, 1983). Evaluation studies have demonstrated that these programs can improve children's problem-solving behavior but there is little evidence that this leads to better behavioral adjustment. Weissberg et al. (1981) suggested that factors other than cognitive problem solving may be influencing adjustment. According to Durlak (1983), the assumption that all children need and will benefit from problem-solving training should be tested.

The limited number of cognitively oriented adult programs makes it difficult to evaluate their impact. As well, evaluation of developmentally oriented problem-solving programs has not linked the development of these skills to interpersonal functioning (see, for example, Urbain & Kendall, 1982).

The review by Durlak (1983) examined the impact of a variety of task-specific problem-solving programs. General conclusions were difficult to make given the differing objectives and methods of the studies, although Durlak's analysis highlighted the promise of the Relationship Enhancement programs (Guerney, 1977) designed to prevent drug taking and adolescent pregnancy.

In the evaluation of problem-solving programs, greater attention needs to be given to follow-up, to control groups, and to more objective outcome data. Because problem solving and role taking have been competing explanations for the development of social competence, comparative studies of problem-solving and non-problem-solving skills would also seem to be appropriate (e.g., problem-solving versus role-taking or other social skills). Durlak (1983) has claimed that parental, premarital, and marital couple programs have not been evaluated sufficiently to come to any conclusions about their potential impact, but family life educators have taken a more optimistic view. Although reports of many of these studies have been relatively inaccessible (found in doctoral dissertations or unpublished material), several recent evaluative reviews have been published (Durlak, 1983; Giblin, Sprenkle, & Sheehan, 1985; Guerney & Maxson, 1990; Gurman & Kniskern, 1987; Hof & Miller, 1981; Wampler, 1982; Zimpfer, 1988).

Of the comprehensive marriage enrichment programs that include communication and problem-solving skills, the Relationship Enhancement procedures developed by Guerney (1977) have been most widely used and most carefully researched. Systematic studies of this program with differing populations have consistently demonstrated positive outcomes (Gurman & Kniskern, 1987), a finding supported in the meta-analysis completed by Giblin et al. (1985).

The Minnesota Couples Communication Program (Miller et al., 1972) has also been widely used and researched. Wampler (1982) reviewed 19 evaluation studies on this program and concluded that evidence from the first 10 years of research indicated that the program was effective, particularly when behavioral measures were considered. Although findings were mixed concerning effects on communication quality and relationship satisfaction, when the best executed studies were considered, there was evidence of a positive impact on both of these aspects.

There has been little well-designed research to evaluate Marriage Encounter programs. Although self-reports from participants have posited positive impacts, several critiques have been published questioning the potential for the program to effect long-term change in marital skills and satisfaction (see, for example, Doherty, McCabe, & Ryder, 1978).

There have also been few studies that have evaluated family enrichment programs that include problem-solving and communication skills. Studies of parent education programs have indicated modest positive results.

Other findings from evaluation studies completed during the 1980s have provided information concerning program format, process, and leadership. The focus, action, intent, function, content, and style of an educator's response can have predictable effects on participants' evaluation of impact (Hammonds & Worthington, 1985). The meta-analysis of 85 enrichment studies by Giblin et al. (1985) concluded that enrichment programs that focused on skills and behavioral practice had more effect than those that did not. Effect sizes were significantly larger for communication and problem-solving variables than for satisfaction or personality measures. In addition, significantly higher effects were found for clinic rather than well-functioning participants. The use of newer techniques such as videotaped skill instruction was helpful in maintaining communication skills (Cleaver, 1987). Specific training in skills like alternative generation in problem-solving education were demonstrated to be more effective than a generic communication skills approach (Warmbrod, 1982).

CONTEMPORARY ISSUES AND CHALLENGES

To improve the means by which they approach and carry out their educational task, family life educators must become aware of and respond to several current issues and challenges. The following appear to be among those most critical for improving programs on communication and problem solving.

Expanding the Family Focus

In practice, though not necessarily by design, family life education programs are more likely to be attended by individuals than by family groups (Bowman & Kieren, 1985). Many reasons are given for this pattern. Some relate directly to the nature of family life, such as time pressures, lack of commitment to learn the interactional skills assumed to be acquired naturally, and disinterest. Additionally, some programs may, in fact, be designed for individuals or couples rather than as family groups. Educational programs included as a part of therapy have had more success in attracting family groups in that the family is already committed to a process designed to resolve a compelling family issue (L'Abate, 1990).

There is, without doubt, some benefit in working with even one family member to build or enrich communication or family problem-solving skills, but, at best, it is an incomplete approach. Individuals cannot be expected to change if the family does not change as well. In an annotated bibliography on prevention by Buckner, Trickett, and Corse (1985), only 19 of a total of 1,009 entries deal primarily with families. L'Abate suggested a central premise: "No matter how much good we do in helping people change, this good will be lost if their immediate families are not part of the process" (1990, p. 7). Family approaches to family life education are needed that will promote the conditions or the context necessary to increase competence and coping skills. Learning these skills with other family members who share identity bonds and a similar emotional history provides the necessary reality and motivation to put these new skills into practice.

To attract family groups may necessitate a reconceptualization of where, when, and how programs are offered. This may mean bringing programs and educational opportunities closer to families within their own communities, for example, in conjunction with other family service programs such as day care or after-school care. Similarly, the entire family could be the focus of a significant part of school family life education or health programs that are typically offered only to children in the family.

L'Abate (1990) suggested that the family center concept might attract more families to family life education. Preventive programs of all types could be offered within communities by building family centers or by using empty school buildings or Sunday school classrooms. Such centers could encompass both informal and formal activities in recreation, social and health services, and educational services. Providing a gathering place for families might help handle the isolation of families and provide them with opportunities to share informally, to learn communication and problem-solving strategies from each other, and to discover that they are not alone in handling difficult interactional issues. As well, family-to-family peer education could be implemented more widely. Marriage and Family Encounter (Calvo, 1975) has used such an approach for a number of years.

Marketing

If family life educators wish to target families for communication and problem-solving educational efforts, marketing issues will need to be addressed. Family life education programs have typically been attended by white middle-class women. Change in this pattern will require asking several important questions: What will attract family groups? Who are the gatekeepers of family activities? What factors limit whole-family participation and how can an educator anticipate these factors? Family life educators need to give more serious attention to the systematic design, collection, analysis, and reporting of data relevant to marketing family life education, in particular problem-solving and communication education (Aid Association for Lutherans, 1987).

Developing a Multicultural Perspective

It is evident that families in North America come from a wide variety of cultural backgrounds. To provide families with meaningful communication and problem-solving learning opportunities, family life educators must become aware of (and, in some cases, rid themselves of) their ethnocentric biases. Culture, class, and race characteristics as these relate to communication and problem-solving vocabulary, rules, rituals, and actual communication patterns need to be recognized and appreciated (see Chapter 7 in Volume 1). Wampler (1982) noted that the research on the first waves of communication programs during the 1960s and 1970s was carried out with white, middle-class families. Communication patterns in these studies were exemplified by a direct interactive style. Wampler noted, however, that communication patterns of many groups do not conform to this direct, interactive model, which has served as the basis for many of the existing program models. Allen (1989), for example, writes poignantly about the narrative storytelling tradition of Native Americans and how that method is at odds with the Western, white middle-class ways of communicating. In addition, family communication programs for aboriginal families will need to be targeted at the extended rather than the nuclear family if they are to be relevant for this particular group.

Boyd-Franklin (1989) affirms previous findings about racial differences in communication. Strong kinship bonds, adaptability of family roles, a strong work orientation, and the power of religion have been recognized as inherent strengths within the black cultural framework. Communication as such is not given the same importance within this group as it is in Caucasian families.

Clearly, communication is necessary in the maintenance of kinship bonds and in balancing family roles, but its preeminence in all families is not evident. Sensitivity to cultural differences is a crucial requirement for family life educators. This includes attention to what is emphasized in programs, how it is marketed, and who is included as well as attention to research that documents the strengths of multiple communication patterns in general or for particular groups. Although Straus (1968) conducted some early studies on family problem solving in different cultures, more needs to be done to identify differences that significantly affect the effectiveness of our educational efforts.

Addressing Gender Issues

Chapter 6 in Volume 1 of this handbook discussed gender issues in family life education. Other references, such as Tannen (1990) and Foss and Foss (1983), are relevant to consideration of gender issues in programs related to family communication and problem solving. Tebes, Grady, and Snow (1989), for example, evaluated a range of parent education programs in light of gender differences and concluded that some of the models that emphasized problem solving and decision making may have a greater appeal and utility for fathers.

L'Abate (1990) discussed the importance of gender differences particularly as these related to coping strategies. He noted most men tend to use problem-focused strategies, whereas most women tend to use emotion-focused strategies (see, for example, Barnett, Biener, & Baruch, 1987). Such gender differences in competence and coping strategies have a significant potential effect on education concerning intimate relationships. Giving specific attention to these differences in educational programs will likely improve the possibility for the resolution of family problems and communication difficulties.

Gender issues in communication interact with those of culture, and family life educators will need to take these into account. For example, the Mexican American cultural group exhibits a particular gender influence in the expression of assertiveness in that machismo prescribes assertiveness for males (Collier, 1986).

Blending Educational and Therapeutic Interests

Both family life educators and therapists have an interest in teaching about communication and problem-solving skills and processes. These two intervention approaches have been clearly distinguished by their objectives, methods, and target audiences, resulting in two different, independent, and sometimes antagonistic approaches to family life education. Therapists like L'Abate (1990) have argued that such an exclusionary view has been debilitating to both educators and therapists and recommended that the two fields should be reconciled and viewed as complementing each other. He has suggested the use of a functionality-to-dysfunctionality continuum to identify families as possible targets for programs: those at risk, those in need, and those in crisis. Several key therapy references (see, for example, Haley, 1977; Olson, 1975) illustrate the commonalities of interest to educators and therapists in the areas of communication and problem solving.

Improving Knowledge About Communication and Problem Solving

It is apparent from this review that there is considerable need to improve the theoretical and empirical knowledge about communication and problem solving in families. In our view, this will require the cooperation of family theorists, family researchers, and family educators.

At the current time, for example, the theoretical propositions that have been generated about communication and problem solving in families are tentative and relatively untested. Family scholars need to subject these propositions to empirical tests to develop increased predictability about these complex processes and thus to provide a better basis for educational programs addressed to these processes. At the same time, educators must become more theoretically and empirically informed so that their educational programs are based on the best knowledge currently available.

As well, there is a need to fill in a number of gaps in understanding of family communication and problem-solving processes. Several of these gaps have already been mentioned, such as those dealing with cultural, racial, and gender differences in these processes. In many cases, these factors should be studied simultaneously. Collier (1986) has suggested, for example, that the rules about assertiveness within cultures may conflict with the rules ascribed to men or to women with respect to assertiveness. This means that people may expect women to be less assertive regardless of cultural membership. Given that behavior tends to be rule governed, Collier posed questions that need to be answered about when sociological, cultural, gender-related, relationship, or personal rules are followed and what contextual circumstances affect this rule hierarchy.

Clearly, gender, cultural, and other rules with respect to the many aspects of communication and problem solving are worthy of further study. Little is known about communication among children and siblings or about communication and problem solving in the latter years of the life cycle. Such information will be essential if educational programs are to be addressed to the needs of the entire family group.

Improving the Evaluation of Programs

In addition to improved understanding of the processes of family communication and problem solving, considerable effort needs to be made to improve the evaluation of the impact of educational programs. According to Giblin et al. (1985), significant short-term effectiveness of programs related to communication and problem solving has been demonstrated, but, as yet, little is known about how to educate for longer term retention of learning. Peer support networks, such as those developed in the Marriage Encounter program (Calvo, 1975), should be investigated for their effectiveness in increasing motivation and commitment to the continued practice and development of skills that might lead to longer term impacts. In addition, tests of different low-cost, nonintrusive booster formats and methodologies such as video or telephone follow-up should be investigated.

In the continuing need to evaluate programs, meta-analysis appears to provide a useful comparative technique (Giblin et al., 1985). Efforts should be made, however, to target previously untested hypotheses. According to Wampler (1982), program evaluation research is characterized by the repeated testing of hypotheses that have been consistently supported (e.g., the effect of communication training on work-style communication) or consistently not supported (e.g., the effect of communication training on perceived self-disclosure). As well, continued use is made of some measurement techniques even though these have been demonstrated to be inappropriate measurement devices.

There is also a need to identify model prevention programs with proven effectiveness. Such models would not only be helpful to practitioners in selecting or developing educational interventions but are of particular importance given dwindling support from funding agencies. To receive funding, family life educators find it increasingly necessary to be able to demonstrate the utility of their programs. Price, Cowen, Lorion, and Ramos-McKay (1989) have identified several effective model prevention programs.

Exploring New Perspectives on Educational Interventions

Dunst, Trivette, and Deal (1988) have challenged the traditional view of many family educational efforts. In this traditional view, the outcome is seen as primarily attributable to the program or the program components. Newer views based on a social systems perspective of intervention have suggested that other sources of informal and formal support also have implications for intervention programs. Family life educators need to conceptualize intervention as an aggregation of many different types of help and assistance and develop new approaches that may not be as focused on skill development as those of the past. For example, Morgaine (1992) has classified skill development in family communication and problem-solving programs as an instrumental/technical approach to learning knowledge and taking action, and she has challenged family life educators to appropriately incorporate two additional approaches: the interpretive approach and the critical/emancipatory approach. The combination of these will provide educators with alternatives for planning communication and problem-solving programs to meet a variety of participant needs.

SUMMARY AND CONCLUSIONS

Although the generic family processes of communication and problem solving remain a central part of most preventive and therapeutic programs dealing with families, theories about family communication and problem solving are relatively recent in origin and in general have not been generated from the empirical study of families engaged in these processes in their own life spaces. As well, theoretical propositions have received little empirical testing with well-functioning family groups. The state of development in this area of study means that family life educators have limited data that describe the nature of family communication and problem solving in a wide range of family circumstances and variations whether based upon cultural, racial, social class, life cycle, or structural factors.

There is no lack of programs, techniques, theories, or ideas about family communication and problem-solving education. Rather, educators are faced with a wide range of possibilities and a limited range of criteria to assess their effectiveness. Although evaluation efforts have increased and have demonstrated the utility of several comprehensive programs incorporating communication and problem-solving education, continuation of these efforts is one of the critical issues facing family life education in the future. The problem-solving task for educators is to use these skills of communication and problem solving to move the field forward and to increase effectiveness for families.

Communication and problem solving as generic skills and processes within family groups no doubt will continue to be central aspects of family life education in the future. The effectiveness of this education will depend largely on the ability of educators to address the critical issues identified in this chapter surrounding how these processes are viewed in terms of total family functioning, what is known about these processes in different family circumstances, and how willing educators are to go beyond traditional methods and target audiences and take a critical look at our intervention efforts.

REFERENCES

Aid Association for Lutherans (AAL). (1987, November). *Marketing strategies for family programs workshop*. Atlanta, GA: National Council on Family Relations.

Aldous, J., Condon, T., Hill, R., Straus, M., & Tallman, I. (1971). *Family problem solving: A symposium on theoretical, methodological and substantive concerns*. Hinsdale, IL: Dryden.

Allen, P. G. (1989). (Ed.). *Spider Woman's granddaughters*. New York: Fawcett Columbine.

Barnett, R., Biener, L., & Baruch, G. (1987). *Gender and stress*. New York: Free Press.

Blechman, E. (1974). The family contract game: A tool to teach interpersonal problem solving. *Family Coordinator, 23*(3), 269-281.

Boscoe, A. (1972). *Marriage Encounter: The rediscovery of love.* St. Meinrad, IN: Abbey.

Bowman, T., & Kieren, D. (1985, December). Underwhelming participation: Inhibitors to family enrichment. *Family Casework,* pp. 617-622.

Boyd-Franklin, N. (1989). *Black families in therapy.* New York: Guilford.

Bright, P., & Robin, A. (1981). Ameliorating parent-adolescent conflict with problem solving communication training. *Journal of Behavioral Therapy and Experimental Psychiatry, 12*(3), 275-280.

Buckner, J., Trickett, E., & Corse, S. (1985). *Primary prevention in mental health: An annotated bibliography* (Publication No. 85-1405). Rockville, MD: U.S. Department of Health and Human Services.

Burr, W. (1990). Beyond "I" statements in family communication. *Family Relations, 38*(3), 266-273.

Calvo, G. (1975). *Marriage Encounter.* St Paul, MN: Marriage Encounter, Inc.

Carnes, P. (1981). *Understanding us: Instructor's manual.* Minneapolis, MN: Interpersonal Communications Program.

Christiansen, A. (1988). Dysfunctional interaction patterns in couples. In P. Noller & M. Fitzpatrick (Eds.), *Perspectives on marital interaction* (pp. 31-52). Philadelphia: Multilingual Matters.

Cleaver, G. (1987). Marriage enrichment by means of an unstructured communication program. *Family Relations, 36,* 49-54.

Collier, M. (1986). Culture and gender effects on assertive behavior and communication competence. In M. McLaughlin (Ed.), *Communication yearbook* (Vol. 9, pp. 576-592). Beverly Hills, CA: Sage.

Dinkmeyer, D., & McKay, G. (1976). *Systematic training for effective parenting (STEP).* Circle Pines, MN: American Guidance Service.

Doherty, W., McCabe, P., & Ryder, R. (1978, October). Marriage Encounter: A critical appraisal. *Journal of Marital and Family Counseling,* pp. 99-106.

Dunst, D., Trivette, C., & Deal, A. (1988). *Enabling and empowering families: Principles and guidelines for practice.* Cambridge, MA: Brookline.

Durlak, J. (1983). Social problem solving as a primary prevention strategy. In R. Felner, L. Jason, J. Moritsugu, & S. Farber (Eds.), *Preventive psychology: Theory, research and practice* (pp. 31-47). New York: Pergamon.

Duvall, E. (1957). *Family development.* Philadelphia: J. B. Lippincott.

D'Zurilla, T., & Goldfried, M. (1971). Problem solving and behavior modification. *Journal of Abnormal Psychology, 78,* 107-126.

Elardo, P., & Caldwell, B. (1979). The effects of an experimental social development program on children in the middle childhood period. *Psychology in the Schools, 16,* 93-100.

Fitzpatrick, M., & Badzinski, D. (1985). All in the family: Communication in kin relationships. In M. Knapp & G. Miller (Eds.), *Handbook of interpersonal communication* (pp. 687-736). Beverly Hills, CA: Sage.

Foss, K., & Foss, S. (1983). The status of research on women and communication. *Communication Quarterly, 31*(3), 195-204.

Giblin, P., Sprenkle, D., & Sheehan, R. (1985). Enrichment outcome research: A meta analysis of premarital, marital and family interventions. *Journal of Marital and Family Therapy, 11*(3), 257-271.

Gordon, I. (1977). Parent education and parent involvement: Retrospect and prospect. *Childhood Education, 54*(2), 71-78.

Gordon, T. (1970). *Parent effectiveness training.* New York: Plume.

Grando, R., & Ginsberg, B. (1976). Communication in the father-son relationship: The parent adolescent relationship development program. *The Family Coordinator, 24*(4), 465-473.

Guerney, B. G., Jr. (1977). *Relationship enhancement.* San Francisco: Jossey-Bass.

Guerney, B., Jr., & Maxson, P. (1990). Marital and family enrichment research: A decade review and look ahead. *Journal of Marriage and the Family, 52*(4), 1127-1135.

Gurman, A., & Kniskern, D. (1987). Enriching research on marital enrichment programs. *Journal of Marriage and Family Counseling, 3,* 3-11.

Hains, A. A., & Hains, A. H. (1987). The effects of a cognitive strategy intervention on the problem solving abilities of delinquent youths. *Journal of Adolescence, 10,* 399-413.

Haley, J. (1977). *Problem solving therapy: New strategies for effective family therapy.* San Francisco: Jossey-Bass.

Hammonds, T., & Worthington, E. (1985). The effect of facilitation utterances on participant responses in a brief ACME type marriage enrichment group. *American Journal of Family Therapy, 13,* 39-49.

Hamner, T., & Turner, P. (1985). *Parenting in contemporary society.* Englewood Cliffs, NJ: Prentice-Hall.

Hof, L., & Miller, W. (1981). *Marriage enrichment: Philosophy, process, and program.* Bowie, MD: Robert J. Brady.

Hoopes, M., Fisher, B., & Barlow, S. (1984). *Structured family facilitation programs: Enrichment, education and treatment.* Rockville, MD: Aspen.

Imber-Black, E., Roberts, J., & Whiting, R. (Eds.). (1988). *Rituals in families and family therapy.* New York: Norton.

Jacob, T. (1975). Family interaction in disturbed and normal families: A methodological and substantive review. *Psychological Bulletin, 32,* 33-65.

Johnson, D., & Johnson, F. (1982). *Joining together* (2nd ed.). Englewood Cliffs, NJ: Prentice-Hall.

Kessen, W. (1965). *The child.* New York: John Wiley.

Kieren, D., Hurlbut, N., Looney, T., Mahaffey, B., & Bowman, T. (1988). *The family problem solving workshop and instructor's guide.* Edmonton: University of Alberta.

Kieren, D., & Poon, J. (1986). The family problem solving diary: A family enrichment technique. *Family Life Educator, 4*(4), 28-33.

Klein, D., & Hill, R. (1979). Determinants of family problem-solving effectiveness. In W. Burr, R. Hill, F. Nye, & I. Reiss (Eds.), *Contemporary theories about the family* (Vol. 1, pp. 493-548). New York: Free Press.

Knopf, J., & Reid, W. (1986). Marital decision making. In J. Conte & S. Briar (Eds.), *The casebook.* New York: Columbia University Press.

L'Abate, L. (1990). *Building family competence.* Newbury Park, CA: Sage.

Lewis, J., Beavers, W., Gossett, J., & Phillips, V. (1976). *No single thread: Psychological health in family systems.* New York: Brunner/Mazel.

Lewis, R., & Spanier, G. (1979). Theorizing about the quality and the stability of marriage. In W. Burr, R. Hill, F. Nye, & I. Reiss (Eds.), *Contemporary theories about the family* (Vol. 1, pp. 268-294). New York: Free Press.

Mace, D. (1975). We call it ACME. In S. Miller (Ed.), *Marriages and families: Enrichment through communication.* Beverly Hills, CA: Sage.

McCubbin, H., & McCubbin, M. (1988). Typologies of resilient families: Emerging roles of social class and ethnicity. *Family Relations, 37*(3), 247-254.

McKeon, R. (1941). *The basic works of Aristotle.* New York: Random House.

Miller, S., Nunnally, E., & Wackman, D. (1972). *Minnesota Couples Communication Program: Couples' handbook.* Minneapolis, MN: MCCP.

Morgaine, C. (1992). Alternative paradigms for helping families change themselves. *Family Relations, 41*(1), 12-17.

Olson, D. (Ed.). (1975). *Treating relationships.* Lake Mills, IA: Graphic.

Olson, D., McCubbin, H., Barnes, H., Larsen, A., Muxen, M., & Wilson, M. (1983). *Families: What makes them work.* Beverly Hills, CA: Sage.

Pangle, T. (1980). *Laws: English/The laws of Plato.* New York: Basic Books.

Papp, P., Silverstein, O., & Carter, E. (1973). Family sculpting in preventive work with well families. *Family Process, 12,* 197-212.

Price, R., Cowen, E., Lorion, R., & Ramos-McKay, J. (1989). The search for effective prevention programs: What we learned along the way. *American Journal of Orthopsychiatry, 59*(1), 49-58.

Quest International. (1985). *Lions Quest programs: Skills for adolescents.* Waterloo, Ontario: Lions Quest Canada.

Rausch, H., Greif, A., & Nugent, J. (1979). Communication in couples and families. In W. Burr, R. Hill, F. Nye, & I. Reiss (Eds.), *Contemporary theories about the family* (Vol. 1, pp. 468-492). New York: Free Press.

Reid, W. (1985). *Family problem solving.* New York: Columbia.

Sawin, M. (1979). *Family enrichment with family clusters.* Valley Forge, PA: Judson.

Schaap, C., Buunk, B., & Kerkstra, A. (1988). Marital conflict resolution. In P. Noller & M. Fitzpatrick (Eds.), *Perspectives on marital interaction* (pp. 203-244). Philadelphia: Multilingual Matters.

Spivack, G., Platt, J., & Shure, M. (1986). *The problem solving approach to adjustment.* San Francisco: Jossey-Bass.

Steinglass, P., Bennett, L., Wolin, S., & Reiss, D. (1987). *The alcoholic family.* New York: Basic Books.

Stinnett, N. (1985). Research on strong families. In G. Rekers (Ed.), *National leadership forum on strong families.* Ventura, CA: Regal.

Straus, M. (1968). Communication, creativity and problem solving ability of middle and working class families in three societies. *American Journal of Sociology, 73,* 417-430.

Tallman, I. (1970). The family as a small problem solving group. *Journal of Marriage and the Family, 32,* 94-104.

Tannen, D. (1990). *You just don't understand.* New York: Ballantine.

Tebes, J., Grady, K., & Snow, D. (1989). Parent training in decision making facilitation: Skill acquisition and relationship to gender. *Family Relations, 38*(3), 243-247.

Urbain, E., & Kendall, P. (1982). Review of social-cognitive problem solving interventions with children. *Psychological Bulletin, 88,* 109-143.

Vincent, C. (1973). *Sexual and marital health.* New York: McGraw-Hill.

Vogelsong, E., & Guerney, B. (1980). Working with parents of disturbed adolescents. In R. Abiden (Ed.), *Parent education and intervention handbook.* Springfield, IL: Charles C. Thomas.

Wackman, D. (1983). Promoting effective communication in families. In D. Mace (Ed.), *Prevention in family services: Approaches for family wellness* (pp. 175-189). Beverly Hills, CA: Sage.

Wampler, K. (1982). The effectiveness of the Minnesota Couple Communication Program: A review of research. *Journal of Marital and Family Therapy, 18*(3), 345-354.

Warmbrod, M. (1982). Alternative generation in marital problem solving. *Family Relations, 31*(4), 503-512.

Watzlawick, P., Beavin, J., & Jackson, D. (1967). *Pragmatics of human communication.* New York: Norton.

Weick, K. (1971). Group processes, family processes, and problem solving. In J. Aldous et al. (Eds.), *Family problem solving: A symposium on theoretical, methodological and substantive concerns.* Hinsdale, IL: Dryden.

Weissberg, R., Gesten, E., Rapkin, B., Cowen, E., Davidson, E., de Apodaca, R., & McKim, B. (1981). The evaluation of a social problem solving training program for suburban and inner city third grade children. *Journal of Consulting and Clinical Psychology, 49,* 251-261.

Zimpfer, D. (1988). Marriage enrichment programs: A review. *Journal for Specialists in Group Work, 13,* 44-53.

7

Family Life Education for Midlife and Later Life Families

Margaret E. Arcus

ALTHOUGH THE CLAIM is often made that education for family life is needed by individuals of all ages (e.g., Arcus, 1987; National Commission on Family Life Education, 1968), historically, family life education has placed a disproportionate emphasis on programs related to the roles and issues of early family life. The earliest form of family life education, for example, was that of parent education designed primarily for the parents of young children (Brock, Oertwein, & Coufal, Chapter 4, this volume). Within the broad field of marriage education (see Chapter 2 in this volume by Stahmann & Salts), programs have typically focused on marriage preparation for the early years of marriage, with attention given only recently to the enrichment of lasting relationships. As well, family life education has since its inception devoted considerable effort to providing family life education for school-aged children and youth.

Although this traditional emphasis on the issues of early family life may create the impression that these are the most important issues for family life education, this chapter is based on the assumption that later life family issues are as important to individuals, to families, and to societies as are those pertaining to the earlier years. Further, it is assumed that programs in family life education for midlife and later life families can sustain and improve the lives of individuals and families at

AUTHOR'S NOTE: Appreciation is expressed to Tim Brubaker of Miami University, Karen Roberto of Colorado State University, and Brian de Vries and David Watt of the University of British Columbia for their suggestions for this chapter.

this stage of the life course. Clearly, the later periods of adulthood are potentially a key time for family life education, as adults not only attempt to meet their own needs for family living but also may bear some responsibility for the family needs of other generations, that is, the needs of their parents, their children, and possibly their grandchildren (see Hennon & Arcus, 1993).

Because of its emphasis on early family life issues, family life education has failed to respond adequately to the growing proportion of older people in nearly all societies. The significance of this group for family life education does not lie just in its numbers, however. At least at the current time, relatively few of those individuals who are now middle aged or older had opportunities to participate in and benefit from family life education programs during their early years. As well, the number of years encompassed by this period of the life course is relatively large, involving (at least for some people) a period of from 30 to 40 years.

It is not the purpose of this chapter to systematically review the growing body of research on midlife and later life families. Several recent reviews have summarized and critiqued some of this research (Bengtson, 1989; Bengtson, Cutler, Mangen, & Marshall, 1985; Brubaker, 1990b; Mancini & Bliezner, 1989), and readers are referred to these references for more detailed information. Rather, this chapter will first provide an overview of midlife and later life issues of particular relevance to family life education and will then review the literature describing family life education programs for this typically underserved audience. The chapter will conclude with a brief summary and a discussion of special considerations to be taken into account when providing family life education for this particular audience.

FAMILY LIFE NEEDS OF MIDLIFE AND LATER LIFE FAMILIES

Because the family life needs of midlife and later life families are often linked, the discussion of these needs will be organized around three broad themes: intergenerational issues, couple issues, and individual issues. These same three themes will be used to review existing programs for adults in family life education.

Intergenerational Issues

To examine intergenerational family issues, it is important to focus both on changes in family structure (e.g., the launching of children and the empty nest, the marriage and/or divorce of children, the addition of grandchildren, the return of adult children to the family home) and on the implications of these changed structures for family roles and relationships (e.g., relationships with in-laws and with grandchildren, changed relationships with adult children and with aging parents).

Midlife and later life families have been defined as those families beyond the child-rearing years who have begun to launch their children (Brubaker, 1990b). There are a number of changes that typically occur in the family structure at this stage of the life course. As children mature and become independent, middle-aged and older couples have fewer persons within their own households. This contraction in the household unit draws attention to the importance of the dyadic relationship in marriage. Many couples may have had a dyadic relationship in marriage for only a relatively short period of time (approximately 2 to 5 years) before the expansion of the household through the arrival of the first child. But once the children leave home at adulthood, a couple can anticipate being a two-person household again for approximately another 15 to 30 years.

At the same time that the household contracts because children leave home, the kinship networks of middle-aged and older couples expand as their children marry and possibly have children of their own. Thus family relationships may become more complex and at times more demanding. Relationships need to be established with a son- or daughter-in-law and with his or her family, relationships that may be even more complex if the son- or daughter-in-law brings children from a previous marriage into the family network.

The expansion of family kinship networks during the middle and later adult years due to the marriage of the children is an anticipated and expected development for most families. In recent years, however, unexpected and nonnormative expansion rather than contraction has occurred in some households. For some older couples, their adult children leave home, only to return after a few years of independence (Suitor & Pillemer, 1987, 1988). With the return of an adult child, both the parents and the adult child need to establish new patterns of interaction within the household. Initially, the adult child's return may be defined as temporary as it is assumed that the adult child will return to an independent household, usually as soon as financial independence is gained or regained. Whether temporary or not, the return of an adult child provides a challenge to both generations and may require strategies to alter previous decision-making patterns and ways of interaction to accommodate not only the needs of the parents but also those of their adult children who are now "guests" within the home.

In addition to relationships with their adult children, the inter-generational relationships of many older people include relationships with grandchildren and possibly with great-grandchildren. Becoming a grandparent is often the first family role associated with later life (Brubaker, 1990a). This new role may signify an important time in the lives of many older persons, but the experience of being a grandparent may vary depending both upon one's gender and upon the age at which one becomes a grandparent (Hagestad, 1988). In particular, becoming a grandparent at an earlier age has been associated with feelings of dis-comfort about this role (Burton & Bengtson, 1985; Hagestad & Burton, 1986). Thus there appears to be more satisfaction with the role if it is "on time" rather than "off time."

The grandparent role has always been loosely defined (Fisher, 1983; Sprey & Matthews, 1982), but recent changes in families have altered the nature of the grandparent role for some individuals. Because the parents of many young children are employed, grandparents have an increased opportunity and in some cases there is increased need for them to assist in the rearing of their grandchildren. Despite the interest of most parents in helping their adult children, however, not all grandparents are pleased to take on the child-rearing role for grandchildren as this may restrict their own freedom and opportunities for development (Connidis, 1989). Today's grandparents may thus face the challenge of balancing their own needs with the needs of their children for assistance in the rearing of the next generation.

Typically, the changes associated with becoming a grandparent are based on continuous patterns of family relationships. This continuity may strengthen the bonds between the generations and may contribute to stability within the extended family network (Bengtson & Robertson, 1985; Fisher, 1981; Hagestad, 1985). In some situations, it may be neces-sary for the middle generation to mediate the grandparent-grandchild relationship. This is particularly evident when an adult child divorces.

Of particular concern to families with aging members are issues revolving around health. Because it mediates so many other aspects of life, health is seen by the elderly as one of the most important aspects of life (Green & Kreuter, 1991). The majority of care for ill and impaired elderly tends to come from family members and can lead to stress and potential crisis in the family (Cantor, 1983). Although women are typi-cally more involved in this caregiving than men (Brody, 1985), caregiv-ing is stressful for both men and women. This stress comes from the competing demands of multiple roles and the need to balance caregiv-ing with other tasks and roles.

One of the disturbing patterns of intergenerational relationships is that of the neglect and physical and/or psychological abuse of elder family members. Lloyd and Emery (1993) have examined the dynamics of such abuse in the family, emphasizing the interplay between a variety of individual, familial, social, and cultural factors. They suggested that patterns of abuse in families will likely persist unless specific efforts are made to intervene in these abusive families. The abuse of elder family members is particularly difficult not only because the abused elderly fail to thrive in such an environment but also because there is little likelihood that they will be able to leave the abusive family environment. In fact, for some elderly, the alternative to abuse may be to move to a nursing home, and this may be so distasteful that abuse is tolerated as the lesser of two evils (M. J. Quinn & Tomita, 1986).

Couple Issues

As suggested above, middle-aged and older married couples may need to relearn how to interact as a dyad and how to meet each other's needs in a household that no longer includes their children (Brubaker, 1990b). "Who does what" around the household may become an issue as the children are no longer available to complete household chores. At the same time, the couple needs to develop satisfying patterns of leisure and recreation that meet both their individual and their couple needs.

Marital satisfaction appears to differ for middle-aged and older couples. Some studies (Anderson, Russell, & Schumm, 1983; Schumm & Bugaighis, 1986; Swanson, Eskew, & Kohlhepp, 1981) have indicated that couples in middle age experience lower marital satisfaction than during the earlier years. It is suggested that the multiple demands placed upon these couples (e.g., children, work, community activities) lessen their opportunities to direct attention toward their marital relationship. As the children leave home, however, and as the couple moves into the retirement years, marital satisfaction appears to increase (Anderson et al., 1983; Johnson, White, Edwards, & Booth, 1986). During these later years, the demands of other roles may have decreased and the couple may now have the opportunity to focus on one another and on their relationship.

Sexuality may be an issue for midlife and later life families but sexuality at this stage of the life span seldom receives serious attention in the family literature. Often the sexual interest or activity of older persons is depicted in humor or satire with little attention directed to its importance in the lives of older people. It is clear that older adults have an interest in and are involved in sexual activity even though the amount of activity may have declined (Garza & Dressel, 1983; Palmore, 1981; Robinson, 1983; Streib & Beck, 1980).

For some couples, the decline in sexual activity may be associated with health problems (Garza & Dressel, 1983; Robinson, 1983). Although health may limit sexual activity temporarily, it does not permanently preclude it. If midlife and later life families equate sexual activity with sexual intercourse, however, they may fail to recognize the importance of intimacy and other forms of sexual expression (touching, caressing, holding hands, massaging, showing affection). Sexuality needs to be recognized as an important element of the lives of midlife and older adults, and the variety of ways to express sexuality and to fulfill sexual needs must be acknowledged, both by the adults and by those around them.

In the past, it was usually assumed that most midlife or later life marriages ended with the death of one of the partners. Recently, however, the increase in the incidence of divorce has included the termination of midlife and later life marriages (Thornton & Freedman, 1983). Coleman and Ganong (1993) have identified several negative effects of divorce in later life: lowered psychological well-being (at least for some individuals), reduced social contacts, reduced physical health, economic disadvantages, and, for some individuals, reduced family contacts and exchange of resources. Because of the increase in the number of divorces, dating and marriage or remarriage have become increasingly important for midlife and later life individuals. The dissolution of decades of shared activities and meanings and the development of a new marriage relationship may create ambivalence for the children in these families.

The family's interaction with the work environment influences some couple issues for midlife and later life families (Voydanoff, 1993). For midlife families, these issues tend to revolve around the need for and problems with balancing work and family demands. Given the increasing number of two-worker families, this is an area in need of considerable attention in family life education. Families need to be clear about goals, priorities, and resource availability as they deal with role overload and stress management.

For midlife and later life families, retirement is usually associated with significant changes in financial resources, role transitions, and changes in spousal interactions, and some individuals may become involved in a search for a self-concept other than that of worker (Connidis, 1989). Spouses may define retirement differently (Szinovacz, 1989), and, although some studies have found no relationship between retirement and marital satisfaction (Lee & Shehan, 1989), some women who continue to work after their husbands have retired report lower marital satisfaction than those who retired with or before their husbands. The responses of family members (spouse and kin) to one's retirement may be crucial in the successful transition to retirement (Ade-Ridder & Brubaker, 1983).

Several gender differences in retirement have been noted. For example, men and women appear to differ in their retirement and marital satisfaction (Lee & Shehan, 1989) and in their preparation for and adjustment to retirement. Women are more likely than men to retire so as to take on additional family responsibility such as caring for an older family member (Szinovacz, 1989).

Individual Issues

Midlife and later life family members must accommodate developmental and health changes, both in themselves and in other family members. Normal physical changes associated with aging may alter one's self-concept and one's interest in sexuality or ability to engage in intercourse. Health is an important issue, especially for older persons, and some have suggested that it is the most important factor associated with an older person's well-being (W. H. Quinn, 1983). As noted earlier in this chapter, other family members may be expected to provide assistance as one's own health difficulties increase.

Individuals in midlife and later life families typically must face the loss of their parents and possibly their spouses. At least some families also may need to face the loss of children or grandchildren. The loss of a parent, particularly if the parent has reached old age, is expected if not specifically anticipated. Even when the death of one's parent is "on time," however, emotional, economic, and relational issues must still be addressed. There is no longer the possibility of addressing unresolved parent-child issues, and sibling conflicts over the parent's estate may surface.

The death of a spouse marks the end of a continuous marital relationship and has a major impact on the life situation of the survivor (Ferraro, 1986; Lopata, 1979; Lund, 1989). Because women traditionally marry men older than themselves and because men typically have shorter life spans than women, the surviving partner is frequently female. Many older women are thus faced with the need to develop a life-style as a single person, because the probability of their remarriage lessens with age. For older women, becoming widows typically reduces their incomes substantially. The loss of a spouse or partner may also have an important influence on health.

Although losing a spouse is more typical for women, this loss is difficult for both men and women. Everyday household needs must still be fulfilled; physical and emotional health must still be addressed; family relationships with children, grandchildren, and other relatives must still continue; and contact with friends and other individuals must still be maintained. Widowed persons may rely on their children for support, although their siblings may also be in a unique position to help.

The loss of an adult child is particularly difficult, as it is usually not expected that parents will survive their children (Edelstein, 1984; Klass, 1988; Rando, 1986). For some, such a loss may have identity implications, as it may call into question their ability as parents to protect their children.

FAMILY LIFE EDUCATION FOR MIDLIFE AND LATER LIFE FAMILIES

The preceding brief overview of intergenerational, couple, and individual issues for midlife and later life families indicates that there is no shortage of issues and transitions where family life educators could be of assistance to these families. Despite the fact that midlife and later life individuals and families are a diverse group with diverse needs and issues, there are sufficient commonalities to serve as the basis for developing family life education programs. Although relatively few programs have been reported in the literature (at least when these are compared with other forms of family life education), those programs that have been will be described in this section to provide a general indication of the current status of family life education for this age group.

Programs Addressing Intergenerational Issues

Several educational programs have been designed to enhance intergenerational family relationships. Roberto (1985), for example, designed a 1-day workshop to increase adult children's knowledge of the aging process and to promote more positive relationships with parents. Topics in the workshop included the myths and realities of aging, physical changes with age, communication skills, alternative housing, and the availability of community programs for older adults. Evaluations of the workshop indicated that participants increased both their knowledge of the aging process and their understanding of the availability of resources for their elderly family members. Although no changes in family communication patterns were reported, it may have been unrealistic to expect changes of this kind as a result of a 1-day workshop.

As part of a larger caregiver educational support group curriculum, Couper and Sheehan (1987) developed an educational model to help adult children understand the dynamics and complexity of the interactions occurring within their family systems. They used a case study approach to help participants identify and deal with competing intergenerational demands within a fictitious family. Discussion of the case study was followed by an assessment of their own family situations. Participants reported that this educational model was beneficial in helping them to understand some of the factors of their own current situations.

Guided autobiography is a useful process that has potential for facilitating intergenerational communication in families, for understanding shifting family roles over time, and for assisting in the search for meaning in one's own life (de Vries, Birren, & Deutchman, 1990). This approach to life review is designed to provide a productive environment for reflection and integration of one's life story and incorporates the use of sensitizing questions, pretested themes, and group processes. Although it is appropriate for individuals of all ages, guided autobiography appears to have particular relevance for the personal and family needs of older individuals.

The work of Strom and Strom (1989, 1990) illustrates the benefits of an educational program for grandparents. The goal of their curriculum ("Becoming a Better Grandparent") was to increase satisfaction in being a grandparent, to improve performance in the grandparent role, to decrease the difficulties and frustrations of grandparents, and to improve awareness of their personal success (Strom, Strom, & Collinsworth, 1990). During the 12, weekly, 90-minute meetings, topics such as sharing feelings and ideas with peers, listening to the views of younger people, learning about life span development, improving family communication skills, and self-evaluating were addressed. The nearly 400 grandparents who participated in the program reported making significant improvements in their attitudes and behaviors, changes that were corroborated by reports from both their grandchildren and their children.

Several educational programs have been developed to meet the needs of individuals faced with the challenge of providing care for a frail, aging relative. Most of these programs are intended for spouses and/or adult children who have assumed primary responsibility for a family member facing physical or cognitive decline. The Center for Rural Elderly at the University of Missouri-Kansas City has identified more than 30 educational programs designed to provide caregivers with a structured forum in which to learn skills and information about the tasks they face in providing care to frail family members. The majority of these programs cover a variety of topics including community resources, sensory changes, communication skills, normal aging, behavioral changes, living arrangements, coping with stress, and chronic illness (Roberto, 1990). Instructor manuals for these programs have been developed by various organizations nationwide to assist family life educators in presenting information to caregivers. The presentation formats are similar (with 2-hour sessions offered over the course of several weeks the most popular model), and almost all programs use a multiple-topic approach. Although the majority of the programs include similar content, most were designed for a specific target audience.

An educational/support group for relatives of patients with dementia was designed to (a) provide accurate information about Alzheimer's disease; (b) teach skills for managing the behavioral, legal, financial, social, and interpersonal problems associated with dementia; and (c) offer support to family members (Glosser & Wexler, 1985). The program was offered for 2 hours per week for a period of 8 weeks and included both formal presentations of information and sharing among support group participants. Overall, the participants rated the program as effective and helpful. A positive feature of the program was the inclusion of family members caring for individuals who were at varying levels of dementia, as this enabled participants to learn what they might expect in the future.

Shulman and Mandel (1988) developed a communication skills workshop to enhance the quality of visits for families of nursing home residents. The workshop consisted of three 2-hour sessions on the nature of normal communication and the causes of impaired communication, the consequences of communication breakdown, and practical techniques for improving communication. Family members reported an increased understanding of their relatives' situation, greater satisfaction with visits, and increased skill in using various communication-facilitating techniques.

To assist families caring for neurologically impaired elders, a 3-hour workshop on legal and financial planning was developed by Pratt, Nayt, Ladd, and Heagerty (1989). The primary goals of the workshop were to introduce families to the legal, procedural, and ethical issues that they faced, to increase their knowledge of relevant legal terms and resources for providing and financing care, and to stimulate actual planning and decision making by families. A 1-year outcome evaluation indicated that more than 90% of the participants had taken planned

action since attending the workshop, with 85% indicating that participation in the workshop had stimulated the planned action.

The workplace can be an effective environment for conducting educational programs for employed caregivers (Ingersoll-Dayton, Chapman,
& Neal, 1990), and education for rural caregivers provided through
extension services is also effective (Epstein & Koenig, 1990). Participants
in these settings reported that the programs in which they participated
were beneficial in helping them to fulfill their caregiving role.

Gold and Gwyther (1989) reported an educational program designed to prevent abuse or neglect in older families. Curriculum mod-
ules in this program address four specific areas of potential conflict:
finances, functional ability, social interaction, and emotional response.
In addition to leader presentations and group discussions on these
topics, scripted dialogue is used to engage participants in the active
generation of plausible alternative solutions to specific conflicts. In the
scripted dialogue, the conflict situation builds until a point of crisis or
climax is reached, and the facilitators then ask the participants: "What
might happen next?" or "How would you end this dialogue?" Short
videotapes (approximately 1 minute in length) are also used to illustrate
conflict situations and to generate discussion around alternative solutions. According to Gold and Gwyther, the curriculum can be used in its
entirety or the specific segments can be used independently. The curriculum is also designed to be used with a variety of audiences and age
groups.

Programs to Address Couple Issues

Marriage enrichment is one of the newest approaches to education
for marriage and is of particular relevance to midlife and later life
families (Mace & Mace, 1986). Programs in marriage enrichment are
based on a dynamic, growth-oriented view of marriage and emphasize
the positive aspects of relationships (Hof & Miller, 1980). Numerous
programs have been developed (see Chapter 2 in this volume for a listing
of some of these programs) and may be delivered either through a series
of weekly meetings or through an intensive weekend retreat. An overview of the typical content and process of marriage enrichment programs is found in Mace (1982). An alternative to these programs that
may be useful for some couples is "self-effort" enrichment, an internally
instigated process of relationship growth and development in which a
couple works privately on their own marital agenda (Arcus & Arcus,
1981).

Because of the large number of divorced families and the potential in these families for disruption and stress, there is a need for preventive mental health programs directed toward divorced or divorcing families. Buehler, Betz, Ryan, Legg, and Trotter (1992) developed a community-based educational prevention program to meet the specific needs of divorcing parents and, indirectly, the needs of their families. This program focuses on several aspects of the divorce experience and is designed to help prevent or minimize divorce-related problems. Themes in the five-session program include the parents' adjustment, common responses of children to marital separation, the legal aspects of divorce, and former-spouse and parent-child relationships, including attention to communication skills and negotiation techniques. Each session is introduced by a brief presentation of information and several handouts. These didactic presentations are then followed by an hour of small group activity that provides participants with the opportunity to practice targeted skills. Role-playing is used to demonstrate the specific skill under discussion. Each session concludes with a discussion involving the entire group regarding the issues that emerged from the small group activities. Most participants in the program reported that they were generally satisfied with the experience, although there were some differences between men and women, between those who had left the family and those who remained, and between those parents who were contesting and those who were not contesting the divorce.

Other preventive educational programs for separated or divorced individuals and families are reported in Bloom, Hodges, and Caldwell (1982), Byrne (1990), Kessler (1978), Stolberg (1988), and Warren et al. (in press). Additional references on programs are cited in Chapter 2 of this volume.

There are few programs that address the sexuality needs of older adults. As part of a larger preventive health care program, Salamon and Charytan (1984) designed a 2-hour, seven-session sexuality workshop for adults. The first three sessions were structured sessions providing information on the myths and realities of sexuality and aging as well as on common medical and emotional problems. Sessions four and five involved open discussions of topics presented by the participants, and session six explored the topic of intimacy. The final session served as a summary session for the workshop. Self-report evaluations indicated that the adults became significantly more knowledgeable about later life sexuality as a result of their participation in this program. According to the authors, participants were also able to communicate their sexual needs and concerns more effectively to members of the health care program following participation in the workshop.

A psychoeducational intervention program focusing on sexuality in later life was developed for older people, adult family members, and nursing home staff (White & Catania, 1982). Topics included in the three lecture/discussion sessions were myths about sexuality and aging, physical and psychological aspects of sexuality and aging, interpersonal intimacy, and the effects of disease, drugs, and the environment on sexuality. To allow for a more personalized approach, the same material was presented separately to the three different target groups. An evaluation of the program indicated positive changes in knowledge about and attitudes toward later life sexuality for all three groups.

Teaching human sexuality through a correspondence course is an innovative approach to sexuality education that may be attractive to midlife and older adults. Developed for adults of all ages, this course was designed to provide individuals with a general overview of the biological, psychological, and social aspects of sexuality (Engel, 1983). An evaluation of the first 100 participants in the course indicated that correspondence study had a significant effect on the sexual knowledge of all groups, including males and females, younger and older adults, and those living in urban and rural areas. These findings suggest that correspondence courses on sexuality can benefit a wide range of older individuals. It also suggests that other family life education programs might consider the use of this delivery system.

Riker and Myers (1990) published brief case studies of various corporate preretirement programs to illustrate particular approaches to employee retirement. In general, each of the six programs described included information on financial planning and retirement income. Health and the use of leisure time were also commonly addressed topics. Although the employee's spouse was included in many of the seminars, a specific focus on interpersonal relations appeared to be limited. Other programs have been described in Imel (1983), Merikangas (1983), Olson (1981), and Tiberi, Boyack, and Kerschner (1978).

Meade and Walker (1989) identified several important issues to be addressed by family life educators providing retirement programs: the theoretical assumptions that underpin the program's rationale, the content of the agenda, the timing of such learning opportunities, the most appropriate teaching methods, and the accessibility of the program. A life-course perspective, with an emphasis on historical and social time, may help older individuals better understand their personal reaction to this later life transition. The authors suggested that the content of preretirement programs needs to be expanded beyond traditional financial planning aspects in order to explore family issues (role changes, spousal expectations) and options for leisure and health maintenance. The location and timing of programs must also be considered, as many women and minorities in particular may lack access to employer-sponsored programs because of the size of their workplace. This suggests that at least some programs need to be made available in the community to reach a wider range of individuals.

Family life educators must also recognize differences in target groups when planning retirement programs. Midlife families are typically in the initial thinking stage of retirement, and topics such as work/leisure options, health maintenance, and financial planning need to be incorporated into programs for this group (Kragie, Gerstein, & Lichtman, 1989). Those who are about to retire will likely have done some financial planning and will need different programs that address their specific concerns about retirement income, health, leisure, and family issues. Older women may need to receive special programs that address their special employment circumstances.

Programs to Address Individual Issues

In the development of programs focusing on the loss of a spouse, it is important to emphasize the continuation of previous patterns of interaction. Contact with friends and a satisfactory social network are associated with positive feelings of well-being for both widows and widowers. Widowed Persons Services is one popular program for recent widows (Bressler, 1986). Cosponsored by the American Association of Retired Persons, this self-help program is intended to aid newly widowed individuals with the adjustment process. Because education is one of the key components of this program, members of the community are often recruited to present information to these groups. Wood (1987) developed a Grief Workshop that combines both educational experiences and the development of a support system to help adults deal with loss and grief. A seminar experience provides the opportunity to gain information, to interact with others who are facing the same experience, and to form support networks. This Grief Workshop is typically organized around holiday periods, a time that is especially difficult for those who have lost loved ones. The Widow-to-Widow program developed by Silverman (1977) emphasizes the provision of support services to the newly widowed by someone who has already faced that experience.

Formal, time-limited programs are also available for bereaved older adults. They provide newly widowed persons with the opportunity to work through their grief, come to terms with their loss, and identify strategies for problem solving (Constantino, 1981; DeBor, Gallagher, & Lesher, 1983). Elderly widowed persons who participated in these programs reported feeling better about themselves and better prepared to confront their new life status. One 14-week program for bereaved adults begins with lectures on the dynamics of grief and the recovery process, while later sessions are less structured and address issues raised by the participants (Sabatini, 1988-1989).

CONCLUSIONS

Although midlife and later life families may be underserved by family life education, the review in this chapter indicates that they are not a totally neglected audience. Particularly in recent years, programs have been developed that address a number of intergenerational, couple, and individual issues for this age group. Clearly, there are a number of important limitations in the programs described in this chapter. Many are relatively short term, involving only a few hours or a limited number of sessions. As well, many of them are focused on a relatively specific problem, resulting in a narrow focus with little attention to the interaction of the problem with other elements of the family context. Most programs also appear to be problem focused rather than preventive. Despite these limitations, however, the current programs provide a basis for what must become a major new direction in family life education.

As family life educators respond to the needs of midlife and later life families, several special considerations will need to be taken into account. There are questions, for example, about who is the best educator for some of these programs. Some programs, such as grief and bereavement programs, have relied primarily on peers (those who have had the same experience), while other programs such as retirement programs are handled primarily by professionals (those who have special training or expertise). It will be important to consider carefully the goals and the intentions of programs for adults so that the most appropriate individuals are used as primary educators. In some cases (and maybe in most cases), efforts may need to be made to combine the special expertise of both peers and professionals.

Family life educators will also need to design their programs based not only on information about midlife and later life families but also on the best knowledge available about adult patterns and processes of learning. Programs that fail to take these adult processes into account may be ineffective, irrelevant, or possibly both. It is important that family life educators not assume that older adults will learn in the same way as younger ones.

Finally, issues arise around the best location in which to provide family life education and about the most appropriate educational medium to use. Midlife families, particularly dual-earner families, may find it difficult to find time to become involved in typical family life education programs, or they may prefer to learn on their own rather than in groups. Older individuals, especially those who have health problems or transportation difficulties, may find it difficult to attend the typical family life education program on a regularly scheduled basis. As well, any sensory decline with aging may influence the ability of older persons to fully engage in many family life education activities.

The issues discussed above will not be easy ones to address in family life education but they should not be insurmountable problems. One thing does seem clear: Any serious attempt to meet the needs of midlife and later life families will require some serious reconsideration of the typical approaches and strategies used in family life education. It is time to undertake that reconsideration.

REFERENCES

Ade-Ridder, L., & Brubaker, T. H. (1983). The quality of long-term marriages. In T. H. Brubaker (Ed.), *Family relationships in later life* (pp. 21-30). Beverly Hills, CA: Sage.

Anderson, S. A., Russell, C. S., & Schumm, W. R. (1983). Perceived marital quality and family life-cycle categories: A further analysis. *Journal of Marriage and the Family, 45,* 127-139.

Arcus, M. (1987). A Framework for Life-Span Family Life Education. *Family Relations, 36,* 5-10.

Arcus, M., & Arcus, P. (1981). A tool for marriage enrichment. In N. Stinnett, J. DeFrain, K. King, P. Knaub, & G. Rowe (Eds.), *Family strengths: Vol. 3. Roots of well-being* (pp. 119-128). Lincoln: University of Nebraska Press.

Bengtson, V. L. (Ed.). (1989). *The course of later life: Research and reflections.* New York: Springer.

Bengtson, V. L., Cutler, N. E., Mangen, D. J., & Marshall, V. W. (1985). Generations, cohorts, and relations between age groups. In R. H. Binstock & E. Shanas (Eds.), *Handbook of aging and the social sciences* (pp. 304-338). New York: Van Nostrand Reinhold.

Bengtson, V. L., & Robertson, J. F. (Eds.). (1985). *Grandparenthood.* Beverly Hills, CA: Sage.

Bloom, B. L., Hodges, W. F., & Caldwell, R. A. (1982). A prevention program for the newly separated: Initial evaluation. *American Journal of Community Psychology, 10,* 251-264.

Bressler, D. (1986). Widowed persons service. *Generations, 10*(4), 21-22.

Brody, E. M. (1985). Parent care as a normative family stress. *The Gerontologist, 25,* 19-29.

Brubaker, T. H. (1990a). Continuity and change in later life families: Grandparenthood, couple relationships and family caregiving. *Gerontology Review, 3,* 24-40.

Brubaker, T. H. (1990b). Families in later life: A burgeoning research area. *Journal of Marriage and the Family, 52,* 959-981.

Buehler, C., Betz, P., Ryan, C. M., Legg, B. H., & Trotter, B. B. (1992). Description and evaluation of the orientation for divorcing parents: Implications for postdivorce prevention programs. *Family Relations, 41*, 154-162.

Burton, L. M., & Bengtson, V. L. (1985). Black grandmothers: Issues of timing and continuity of roles. In V. L. Bengtson & J. J. Robertson (Eds.), *Grandparenthood* (pp. 61-80). Beverly Hills, CA: Sage.

Byrne, R. C. (1990). The effectiveness of the beginning experience workshop: A paraprofessional group marathon workshop for divorce adjustment. *Journal of Divorce, 13*(4), 101-120.

Cantor, M. H. (1983). Strain among caregivers: A study of experience in the United States. *The Gerontologist, 23*, 597-604.

Coleman, M., & Ganong, L. H. (1993). Families and marital disruption. In T. H. Brubaker (Ed.), *Current issues in the family: Vol. 1. Family relations: Challenges for the future* (pp. 112-128). Newbury Park, CA: Sage.

Connidis, I. A. (1989). *Family ties and aging.* Vancouver, BC: Butterworths Canada.

Constantino, R. (1981). Bereavement crisis intervention for widows in grief and mourning. *Nursing Research, 30*, 351-353.

Couper, D., & Sheehan, N. (1987). Family dynamics for caregivers: An educational model. *Family Relations, 36*, 181-186.

DeBor, L., Gallagher, D., & Lesher, E. (1983). Group counseling with the bereaving elderly. *Clinical Gerontologist, 1*, 81-90.

de Vries, B., Birren, J. E., & Deutchman, D. E. (1990). Adult development through guided autobiography: The family context. *Family Relations, 39*, 3-7.

Edelstein, L. (1984). *Maternal bereavement: Coping with the unexpected death of a child.* New York: Praeger.

Engel, J. (1983). Sex education of adults: An evaluation of a correspondence course approach. *Family Relations, 32*, 123-128.

Epstein, B., & Koenig, M. (1990). Educating elderly caregivers. *Journal of Extension, 28*, 8-10.

Ferraro, K. F. (1986). The effect of widowhood on the health status of older persons. *International Journal of Aging and Human Development, 21*, 9-25.

Fisher, L. R. (1981). Transitions in the mother-daughter relationship. *Journal of Marriage and the Family, 43*, 613-622.

Fisher, L. R. (1983). Transition into grandparenthood. *International Journal of Aging and Human Development, 16*, 67-78.

Garza, J. M., & Dressel, P. L. (1983). Sexuality and later life marriages. In T. H. Brubaker (Ed.), *Family relationships in later life* (pp. 91-108). Beverly Hills, CA: Sage.

Glosser, G., & Wexler, D. (1985). Participants' evaluation of educational/support groups for families of patients with Alzheimer's disease and other dementias. *The Gerontologist, 25*, 232-236.

Gold, D. T., & Gwyther, L. P. (1989). The prevention of elder abuse: An educational model. *Family Relations, 38*, 8-14.

Green, L. W., & Kreuter, M. W. (1991). *Health promotion planning: An educational and environmental approach.* Toronto: Mayfield.

Hagestad, G. O. (1985). Continuity and connectedness. In V. L. Bengtson & J. F. Robertson (Eds.), *Grandparenthood* (pp. 31-48). Beverly Hills, CA: Sage.

Hagestad, G. (1988). Demographic change and the life course: Some emerging trends in the family realm. *Family Relations, 37*, 405-410.

Hagestad, G. O., & Burton, L. (1986). Grandparenthood, life context and family development. *American Behavioral Scientist, 29*, 471-484.

Hennon, C. B., & Arcus, M. (1993). Life-span family life education. In T. H. Brubaker (Ed.), *Current issues in the family: Vol. 1. Family relations: Challenges for the future* (pp. 181-210). Newbury Park, CA: Sage.

Hof, L., & Miller, W. R. (1980). Marriage enrichment. *Marriage and Family Review, 3,* 1-27.

Imel, S. (1983). *Retirement education programs: Overview.* (ERIC Digest No. 29 [microform]; ERIC Document No. ED 240 399, Microform Division)

Ingersoll-Dayton, B., Chapman, N., & Neal, M. (1990). A program for caregivers in the workplace. *The Gerontologist, 30,* 126-130.

Johnson, D. R., White, L. K., Edwards, J. N., & Booth, A. (1986). Dimensions of marital quality: Toward methodological and conceptual refinement. *Journal of Family Issues, 7,* 31-49.

Kessler, S. (1978). Building skills in divorce adjustment groups. *Journal of Divorce, 2*(2), 209-216.

Klass, D. (Ed.). (1988). *Parental grief: Solace and resolution.* New York: Springer.

Kragie, E., Gerstein, M., & Lichtman, M. (1989). Do Americans plan retirement? *The Career Development Quarterly, 37,* 232-239.

Lee, G. R., & Shehan, C. L. (1989). Retirement and marital satisfaction. *Journal of Gerontology, 44,* S226-S230.

Lloyd, S. A., & Emery, B. C. (1993). Abuse in the family: An ecological, life-cycle perspective. In T. H. Brubaker (Ed.), *Current issues in the family: Vol. 1. Family relations: Challenges for the future* (pp. 129-152). Newbury Park, CA: Sage.

Lopata, H. Z. (1979). *Women as widows: Support systems.* New York: Elsevier.

Lund, D. A. (Ed.). (1989). *Older bereaved spouses.* New York: Hemisphere.

Mace, D. (1982). *Close companions: The marriage enrichment handbook.* New York: Continuum.

Mace, D., & Mace, V. (1986). The history and present status of the marriage and family enrichment movement. In W. Denton (Ed.), *Marriage and family enrichment* (pp. 7-18). New York: Haworth.

Mancini, J. A., & Bliezner, R. (1989). Aging parents and adult children: Research themes in intergenerational relationships. *Journal of Marriage and the Family, 51,* 275-290.

Meade, K., & Walker, J. (1989). Gender equality: Issues and challenges for retirement education. *Educational Gerontologist, 15,* 171-185.

Merikangas, M. (1983). Retirement planning with a difference. *Personnel Journal, 62*(5), 420, 422-427.

National Commission on Family Life Education (Task Force of the National Council on Family Relations). (1968). Family life education programs: Principles, plans, procedures. *The Family Coordinator, 17,* 211-214.

Olson, S. K. (1981). Current status of corporate retirement preparation programs. *Aging and Work, 4*(3), 175-187.

Palmore, E. (1981). *Social patterns in normal aging: Findings from the Duke longitudinal study.* Durham, NC: Duke University Press.

Pratt, C., Nayt, T., Ladd, L., & Heagerty, B. (1989). Model legal-financial education workshop for families caring for neurologically impaired elders. *The Gerontologist, 29,* 258-262.

Quinn, M. J., & Tomita, S. K. (1986). *Elder abuse and neglect: Causes, diagnosis, and intervention strategies.* New York: Springer.

Quinn, W. H. (1983). Personal and family adjustment in later life. *Journal of Marriage and the Family, 45,* 57-73.

Rando, R. A. (1986). *Parental loss of a child.* Champaign, IL: Research Press.

Riker, H., & Myers, J. (1990). *Retirement counseling: A practical guide for action.* New York: Hemisphere.

Roberto, K. (1985). Adult children and aging parents: A report of a program design and evaluation. *Activities, Adaptation, & Aging, 6,* 89-101.

Roberto, K. (1990, April). *Education and training of family caregivers in rural areas.* Paper presented at the meeting of the National Council on Aging, Washington, DC.

Robinson, P. (1983). The sociological perspective. In R. B. Weg (Ed.), *Sexuality in later life.* New York: Academic Press.

Sabatini, L. (1988-1989). Evaluating a treatment program for newly widowed people. *Omega, 19,* 229-238.

Salamon, M., & Charytan, P. (1984). A sexuality workshop program for the elderly. *Clinical Gerontologist, 2,* 25-34.

Schumm, W. R., & Bugaighis, M. A. (1986). Marital quality over the marital career: Alternative explanations. *Journal of Marriage and the Family, 48,* 165-168.

Shulman, M., & Mandel, E. (1988). Communication training of relatives and friends of institutionalized elderly persons. *The Gerontologist, 28,* 797-799.

Silverman, P. R. (1977). Widowhood and preventive intervention. In S. H. Zarit (Ed.), *Readings in aging and death: Contemporary perspectives* (pp. 175-182). New York: Harper & Row.

Sprey, J., & Matthews, S. H. (1982). Contemporary grandparenthood: A systemic transition. *The Annals of the American Academy of the Political and Social Sciences, 464,* 937-956.

Stolberg, A. L. (1988). Prevention programs for divorcing families. In L. A. Bond & B. M. Wagner (Eds.), *Families in transition* (pp. 225-251). Beverly Hills, CA: Sage.

Streib, G. F., & Beck, R. W. (1980). Older families: A decade review. *Journal of Marriage and the Family, 42,* 937-956.

Strom, R., & Strom, S. (1989). Grandparents and learning. *International Journal of Aging and Human Development, 29,* 163-169.

Strom, R., & Strom, S. (1990). Raising expectations for grandparents: A three generational study. *International Journal of Aging and Human Development, 30,* 161-167.

Strom, R., Strom, S., & Collinsworth, P. (1990). Improving grandparent success. *Journal of Applied Gerontology, 9,* 480-491.

Suitor, J. J., & Pillemer, K. (1987). The presence of adult children: A source of stress for elderly couples' marriages. *Journal of Marriage and the Family, 49,* 717-723.

Suitor, J. J., & Pillemer, K. (1988). Explaining intergeneration conflict when adult children and elderly parents live together. *Journal of Marriage and the Family, 50,* 1037-1047.

Swanson, C. H., Eskew, R. W., & Kohlhepp, K. A. (1981). Stage of family life cycle, ego development and the marriage relationship. *Journal of Marriage and the Family, 43,* 841-853.

Szinovacz, M. (1989). Decision-making on retirement training. In D. Brinberg & J. Jacard (Eds.), *Dyadic decision making* (pp. 286-310). New York: Springer.

Thornton, A., & Freedman, D. (1983). The changing American family. *Population Bulletin, 38,* 1-44.

Tiberi, D. M., Boyack, V. L., & Kerschner, P. A. (1978). A comparative analysis of four preretirement education models. *Educational Gerontology: An International Quarterly, 3,* 355-374.

Voydanoff, P. (1993). Work and family relationships. In T. H. Brubaker (Ed.), *Current issues in the family: Vol. 1. Family relations: Challenges for the future* (pp. 98-111). Newbury Park, CA: Sage.

Warren, N. J., Grew, R. S., Ilgen, E. R., Konanc, J. T., Van Bourgondien, M. E., & Amara, I. A. (in press). Parenting after divorce: Preventive programs for divorcing families. In E. J. Flynn, E. F. Hurst, & E. Breckinridge (Eds.), *Impact of divorce on children.* Bethesda, MD: National Institute of Mental Health.

White, C., & Catania, J. (1982). Psychoeducational intervention for sexuality with the aged, family members of the aged, and people who work with the aged. *International Journal of Aging and Human Development, 15,* 121-138.

Wood, B. (1987). Survival KIT for the holidays: A grief workshop approach. *Family Relations, 36,* 235-241.

8

Family Life Education

Current Status and New Directions

Margaret E. Arcus

Jay D. Schvaneveldt

J. Joel Moss

THE PURPOSE OF VOLUME 2 of the *Handbook of Family Life Education* has been to examine some of the major topic areas in the practice of family life education. In the introductory chapter, an overview of the nature of family life education as a field of study and practice was provided, and several key elements and processes of family life education practice were discussed and critiqued. Individual chapters then focused on selected major topic areas in family life education (marriage and intimate relationships, sexuality, parenting, family resource management, and communication and problem solving). One chapter also examined family life education directed toward a specific audience (midlife and later life families). In each of these chapters, authors provided an overview of the current status of education related to these topic areas or audiences, including relevant theoretical and empirical foundations, major approaches to educational practice, trends and new directions, areas in need of scholarly and practical attention, and current issues and challenges.

In this final chapter of Volume 2, the information from the previous chapters will be integrated and discussed to provide a summary over-

view of the current status of family life education practice and to identify the major issues and challenges facing family life educators as they
seek to extend and improve the practice of family life education.

THE CURRENT STATUS OF FAMILY LIFE EDUCATION PRACTICE

Before integrating information across the chapters, it is useful to
provide brief overviews of the current status of the practice of family life
education related to each of the topic areas discussed in this volume.
These chapters will be discussed in the order in which they appeared in
the volume.

Marriage and Intimate Relationships

In Chapter 2, Stahmann and Salts noted that education for marriage
and intimate relationships is a well-established form of family life education, with the first programs developed more than 50 years ago. From
their inception, these programs were designed to provide information
about marriage to couples and to help them work out their interpersonal
difficulties. Both the emergence of relationship education and its continued relevance at the current time reflect the centrality of marital and
intimate relationships in family life. In addition to the need for information about relationships, indicators such as the potential for interpersonal difficulties, the changing roles of women, and the increasing
probability of divorce suggest that this form of family life education will
likely continue to be important well into the future.

Of the four broad approaches to education for marriage and intimate
relationships identified by Stahmann and Salts, only three are directly
relevant to family life education: general marriage education programs,
premarital counseling programs, and enrichment programs. The fourth
approach (marital and premarital therapy) is designed primarily to help
couples address their specific relationship problems. Because most family life educators do not have the necessary skills to provide therapy, this
approach generally lies outside the province of family life education.

General marriage education courses or programs tend to be offered
in high schools and colleges/universities and, more recently, through
community adult education and extension programs. The specific goals
and structured educational experiences in these programs differ depending upon the age level of the participants, but most programs focus
on helping participants obtain information about relationships, gain
relevant relationship skills, and explore attitudes and values. Although

considerable general marriage education is provided, particularly at the high school level, little is known about these programs beyond their various curriculum guidelines. A major question is in need of research attention: Does general relationship education at the high school and college/university level make a difference in relationships later on?

Premarital counseling programs are usually offered to couples and tend to provide educative counseling or personalized training in relationships rather than using the traditional problem-oriented approach associated with counseling. The aim in these programs is to enhance the couple's relationship through building insights and communication skills and assessing the strengths and weaknesses of the relationship. Many different premarital counseling programs have been developed, with some designed for individual couples and others for groups of couples. The advantages and disadvantages of each approach have been identified, but to date the limited research on premarital counseling has not addressed their comparative effectiveness. It does appear, however, that programs that include relationship skill development or a focus on process are more effective than those that emphasize lectures and discussions.

According to Stahmann and Salts, enrichment programs are the newest of the marriage education programs, first appearing around the 1960s. Numerous specific enrichment programs are available, either for general audiences or for specific target groups. These programs are typically experiential, positive, growth oriented, and preventive. Differences in the programs reflect differing expectations regarding time commitments, the amount of structure provided in the program, and the amount of input encouraged from either the leaders or the participants. Reviews of evaluation research have indicated that marriage enrichment programs do make a difference, although their effects appear to diminish over time.

Several trends in marriage education have been identified: (a) the shift in focus from marriage problems to building strengths for relationships, (b) the importance of providing marriage education beyond the premarital stage, and (c) the importance of education for relationship dissolution (e.g., divorce adjustment education). This latter trend is particularly significant given that the quality of relationship dissolution is an essential component of education for remarriage, an area within marriage education for which there appears to be increasing need.

Several issues and challenges in educating for relationships were identified by Stahmann and Salts. There is a need for input from the premarital couples themselves, input that is currently lacking in most programs. Research is needed to determine the credibility of the numerous self-help books available on relationships so that both family life educators and marriage education participants might become better consumers of these publications. More attention needs to be given to later life families and their marital and intimate relationships and to the educational level, ethnicity, and gender of the marriage education participants. Attention also needs to be directed toward the educator's own personal values, beliefs, expectations, and stereotypes and to the influence of these on programs. Questions and issues regarding the best timing for relationship education (especially premarital education) need to be addressed, and there is a need to expand the knowledge base regarding relationships. A major challenge in relationship education will be to determine what kinds of marriage education programs work best for which populations. Evaluation is an important issue and will need to overcome two major problems: (a) the self-selection of the participants and (b) the lack of definition of what is meant by the "success" of marriage education programs.

Sexuality

Sexuality is also an important dimension and foundation of family life, and thus sexuality education is a critical component of family life education. Although sexuality is a life span concept, Engel, Saracino, and Bergen noted in Chapter 3 that the majority of programs in sexuality education have been designed for children and youth. Most of these programs are offered in school settings, but programs may also be provided by nonschool agencies and organizations. Some programs are general sexuality education programs (that is, they include a range of physical, social, and psychological concepts), while others focus on specific elements of sexuality, usually problematic ones (that is, adolescent pregnancy, sexually transmitted diseases, and child sexual abuse).

Considerable effort has been devoted to evaluating the impact of these sexuality education programs on children and adolescents. There is some evidence that formal sexuality education programs can increase knowledge, although this knowledge may not be retained without reinforcement. The evidence is contradictory, however, concerning whether or not sexuality education changes an individual's beliefs or attitudes and whether or not it delays or reduces sexual activity. Despite the extensive body of evaluative research in sexuality education, Engel et al. indicated that much of this research suffers from various methodological and conceptual deficiencies, and they called for more and better research on sexuality education programs. In particular, attention needs to be directed toward determining what is effective, when, and for whom.

There is a trend toward requiring or recommending some form of sexuality and/or AIDS education in public schools, and most young people now appear to receive some sexuality education. Significant questions have been raised, however, about both the quality and the timing of this education. School curricula have been found to vary considerably in terms of their comprehensiveness, currency, accuracy, and tone or attitude. Although sexuality education that is either too early or too late is unlikely to be effective, providing developmentally appropriate educational programs is complicated by the diverse timing of adolescent sexual development. There is some evidence that the most negative reactions to sexual developments during puberty and adolescence are associated with the absence of appropriate preparatory sexuality education. At the current time, there appears to be no consensus among either professionals or the general public regarding the most appropriate goals for sexuality education. It is increasingly clear, however, that the negative focus of many programs is too limited and perhaps even harmful. Thus some educators have begun to focus their attention on the development of comprehensive, health-focused sexuality education programs to replace the more typical narrow and problem-oriented focus.

According to Engel et al., family life educators involved in sexuality education face a number of challenges. Attention needs to be given to integrating sexuality education across multiple contexts (e.g., schools, health clinics, homes, and the broader community). Many political challenges must be addressed if family life educators are to gain support for and overcome opposition to comprehensive sexuality education for young people. With the earlier onset of sexual activity, ways will need to be found to help children and youth face issues of responsibility and safety, possibly before they are developmentally ready to take this responsibility. Attention also needs to be directed toward neglected or underserved audiences. In particular, there is a dearth of preventive, health-focused sexuality education programs designed for adults of all ages, either to meet their own needs or to assist them in their role as the primary sexuality educators for their children. Finally, because what is learned in sexuality education is mediated by the process itself, the comfort and the attitudes of the educators and the participants are important variables in sexuality education. This highlights the importance of well-qualified sexuality educators.

Parenting

One of the earliest developments in family life education was that of parent education. Parenting plays a central role in family life, and thus education for parenting is a central theme in family life education. Most people become parents, most take the role seriously, most want to be successful at it, and most seek some kind of guidance as they carry out this family role.

In Chapter 4, Brock, Oertwein, and Coufal indicated that, despite the long history of parent education, there is little consensus on a definition of parenting education. Thus there is considerable variation in parent education programs with respect to their goals, their methods, and their thematic emphasis. Three different modes of parent education have been identified: the individual mode, the group mode, and the mass mode. The individual mode (working directly with individual parents) is an important means of parent education, but it is typically associated with counseling and guidance rather than with family life education. At the current time, little attention has focused on the mass mode (addressing anonymous, mass audiences through media such as books, pamphlets, magazines, newspapers, radio, and TV), although some surveys have indicated that this is the mode most preferred by many parents.

The group mode, however, is practically synonymous with parent education. In this mode, educational efforts are directed toward an audience organized into specific learning groups. There are many different kinds of group parent education programs (as discussed in Chapter 4) and little evidence that one approach or model is more effective than another. According to Brock et al., most of the current parent education group programs appear to be based on the Baumrind authoritative model of parenting. This raises an important question for family life education as it seeks to meet the needs of diverse audiences: Is the authoritative model of parenting applicable to all cultural groups? If not, how do parent educators address the needs of culturally diverse groups?

Although most parent education has been targeted to adult populations, two different kinds of programs have been designed specifically for adolescents. Programs developed for those adolescents who are already parents may be home visitor programs, center-based programs, or a combination of the two. Some programs include attention to the adolescent's educational and occupational needs in addition to their parenting needs. More general programs in parent education for adolescents have been available in some schools for some time. There is some suggestion that these programs might be more effective if the emphasis was placed on the precursors of parenting (e.g., on adolescent identity issues) rather than on specific parenting skills. Thus it might be more appropriate to label such programs "preparental education."

Brock et al. suggested that, because all group parent education programs appear to be effective, other variables (cost, format, thematic emphasis) may be the most appropriate criteria for selecting and implementing a program. Regardless of the kind of program chosen, however, they noted the importance of making a good match between the needs of the parents and their children and the design and focus of a specific program.

The use in parent education of numerous packaged programs (programs intended to be implemented as designed by the program developer) presents a major challenge to family life educators, as many parents can't or won't commit to the time requirements of these programs or are interested in particular parenting issues rather than in general parenting skills. Although the earliest parent education programs were presented as appropriate for all parents of all children, the recent trend is toward greater specificity in programs, that is, toward adapting programs for children of different ages and for parents of different backgrounds and needs.

Some contemporary programs have recognized the importance of family systems theory in understanding parent-child interaction. Systems theory, however, has not been adequately incorporated into or used in many programs. Most programs also do not adequately address common family problems related to divorce and remarriage.

Family Resource Management

As shown by Rettig, Rossmann, and Hogan in Chapter 5, although it is well established as an academic area of study, the relevance and role of family resource management in family life education is not well understood by many family life educators. The focus in family resource management education is on the internal dynamics of family decision-making processes and on the goal-directed behaviors of families in improving their quality of life, such as decision making, valuing, planning, communicating, and organizing activities to guide resource use. Through family resource management education, individuals and families are assisted in gaining some degree of control over the events of their everyday living, to mobilize resources toward their values and central life purposes, and to address consciously their changing goals and concerns over the life span. Thus, whenever family life educators help participants to prioritize goals, develop resource awareness, address value conflicts, and strengthen decision-making responsibilities, they are involved in family resource management education.

Family resource management is apparent in family life education in two ways: (a) directly, when the specific educational focus is on family resource management concepts and processes, and (b) indirectly, when the family resource management perspective is incorporated into other topic areas. When taught directly, family resource management education is typically offered in formal settings such as high schools and colleges/universities or in informal settings such as the Cooperative Extension Service. Indirect family resource management education is incorporated into and becomes an integral part of topic areas such as marriage preparation and marriage enrichment or planning for retirement. There is some controversy in the field regarding whether the best way to deliver family resource management education is to maintain its separate identity or to integrate it into other content areas. At the current time, however, the indirect approach appears to be more typical, possibly reflecting both the centrality of resource management concepts and processes in all aspects of family living and the difficulty of isolating these themes from subject matter content.

The importance of the human ecological approach in family resource management education has been noted for some time. Other relevant conceptual frameworks include the practical problems framework and critical thinking. Central issues in resource management education include the lack of guidelines on how to integrate family resource management into other family life education topics, inadequate preparation of the educators, motivating students to learn, and generating a curriculum that is sensitive to cultural values and gender issues. It is likely that the resource management problems of future families will center on global issues regarding resource availability, and this will present major challenges for family life educators.

Communication and Problem Solving

Chapter 6 is based on two premises: (a) that communication and problem solving are generic family life skills or processes and thus essential elements of effective family functioning and (b) that family life education can empower and enhance these processes. Communication is seen as the basis of all human interaction, with the success of any family group dependent upon the ability to exchange information and transmit meaning to one another. Because family life is dynamic, problem solving is essential in helping family units generate solutions to various problems and meet their adaptive functions. Although these two processes are discussed separately in Chapter 6, the processes are inextricably linked.

Kieren and Doherty-Poirier identified three different program emphases in communication and problem-solving education. Some programs focus on the entire process. These programs are more likely to be found in schools than in community programs, with communication and problem solving identified as key components in diverse school subject matter areas. Other programs focus on one step or one skill in the process. These programs are more likely to be found in adult education programs such as family communication programs. Still other programs are situation specific, such as might be found in many marriage and family enrichment programs. The importance of experiential methods is common across all types of programs. According to Kieren and Doherty-Poirier, there is no lack of programs on communication and problem solving, and family life educators are faced with a wide range of possibilities and a limited range of criteria with which to assess the effectiveness of the programs.

There are a number of important issues to be addressed to improve family life education on these processes. Many programs are more likely to be attended by an individual family member than by family groups. Thus, if this form of education is intended to improve family functioning, it is potentially incomplete. Although some of the programs have been designed specifically for individuals, an important new direction for family life education would be to expand the number of family-focused programs. Such a direction will likely necessitate a reconceptualization of where, when, and how programs are offered.

Because cultural patterns of communication and problem solving differ, there is a need for family life educators to give attention to and develop programs from a multicultural perspective and to become aware of (and possibly get rid of) their own ethnocentric biases. Gender differences in communication and problem solving will also need to be addressed. Other issues in need of attention include improving theoretical and empirical knowledge about these processes, improving program evaluation, and giving systematic attention to program marketing issues.

Midlife and Later Life Families

Chapter 7 differs from the preceding chapters in that it focuses on a particular audience rather than a specific topic area. Attention in this chapter is drawn to family life issues and the family life education needs of midlife and later life families (defined in the chapter as those families beyond the child-rearing years who have begun to launch their children).

Although it has been widely accepted that family life education is needed by individuals and families of all ages, historically, little attention has been given to providing specific relevant programs for midlife and later life families. Clearly, family life education for this age group is important. Not only is it a large and growing proportion of the population, but few of those in this age group have had opportunities to participate in and benefit from family life education during their earlier years. As well, the period of adulthood that follows the launching of children includes an extended period of time (potentially 30 to 40 years), a period during which many adults must not only meet their own needs for family living but may also bear some responsibility for the family life needs of other generations (parents, children, grandchildren).

In Chapter 7, three broad themes (intergenerational issues, couple issues, individual issues) were used to discuss both the family life issues of midlife and later life families and the family life education programs related to these issues. To some extent, these are artificial categories in that these issues are often overlapping. For example, although involvement in caregiving is typically an intergenerational issue, it also has implications for couple issues and for individual issues. Nevertheless, these categories provide a useful heuristic for identifying and discussing both family life issues and family life education programs for midlife and later life families.

The intergenerational needs of midlife and later life families are related to changes in both family structures and family relationships. Typically, the households of midlife and later life families contract as children leave home, while the kinship network expands as adult children marry and possibly have children of their own. In some cases, the household expands rather than contracts when adult children return home for financial or other reasons. Becoming a grandparent may be the first family role associated with later life, and some grandparents may need to assist in the rearing of their grandchildren. Caring for elderly family members is a major and often stressful issue for midlife and later life families, and the physical and psychological abuse of these elderly members is a matter of considerable concern.

Couple issues for midlife and later life families include the need to learn how to interact again as a dyad and how to accommodate changing sexuality needs and interests. The termination of marriages at this stage of the life course is increasingly common, with potentially negative impacts on individual well-being and on other family relationships. Balancing work and family and dealing with the retirement of one or both partners are also important midlife and later life couple issues.

Facing the loss of a loved one may occur at any time of the life course, but it is more typically associated with mid- and later life. These losses may include the loss of a parent, one's spouse, or possibly one's children. Each of these losses has an impact on individual well-being and may also influence couple and intergenerational issues.

Because family life education programs for midlife and later life families are relatively new, any review of programs is necessarily less systematic than in other areas such as marriage education, sexuality education, or parent education. Some issues have received more attention than others. For example, marriage enrichment is a recent though increasingly well-established subset of marriage education. A growing number of programs have been developed around themes such as divorce adjustment, retirement preparation, loss and grief, and caregiving for the elderly. As yet, few programs appear to be available on positive preventive programs related to sexuality education, to the nature of changing parent-child relationships during the later years, or to the prevention of elder abuse.

Even for those programs that are available, many are relatively short term and typically problem oriented; that is, many of the programs tend to focus on a narrow and relatively specific problem. Few evaluation studies have been carried out, and most of these are "consumer satisfaction" studies rather than studies of the impact of the program. Little attention has been given to issues of cultural diversity in programs for midlife and later life families. Given the differences in cultural views toward aging and the aged and differences in communication patterns and processes, attention to this issue in the future will be important.

MAJOR ISSUES AND CHALLENGES FOR FAMILY LIFE EDUCATION

Several common issues and challenges for family life education emerge from the preceding discussion. These commonalities help to indicate the current status of the field and suggest some directions for future developments in family life education.

One of the tenets of family life education is the need to base programs on strong scholarly foundations. Chapters in this volume have provided useful summaries of theoretical and empirical bases for determining goals, for selecting content and learning experiences, and for designing evaluation strategies. As is apparent in these chapters, the knowledge base for family life education is expanding but is still incomplete and, in some cases, contradictory. Thus a key implication for enhancing family life education practice is to continue to expand the knowledge base for the field.

It will not be enough to expand this knowledge base, however, unless this knowledge is actually used to better inform family life education practice. As noted in several chapters throughout this volume, many family life educators have not kept up with the current state of knowledge in many areas. Chapter 1, for example, identified the continued use in family life education of Values Clarification, an approach to values education that has been found to be inadequate both conceptually and empirically. In Chapter 4, the authors noted the failure to adequately incorporate family systems theory into parent education programs even though the relevance of this theory is well understood and well accepted. Because its knowledge base continues to expand, family life education is a dynamic field of study and practice, and family life programs must continually be modified to build upon the best scholarship currently available about both the subject matter and the educational processes. Given the growing body of relevant knowledge and the many demands placed on family life educators, this will not be an easy challenge to meet. But programs based on outdated knowledge may be irrelevant, ineffective, and possibly misleading and may seriously undermine the potential of family life education to accomplish its goals.

The chapters have provided some evidence that some aspects of some family life education programs "work." Taken as a whole, however, the body of evidence concerning the impact of family life education is limited and, at least in some cases, appears to be limited to relatively easy questions (e.g., Can participants gain knowledge as a result of a particular program, or can they learn new skills given a particular kind of training?). A common theme across these chapters is thus the need for more and better evaluation research. This is not a new concern, however, as many authors also indicated that it has been discussed in the literature for some time.

The need for more and better research should not be interpreted to mean "more of the same but better." There is no doubt that better research is needed to address the many methodological limitations of current evaluation studies (e.g., small samples, simplistic analysis of data, inadequate conceptualization and measurement). Family life education has typically emphasized quantitative methods, however, and it is likely that the field would benefit from the use of additional research methodologies to address different kinds of questions. At the current time, central questions in need of research attention include these:

Which programs work best for whom and under what conditions? Are those who take family life education courses different than those who don't? Does early preparation in family life education make a difference later on, that is, is it truly preventive?

Chapters in this volume identified several important challenges regarding the preparation of family life practitioners. As noted in Chapter 1, appropriately prepared and qualified family life educators are crucial to the successful realization of the goals of family life education, as it is these individuals who bear responsibility for the shaping of a program and for the nature of the educational experience. Specific suggestions for improving the preparation of family life educators made by the authors of these chapters include (a) the need to address personal awareness issues more systematically, by helping educators to understand their own personal values and expectations regarding family living, to challenge their biases and stereotypes, and to understand the potential influence of these on their own practice; (b) the need to become more comfortable with sensitive topics, especially in the area of sexuality, and to find ways to help family life education participants also become comfortable with these topics; (c) the need to learn new ways of creating a learning environment, including attention to interactive and reflective learning; and (d) the need to learn how to adapt packaged curricula or programs appropriately to meet the needs, interests, and characteristics of a particular audience. With respect to this latter point, it is somewhat ironic that the literature of family life education tends to emphasize program rationales and descriptions but gives little attention to helping educators make sound decisions about program adaptation. Several authors also recognized the need to expand the repertoire of skills and abilities necessary for family life educators to include fundraising, political action, and administration. These challenges call for a serious rethinking of how and when to prepare family life educators.

Because traditional group modes may not work for all audiences (or potential audiences), it is time to rethink and to expand delivery methods and settings in family life education. In particular, more serious attention needs to be given to the mass mode of family life education and to the possibilities that emerge from new educational technologies (e.g., computers, interactive videos). In some cases, it may be necessary to take family life education into nontraditional settings (e.g., the workplace) to facilitate participation in programs. As suggested earlier, if families as whole units are to be the target group, there will be a need to reconceptualize how, when, and where family life education is to be offered.

Finally, most authors in this volume directed attention to un-derserved or neglected audiences and suggested that it is time for family life education to move away from the traditional (though possibly unintended) focus on programs for middle-class Caucasian females. Among the underserved or neglected audiences that were identified by these authors are diverse cultural and socioeconomic groups, men, families as groups, and midlife and later life families and family members. Some of the issues surrounding gender, class, and ethnicity have begun to be recognized in family life education but as yet there is limited attention in the literature to the ways practitioners might address these issues. (For critical overviews of the issues and literature relevant to these issues, see both the various chapters in this volume and those in Volume 1 of the *Handbook of Family Life Education*.)

CONCLUSION

Since its inception around the turn of this century, the movement called family life education has experienced considerable growth in the number and kinds of programs offered, in the body of knowledge that underlies these programs, and in the number of individuals and families who are served by family life education. There also has been an expansion in the focus of family life education from its early emphasis on solving family problems to the more contemporary focus on building family strengths. There is thus some reason for family life educators to take pride in the growth and development of this field of study and practice.

As the end of this century nears, however, it is important not only to reflect on the progress of the field but also to consider seriously its limitations and to refocus the efforts of the field in light of this reflection. Despite the many signs of progress in family life education, this is not the time for complacency. Growth in programs and in program areas has been uneven, with some areas well developed and others still in their infancy. There are still many gaps in the literature about families and about family life education, with many questions unresolved or unex-amined. Of major concern is the fact that the family life education needs of many segments of the population, both individuals and families, remain neglected or underaddressed.

The intent of the *Handbook of Family Life Education* has been to reflect critically on developments in family life education over time and to establish some baseline information on which family life education might plan its next steps. Volume 1 of the *Handbook of Family Life*

Education identified a major scholarly agenda that lies ahead for this field. This volume has suggested a similar agenda for family life education practice. Among other things, it is time to address more difficult and more complex evaluation questions; it is time to give more systematic attention to the preparation of educators; and it is time to address critical issues related to gender, class, and ethnicity.

In short, it is time to refocus the efforts of family life education practice and scholarship so that it might more effectively serve the individuals and families for which it is intended.

Appendix

SINCE ITS INCEPTION, the National Council on Family Relations (NCFR) has had an ongoing interest in promoting and supporting quality family life education. Although the NCFR has been concerned with all aspects of family life education, including program development, delivery, and evaluation, special attention has been given to the preparation of family life educators. A committee that was established by the NCFR in 1968-1970 identified the major subject matter areas needed by family life educators (Committee on Education Standards and Certification for Family Life Educators, 1970). A second committee, established in 1975, examined issues related to the certification of family life teachers (Kerckhoff & O'Connor, 1978). The work of each of these committees has been important in developing preparation for family life educators.

In 1980 the NCFR established the Committee on Standards and Criteria for the Certification of Family Life Education "to take additional steps toward addressing the many questions involved in the delivery of quality training for family life educators" (Davidson, 1989, p. 128). This committee explored the feasibility of developing and implementing certification for family life educators and eventually recommended such a program to the NCFR Board of Directors in 1984 (Davidson, 1989), which acted on the recommendations, and a certification program for family life educators was initiated in 1985. (Information regarding the details of this program may be obtained from the National Council on Family Relations.)

In addition to its recommendations regarding a certification program for family life educators, the Committee on Standards and Criteria for the Certification of Family Life Educators (1984) also made two other important contributions. First, they developed curriculum guidelines for college/university preparation programs, guidelines that not only identified the broad subject areas that should be included in these preparation programs but that also provided more detailed information regarding essential themes within each of these subject areas.

The committee also developed an overview of the major content areas in family life education. This overview is known as the Framework for Life-Span Family Life Education (Arcus, 1987) and is reproduced here in its entirety. The framework was based on the assumption that people of all ages need to learn about the many aspects of family life and was developed to help stimulate the development and expansion of quality programs in family life education. It was believed that this specification of appropriate content for life-span family life programs would meet a critical need in the field and would help to advance both the practice and the scholarship of family life education.

Several key principles guided the development of the framework (Arcus, 1987). It was intended that the framework reflect a broad conception of family life education and that it be consistent with other writings in the field. At the same time, however, the number of topics was limited to make the framework more concise. This was accomplished by combining some related topic areas that in other documents might be listed separately. For example, "Human Development and Sexuality" was listed as one topic area rather than two, and friendships, dating, and marriage were combined into the broader topic area of "Interpersonal Relationships." It was hoped that this consolidation would make the framework more manageable without losing important concepts or ideas. Three key processes (communicating, decision making, problem solving) were not listed as separate topics but were incorporated into all of the topic areas.

It was also intended that the framework include all dimensions of learning: knowledge, attitudes, and skills. Although key concepts related to these dimensions were not designated separately under each topic area, a review of the framework will indicate that all three dimensions were included.

The developers of the framework believed that readiness to learn about family life was not tied to specific ages and that it was thus more appropriate to organize the content into broad, general age categories rather than specific ones. The framework was intended to illustrate that each topic area may be addressed at each age level by varying the focus and the complexity of the key concepts. Family life educators will need to become familiar with the entire framework to satisfactorily meet the diverse developmental needs of their program participants. Because not all adolescents are alike, for example, one would need to understand the concepts listed under "Children" to respond to the needs of the early adolescent, while the concepts listed under "Adults" would be important in meeting the needs of those adolescents who are more mature and verging upon adulthood.

The framework may be used by family life educators in a number of ways. Although it was not intended to be a curriculum, family life educators might use the framework as an aid in program development, helping to determine the content appropriate for a particular program. It might also be of value in assessing the breadth of content in an existing family life program; that is, it might assist family life educators in identifying those areas that are "missing" or that might need strengthening.

Additionally, the framework could be used to assess the comprehensiveness of program offerings in an agency, an organization, or a community. Are there particular content areas that have been ignored or that have received less attention than they deserve? For those involved in the preparation of family life educators, the framework might be used as the basis for class assignments (e.g., to critique an existing program for its breadth) or as a means to assess the continuing education needs of family life educators. Family life education scholars may also find the framework of value as they develop and test theory in family life education. There are also likely to be other creative uses of the framework.

The NCFR Committee on Standards and Criteria for Certification of Family Life Educators responsible for the development of the Framework included J. Kenneth Davidson, Sr., Committee Chair; Sharon J. Alexander; Virginia Anderson; Margaret E. Arcus; Betty L. Barber; Carol A. Darling; Sally Hansen; Judith O. Hooper; Stephen R. Jorgensen; Terrance O. Olson; Marie F. Peters; Sharon Price-Bonham; and Joanne D. Wall. More than 25 other NCFR members served as consultants during the revision of the various drafts of the framework, and their names are listed in the 1983 report presented to the NCFR Board of Directors.

REFERENCES

Arcus, M. (1987). A Framework for Life-Span Family Life Education. *Family Relations, 36,* 5-10.

Committee on Education Standards and Certification for Family Life Educators. (1970). Family life and sex education: Proposed criteria for teacher education. *The Family Coordinator, 9,* 183-185.

Committee on Standards and Criteria for the Certification of Family Life Educators. (1984). *Standards and criteria for the certification of family life educators, college/university curriculum guidelines, and an overview of content in family life education: A framework for planning life span programs.* Minneapolis, MN: National Council on Family Relations.

Davidson, J. K., Sr. (1989). The certification of family life educators: A quest for professionalism. *Family Science Review, 2,* 125-136.

Kerckhoff, R., & O'Connor, T. (1978). Certification of high school family life teachers. *The Family Coordinator, 27,* 61-64.

TABLE A.1. Framework for Life-Span Family Life Education*

	Topic Areas and Key Concepts**	
Age Levels	Human Development and Sexuality	Interpersonal Relationships
Children	• Physical, emotional, social, and sexual development • Similarities and differences in individual development • Perceptions about older people (adolescents, adults, elderly) • Understanding people with special needs • Uniqueness of each person • Responsibility for keeping healthy (nutrition, personal hygiene) • Social and environmental conditions affecting growth and development • Aspects of human reproduction (prenatal development, birth, puberty) • Body privacy and protection against sexual abuse	• Building self-esteem • Identifying and enhancing personal strengths • Respecting self and others • Dealing with emotions • Communicating with others • Sharing feelings constructively • Learning from and teaching others • Making, keeping, and ending friendships • Sharing time, friends, and possessions • Handling problems with others • Acting with consideration for self and others

continued

TABLE A.1. (*continued*)

Topic Areas and Key Concepts

Age Levels	Human Development and Sexuality	Interpersonal Relationships
Adolescents	• Types of development: physical, cognitive, emotional, personality, moral, social, and sexual • Patterns of development over the life span (conception to death) • Interaction among types of development (e.g., social and sexual development) • Accepting individual differences in development • Stereotypes and realities about adulthood and aging • Developmental disabilities • Social and environmental conditions affecting growth and development • Effects of chemical substances on physical health and development • Responsibility for personal health (nutrition, hygiene, exercise) • Body privacy and protection against sexual abuse • Communicating about sexuality (personal values, beliefs) • Normality of sexual feelings and sexual responses • Human reproduction and contraception • Varying family and societal beliefs about sexuality • Choices, consequences, and responsibilities of sexual behavior	• Building self-esteem and self-confidence • Assessing and developing personal abilities and talents • Respecting self and others • Changing and developing one's thoughts, attitudes, and values • Dealing with emotion • Dealing with success and failure • Communicating information, thoughts, and feelings • Initiating, maintaining, and ending relationships • Assessing compatibility in interpersonal relationships • Understanding the effects of self-perceptions of relationships • Understanding the needs and motivations involved in dating • Accepting responsibility for one's actions • Acting in one's own and others' best interests • Understanding the bases for choosing a family life-style (values, heritage, religious beliefs) • Factors influencing mate selection (social, cultural, personal) • Understanding the dimensions of love and commitment • Exploring the responsibilities of marriage

Adults	
• Dimensions of development: physical, cognitive, affective, moral, personality, social, and sexual	• Building self-esteem and self-confidence in self and others
• Patterns of development over the life span (conception to death)	• Establishing personal autonomy
• Interaction among dimensions of development (e.g., social and sexual development)	• Achieving constructive personal change
• Factors influencing individual differences in development	• Communicating effectively
• Promoting development in self and others	• Dealing with emotions
• Myths and realities of adulthood and aging	• Dealing with crises
• Dealing with disabilities	• Types of intimate relationships
• Social and environmental conditions affecting growth and development	• Exercising initiative in relationships
• Responsibility for personal and family health	• Developing, maintaining, and ending relationships
• Communicating about sexuality (personal values, beliefs, shared decision making)	• Understanding the effects of self-perceptions of relationships
• Normality of sexual feelings	• Varying influences on roles and relationships (ethnic, racial, social)
• Human sexual response	• Recognizing factors associated with quality relationships
• Contraception, infertility, and genetics	• Taking responsibility and making commitments in relationships
• Responsible sexual behavior (choices, consequences, shared decision making)	• Evaluating choices and alternatives in relationships
• Prevention of sexual abuse	• Changes in the marital relationship over time
• Varying societal beliefs about sexuality	• Acting in accordance with personal beliefs with consideration for others' best interests
	• Creating and maintaining a family of one's own

continued

TABLE A.1. (*continued*)

Topic Areas and Key Concepts

Age Levels	Human Development and Sexuality	Interpersonal Relationships
Children	• Families as sources of protection, guidance, affection, and support • Families as possible sources of anger and violence • Family similarities and differences • Individuality and importance of all family members • Responsibilities, rights, and interdependence of all family members • Changes in families (births, separations, deaths) • Family members as individuals • Getting along in the family • Expressing feelings in families • Family rules • Family problems • Impact of change on families • Family traditions and celebrations • Personal family history	• Taking care of possessions • Learning about time and schedules • Helping with family tasks • Developing talents and abilities • Using and saving human and nonhuman resources • Importance of space and privacy • Learning to choose • Selecting and consuming (food, clothing, recreation) • Using money • Influences on consumer decisions (wants, costs, media, friends)

	Family Interaction	Family Resource Management
Adolescents	• Families as sources of protection, guidance, affection, and support • Families as possible sources of anger and violence • Family differences (membership, economic level, role performance, values) • Different needs and expectations of all family members • Rights, responsibilities, and interdependence of family members • Becoming an adult within the family • Interaction between family members • Communication in families • Managing feelings in families • Family rules • Coping with internal change and stress in the family • Personal and family decision making • Intergenerational relationships • Interaction of friends and family • Influence of family background and history • Family traditions and celebrations • Changes in family composition (births, divorce, death)	• Using personal resources • Assessment of and changes in personal and family resources • Selection of resources to meet personal needs (food, clothing, recreation) • Allocating time for work, school, and leisure • Negotiating privacy and independence • Developing leisure interests • Values as bases for choices • Choosing long- and short-term goals • Responsibility for decisions • Exploring career choices • Earning, spending, and saving money • Influences on consumer decisions (personal values, costs, media, peers)

continued

TABLE A.1. (*continued*)

Topic Areas and Key Concepts

Age Levels	Family Interaction	Family Resource Management
Adults	• Families as sources of protection, guidance, affection, and support • Families as possible sources of anger and violence • Differences in families (membership, economic level, role performance, values) • Changing needs and expectations of all family members • Rights, responsibilities, and interdependence of family members • Family transitions (marriage, birth, divorce, remarriage, death) • Individual and family roles • Individual development in the family • Intimate relationships in the family • Effects of family on self-concepts of its members • Factors affecting marital and family relationships • Giving and receiving affection • Power and authority in the family • Family rules—overt and covert • Sources of stress and coping with stress • Intergenerational dynamics throughout the life span • Life-style choices • Family history, traditions, and celebrations • Varying influences on family interaction patterns (ethnic, racial, social)	• Developing personal resources • Resource consumption and conservation—material and nonmaterial • Using resources to meet basic needs of family (food, clothing, shelter) • Expendability of human energy • Balancing family and work roles • Developing leisure interests • Varying needs of family members for privacy and independence • Financial planning • Values as bases for choices • Establishing long- and short-term goals • Differing views about uses of family resources • Development of personal resources through career choices • Influences on consumer decisions (personal values, costs, media, peers) • Retirement planning

	Education About Parenthood	Ethics
Children	• Responsibilities of parents • Responsibilities of children • Rewards and difficulties of parenthood • Meeting the needs of children of different ages • Different parenting styles and behavior • Safety for children • Problems of family violence, abuse, and neglect • Different types of caregivers • Sources of help for parents (family, neighborhood, community) • Parents who live away from children	• Respect for all persons • Rights of all persons • Gaining new rights and responsibilities with age • Consequences of actions for self and others • Taking responsibility for actions
Adolescents	• Understanding marital and parental roles • Meeting children's needs at different stages of development • Responding to individual differences in children • Rewards and difficulties of parenting • Child-rearing practices • Parent-child communication • Family conflict and conflict resolution • Teaching life skills to children (self-sufficiency, safety) • Problems of family violence, abuse, and neglect • Varied parenting situations (single parenting, stepparenting, adoption) • Sources of help for parents (family, neighborhood, community) • Parents living away from children • Factors to consider in deciding if and when to become a parent	• Ethical principles as one kind of values • Ethical values as guides to human social conduct • Interrelationship of rights and responsibilities • Self-responsibility and social responsibility • Complexity and difficulty of ethical choices • Ethical implications of social and technological change • Developing a personal ethical code

continued

TABLE A.1. (*continued*)

Topic Areas and Key Concepts

Age Levels	Education About Parenthood	Ethics
Adults	• Changing parental responsibilities as children become independent • Changing parent-child relationships over the life span • Preparation for birth and parenthood • Demands and rewards of parenthood • Child-rearing practices, guidance, and parenting strategies • Importance of parental communication regarding child-rearing practices • Parent-child communication • Family conflict and conflict resolution • Providing a safe environment for children • Teaching life skills to children (self-sufficiency, decision making) • Problems of family violence, abuse, and neglect • Varied parenting situations (single parenting, stepparenting, adoption) • Sources of help for parents (family, neighborhood, community) • Factors to consider in deciding if and when to become a parent • Influences on parenting styles (ethnic, racial, social)	• Ethical principles as one kind of values • Ethical values as guides to human social conduct • Acting in accordance with personal beliefs with consideration for others • Interrelationship of rights and responsibilities • Personal autonomy and social responsibility • Establishing an ethical philosophy of life • Complexity and difficulty of ethical choices and decisions • Ethical implications of social and technological change • Assisting in the formation of ethical concepts and behavior in others

Family and Society

Children
- Understanding and respecting the law
- Laws and policies affecting families
- Children's legal rights
- Programs that support individuals and families
- Importance of families, neighborhood, and the community
- Families and schools working together
- Jobs, money, and the family
- Differing religious beliefs and practices of families

Adolescents
- Understanding laws affecting families
- Families and the justice system
- Impact of laws and policies on families
- Respecting the civil rights of all people
- Individual and family legal protection, rights, and responsibilities
- Family conflict and legal protection of family members
- Support for families with special needs and problems
- Importance of family to society
- Individual and family responsibility in the community
- Functioning in the school system
- School as preparation for the future
- Education throughout the life span
- Reciprocal influences of technology and families
- Reciprocal influences of the economy and families
- The influence of religion on families
- Families and the workplace
- Population issues and resource allocation

continued

TABLE A.1. (*continued*)

Age Levels	Topic Areas and Key Concepts Family and Society
Adults	• Understanding and affecting laws and policies • Transmitting values regarding education, justice, and the law • Protecting the civil rights of all people • Family conflict and legal protection of family members • The influence of religion on families • Understanding and obtaining community support services • Supportive networks (family, friends, religious institutions) • Role of family in society • Individual and family responsibility in the community • Utilizing the educational system • Family participation in the education of children • Education throughout the life span • Reciprocal influences of technology and families • Economic fluctuations and their impact on families • Interrelationship of families, work, and society • Population issues and resource allocation

*A wall poster of this framework is available from the National Council on Family Relations.

**Communicating, decision making, and problem solving have not been listed as separate concepts but should be incorporated into each topic area.

SOURCE: From "A Framework for Life-Span Family Life Education" by M. Arcus, 1987. *Family Relations, 36,* pp. 5-10. Copyrighted © 1987 by the National Council on Family Relations, 3989 Central Ave. N.E., Suite #550, Minneapolis, MN 55421. Reprinted by permission.

Author Index

Subject Index

About the Authors

Margaret E. Arcus is Professor of Family Science and Acting Director of the School of Family and Nutritional Sciences at the University of British Columbia. She is also a Fellow of the Association for Values Education and Research. She has been active in family life education as a secondary school teacher, university teacher educator, and community consultant. Her major areas of interest include conceptual issues, ethics and values, and teacher education, and she has published articles in journals such as *Family Relations, International Journal of Sociology of the Family, Journal of Home Economics,* and the *Canadian Home Economics Journal.* She is a certified family life educator and was a member of the committee that developed the Family Life Education Certification Program for the National Council on Family Relations.

M. Betsy Bergen (Ph.D.) is Associate Professor in the Department of Family and Child Development at Kansas State University. She has been certified as a family life educator by the National Council on Family Relations and as a sex educator and counselor by the American Association of Sex Educators, Counselors and Therapists. Her research and publications focus on family relations, adolescents and young adults, sexual attitudes and behaviors, and sexuality and AIDS education.

Gregory W. Brock obtained his Ph.D. from Pennsylvania State University and is currently Chair of the Department of Family Studies at the

University of Kentucky. His research interests include professional ethics and marriage and family therapy treatment evaluation, and his most recent publications are *Procedures in Marriage and Family Therapy* (second edition) and *Ethics, Legalities, and Professional Practice Issues in Marriage and Family Therapy.* He is a Clinical Member and Approved Supervisor of the American Association for Marriage and Family Therapy (AAMFT), Chair of the AAMFT Ethics Committee, and founder and manager of the Family Science Network, a computer electronic mail and communication system for family scientists and family researchers.

Jeanette D. Coufal obtained her Ph.D. from Pennsylvania State University. She has served as a faculty member at Texas Tech University and the University of Wisconsin-Stout and is currently Director of BlueGrass Impact in Lexington, Kentucky. She is a Clinical Member and Approved Supervisor of the American Association for Marriage and Family Therapy and a long-standing member of the National Council on Family Relations. She has a number of family life education-related publications on topics such as marital therapy and enrichment and parent education.

Maryanne Doherty-Poirier is an assistant professor in the Department of Family Studies at the University of Alberta, Edmonton, where she is responsible for teaching undergraduate and graduate courses in family life education. She has worked and researched in family life education program design, development, implementation, and evaluation. Most recently, she completed an evaluation research project of HIV/AIDS instruction offered throughout the province of Alberta.

John W. Engel obtained his Ph.D. from the University of Minnesota and is currently Professor in the Department of Human Resources at the University of Hawaii, Honolulu. His research and publications focus on family life education and counseling, work/family interface, and cross-cultural differences. He has been certified as a family life educator by the National Council on Family Relations and as a sex educator and counselor by the American Association of Sex Educators, Counselors and Therapists.

M. Janice Hogan is Professor in the Department of Family Social Science at the University of Minnesota. She is a former President of the National

Council on Family Relations and former Chair of the Family Economics and Management Section of the American Home Economics Association. Her professional work has included County Extension work in New York State and a faculty position at Arizona State University. International collaborative efforts include involvement in a Russian project on family and child policy as well as coediting a book on Russian and U.S. families, an exchange project between university home economics programs in Thailand and Taiwan, and directing the College of Human Ecology's international program. Her major research agenda is a longitudinal study of couples' gender roles, conflict resolution, and resource issues.

Dianne K. Kieren is Professor of Family Studies at the University of Alberta in Edmonton, Alberta, Canada. During her Ph.D. studies at the University of Minnesota, she developed a keen interest in the nature and process of family problem solving. She is a professional home economist and certified family life educator who has been a university professor and community family life educator for more than 20 years. She is the author of six junior high school health and sexuality textbooks and two university-level books that use the problem-solving framework as their conceptual structure.

J. Joel Moss received his Ph.D. in sociology from the University of North Carolina and is Professor Emeritus of the Family Science Department of Brigham Young University. He has published many articles on family life education and served as Guest Editor (with Ruth Brasher) of "A Special Issue: Family Life Education" for *Family Relations*. Other editorial responsibilities include the positions of Associate Editor for the *Journal of Marriage and the Family*, Associate Editor of *Family Perspective*, Managing Editor for *Family Science Review*, and external referee for the *Journal of Home Economics*. He has served as a consultant to Project Head Start. Currently, he is teaching English at a university in the People's Republic of China.

Mary Oertwein obtained her M.S. in marriage and family therapy from the University of Kentucky. She is currently the Flexible Response Coordinator for BlueGrass Impact in Lexington, Kentucky.

Kathryn D. Rettig is Professor in the Department of Family Social Science at the University of Minnesota, where she teaches in the area of family economics and management. She has also taught at the University of Illinois, Michigan State University, Iowa State University, and Glassboro State College. She is currently developing a conceptual framework of management with emphasis on perceptual and personal variations of decision makers. Her research interests have centered on measures of family life quality and adjustments of families to strains such as divorce and mandatory farm credit mediation. Her recent work involves policy evaluation concerning the income adequacy of child support guidelines for the economic well-being of children.

Marilyn Martin Rossman is Associate Professor of Home Economics Education at the University of Minnesota, where she teaches courses in family life education. She is currently working on research projects in the areas of parent and school collaboration, work and family interaction, and parents as sexuality educators of their children. She is a former President of the Minnesota Council on Family Relations and the National Association of Teacher Educators of Vocational Home Economics.

Connie J. Salts received her Ph.D. from Florida State University. She is currently Associate Professor and Director of the Marriage and Family Therapy Program, Department of Family and Child Development at Auburn University. Her areas of research interest and her publications focus on premarital issues, divorce adjustment, and marital and family therapy training and supervision. Dr. Salts is a Clinical Member and Approved Supervisor of the American Association for Marriage and Family Therapy.

Marie Saracino (Ph.D.) is Assistant Professor in the Department of Home Economics at Steven F. Austin State University. She has conducted research and published on a wide variety of topics, including sexuality education, adolescent pregnancy and parenthood, AIDS-related beliefs and behaviors, remarriage and stepparenting, and marital satisfaction over the life cycle.

Jay D. Schvaneveldt is Professor in and Head of the Department of Family and Human Development at Utah State University. He obtained his Ph.D. from Florida State University and completed a postdoctorate at the University of Minnesota. He has published in family, child, adolescent, human development, and biological journals dealing with family relations, marriage, parent-child interaction, social change, and family life education. He is coauthor of *Understanding Research Methods* and author or coauthor of several chapters in various handbooks on marriage and the family and theory. He was a Fulbright Scholar in sociology and anthropology to the nation of Thailand, Khon Kaen University.

Robert F. Stahmann received his Ph.D. from the University of Utah and is currently a professor in the Department of Family Sciences at Brigham Young University in Provo, Utah. He has special qualifications as a Certified Family Life Educator in the National Council on Family Relations; a Certified Sex Therapist in the American Association of Sex Educators, Counselors, and Therapists; and a Fellow and Approved Supervisor in the American Association for Marriage and Family Therapy. His research and publications are in the areas of couples therapy and premarital and re-marital counseling. He is co-author of *Premarital Counseling: The Professional's Handbook* (2nd edition) and author of *Dynamic Assessment in Couples Therapy*. He also has numerous publications in professional journals.

Jane Thomas is a curriculum consultant with the Vancouver School Board, Vancouver, B.C. She completed her Ed.D. in the Faculty of Education at the University of British Columbia and has been a sessional instructor at that university for the School of Family and Nutritional Sciences and for the Faculty of Education. She has had experience as a family life education teacher in the secondary schools and as a teacher educator at the university level and has been involved in both local and provincial family life education curriculum development. She is a certified family life educator and is currently the Provincial Coordinator for the CLFE program in British Columbia. She has completed two qualitative studies of family life education and is currently coinvestigator on a national survey of family life education in Canada.